Workplace Studies

Recovering Work Practice and Informing System Design

Workplace studies are of growing significance to people in a broad range of academic disciplines and professions, in particular those involved in the development of new technologies. This book brings together key researchers in Europe and the USA to discuss critical issues in the study of the workplace and to outline recent developments in the field. The collection is divided into two parts: part 1 contains a number of detailed case studies that not only provide an insight into the issues central to workplace studies but also highlight some of the problems involved in carrying out such research. Part 2 focuses on the interrelationship between workplace studies and the design of new technologies. This book provides a valuable, multidisciplinary synthesis of the key issues and theoretical developments in workplace studies and a guide to the implications of such research for technology design and the workplace.

PAUL LUFF is a Senior Research Fellow in the Work, Interaction and Technology Research Group at King's College London.

JON HINDMARSH is a Research Fellow in the Work, Interaction and Technology Research Group at King's College London.

CHRISTIAN HEATH is Professor in the Work, Interaction and Technology Research Group at King's College London.

D0107339

Workplace Studies

Recovering Work Practice and Informing System Design

Edited by

Paul Luff

Jon Hindmarsh

Christian Heath

CAMBRIDGE
UNIVERSITY PRESS

PUBLISHED BY THE PRESS SYNDICATE OF THE UNIVERSITY OF CAMBRIDGE
The Pitt Building, Trumpington Street, Cambridge CB2 1RP, United Kingdom

CAMBRIDGE UNIVERSITY PRESS
The Edinburgh Building, Cambridge CB2 2RU, UK http://www.cup.cam.ac.uk
40 West 20th Street, New York, NY 10011-4211, USA http://www.cup.org
10 Stamford Road, Oakleigh, Melbourne 3166, Australia

© Paul Luff, Jon Hindmarsh, Christian Heath 2000

First published 2000

Printed in the United Kingdom at the University Press, Cambridge

Typeset in Plantin 10/12 pt in QuarkXPress™ [SE]

A catalogue record for this book is available from the British Library

Library of Congress cataloguing in publication data

Luff, Paul.
    Workplace studies: recovering work practice and informing system
design/Paul Luff, Jon Hindmarsh, Christian Heath.
        p.   cm.
    Includes bibliographical references and index.
    ISBN 0 521 59186 4 (hardback) – ISBN 0 521 59821 4 (paperback)
    1. Organisational change – Management.   2. Technological
innovations – Management.   3. Technological innovations – Employee
participation.   4. Communication in design.   5. Communication and
technology.   I. Hindmarsh, Jon.   II. Heath, Christian, 1952–   .
III. Title.
HD58.8.L84   2000   99-30983   CIP

ISBN 0 521 591864 hardback
ISBN 0 521 598214 paperback

Contents

Contributors

BOB ANDERSON
ProVice-Chancellor,
Research and Business
Development,
Sheffield Hallam University,
Sheffield S1 1WB
United Kingdom
Email: r.anderson@shu.ac.uk

LIAM J. BANNON
Interaction Design Centre
University of Limerick
Ireland
Email: liam.bannon@ul.ie

GRAHAM BUTTON
Xerox Research Centre Europe
Cambridge Laboratory
Ravenscroft House
61 Regent Street
Cambridge CB2 1AB
United Kingdom
Email: button@xrce.xerox.com

YRJÖ ENGESTRÖM
Marjatantie 22 A
00621 Helsinki
Finland
Email: yrjo.engestrom@helsinki.fi

THOMAS ERICKSON
IBM T. J. Watson Research Center
Research Remote Office
3136 Irving Ave. S.
Minneapolis MN 55408
USA
Email: snowfall@acm.org

GENEVIEVE FILIPPI
EFD/DER/ESF
1 Avenue du General de Gaulle
92141 Clamart
France
Email: genevieve.filippi@edf.fr

RICHARD H. R. HARPER
Digital World Research Centre
School of Human Sciences
University of Surrey
Guildford GU2 5XH
United Kingdom
Email: r.harper@surrey.ac.uk

CHRISTIAN HEATH
Work, Interaction and Technology
    Research Group
King's College London
Franklin-Wilkins Building
London SE1 8WA
United Kingdom
Email: Christian.Heath@kcl.ac.uk

JON HINDMARSH
Work, Interaction and Technology
    Research Group
King's College London
Franklin-Wilkins Building
London SE1 8WA
United Kingdom
Email: Jon.Hindmarsh@kcl.ac.uk

JOHN HUGHES
Sociology Department
Lancaster University
Lancaster LA1 4YR
United Kingdom
Email: j.hughes@lancaster.ac.uk

MARINA JIROTKA
Oxford University Computing
    Laboratory
Wolfson Building
Parks Road
Oxford OX1 3QD
United Kingdom
Email:
Marina.Jirotka@comlab.oxford.ac.uk

PAUL LUFF
Work, Interaction and Technology
    Research Group
King's College London
Franklin-Wilkins Building
London SE1 8WA
United Kingdom
Email: Paul.Luff@kcl.ac.uk

JON O'BRIEN
Xerox Research Centre Europe
Cambridge Laboratory
61 Regent Street
Cambridge CB2 1AB
United Kingdom
E-mail: jon.obrien@xrce.xerox.com

TOM RODDEN
Computing Department
Lancaster University
Lancaster LA1 4YR
United Kingdom
E-mail: tom@comp.lancs.ac.uk

MARK ROUNCEFIELD
Computing Department
Lancaster University
Lancaster LA1 4YR
United Kingdom
Email:
m.rouncefield@lancaster.ac.uk

KJELD SCHMIDT
Center for Tele-Information
Technical University of Denmark
Building 371
DK-2800 Lyngby
Denmark
Email: schmidt@cti.dtu.dk

WES SHARROCK
Sociology Department
University of Manchester
Oxford Road
Manchester M13 9PO
United Kingdom
Email: Wes.Sharrock@man.ac.uk

LUCY SUCHMAN
Xerox Palo Alto Research Center
3333 Coyote Hill Road
Palo Alto CA 94304
USA
Email: suchman@parc.xerox.com

JACQUES THEUREAU
Philosophy, Technology &
  Cognition
Université Technologique de
  Compiègne
K 103 Centre Pierre Guillaumat
BP 649
60206 Compiègne
France
Email:
jacques.theureau@hds.utc.fr

ERIK VINKHUYZEN
Xerox Palo Alto Research Center
3333 Coyote Hill Road
Palo Alto CA 94304
USA
Email: evinkhuy@parc.xerox.com

LINCOLN WALLEN
Oxford University Computing
  Laboratory
Wolfson Building
Parks Road
Oxford OX1 3QD
United Kingdom
Email:
Lincoln.Wallen@comlab.oxford.ac.uk

JACK WHALEN
Xerox Palo Alto Research Center
3333 Coyote Hill Road
Palo Alto CA 94304
USA
Email: jwhalen@parc.xerox.com

Figures

Preface

It is widely recognised that new technology has had a profound impact on our working lives. It is argued that the so-called digital revolution has transformed the ways in which we communicate with each other, how we store and handle information, the ways in which we classify people and events, how we calculate products and value, and how we market goods and services. Social scientists discuss new forms of organisation, the transformation of contemporary culture and, among many other things, globalisation and emergence of the network society. Despite our attempts to remain optimistic in the face of the inevitable pursuit for more advanced and sophisticated technologies, often at the expense of employment, there is a growing recognition that complex systems may not necessarily enhance work practice, human relations or even efficiency within organisations. Poor performance, mishaps and technological failures are encouraging those within industry to begin to reconsider the advantages of technology for technology's sake, and to recognise that there is more to the design and deployment of complex systems than simply identifying new functionalities for computer systems. There is also a corresponding change within academia, a recognition that for all our discussion of technology we actually know very little as to how ordinary people in their daily working lives go about using the tools of their trades.

Over the past few years, there have been a number of research projects concerned with the ways in which new tools and technologies feature in everyday organisational conduct. These investigations have come to be known as 'workplace studies'. They consist of ethnographies, field studies, sometimes augmented by video recordings, of work and communication in complex organisational environments. So for example we find studies of command and control centres, news rooms, architectural practices, medical consultations and financial institutions. In various ways these studies are concerned with the social and interactional organisation of technology in the workplace. They direct attention towards the fine details of human conduct and coordination, and demonstrate how technologies, ranging from paper documents through to complex multimedia systems, rely upon the working procedures and practical reasoning of the members of particular settings and organisations. They are concerned, in a sense, with the work to make technologies work; with the tacit and 'seen but unnoticed' resources through which organisational activities are accomplished in and through tools and technology.

In this book we bring together a collection of these studies, coupled with discussion papers concerning their intellectual and practical implications. The investigations reflect the diversity of approaches that we find within workplace studies. So for example we find studies informed by ethnomethodology and conversation analysis, by activity theory and by analytic developments in cognitive science, such as course-of-action analysis. The investigations also address a range of substantive issues and domains. These include, for example, the role of documents in the International Monetary Fund (IMF), the organisation of software design meetings, the interaction between call centres and clients, the practical scrutiny of documents in large-scale legal cases, and the management of crises in the operations room of the RATP in Paris. In each of these investigations, the authors examine, from their particular analytic perspective, the practices and procedures, the *in situ* reasoning and knowledge, relied upon by participants in accomplishing their practical actions and activities. In various ways, therefore, the studies reveal the complex array of resources that inform the production and coordination of workplace activities – resources on which the participants rely and yet remain largely tacit and unexplicated.

The investigations discussed in the book, and workplace studies more generally, are providing an important contribution to our understanding of work, technology and interaction. They are generating a rich and diverse body of observations and findings, based on detailed empirical research, about how individuals in organisations use technologies to inform the production and coordination of their actions and activities. In one sense, workplace studies can be seen as a reflowering of the sociology of work, as contributing to, and developing, the rich body of research on organisations and interaction, which emerged in Chicago following the Second World War. But they have a broader relevance, and perhaps raise issues which lie beyond their purely empirical contribution. For example, some workplace studies, including chapters within this volume, are developing insights and analytic considerations which extend and enhance the growing body of research concerned with language use and interaction, or consider for example how demonstrations of interdependent courses of action in the workplace contribute to our understanding of shared and distributed cognition. But it is perhaps in disciplines such as human–computer interaction (HCI) and Computer Supported Cooperative

Work (CSCW) that workplace studies are having their most profound impact. They are for example challenging long-standing assumptions concerning how individuals use or interact with computers and the nature of the resources on which they rely in performing even the most seemingly mundane, individual activities. They also demonstrate how traditional ideas concerning group behaviour and roles, ideas which informed early work in CSCW, provide a relatively inflexible and impoverished understanding of collaborative work.

The contribution of workplace studies, therefore, to contemporary research and debates within various fields is not simply empirical. Rather, through wide-ranging yet detailed naturalistic research, workplace studies are beginning to readdress or, to use Garfinkel's term, 'respecify' many of the key concepts and ideas that currently infuse our understanding of technology in action. Take for example the idea of the 'user', and the individual's cognitive resources which have served to inform a substantial body of research in HCI. In various ways workplace studies have demonstrated not only how individual actions and activities are routinely produced with regard to the real-time contributions of others, but also that the competent and accountable use of a system in an organisation is inseparable from a body of local knowledge and reasoning through which technologically informed actions and activities are produced and rendered intelligible. Similarly, traditional ideas concerning the character of such concepts as 'information', 'communication', 'collaboration', 'cognition' and even 'technology' are being questioned and reconsidered in the light of detailed empirical studies of work and interaction in organisational environments. The contribution of workplace studies, therefore, in part derives from the ways in which they are building a new and distinct foundation for our understanding of technology and social action.

These empirical and conceptual contributions are also of some practical relevance. For example they provide an array of observations and findings concerning both generic and local features of collaborative work and thereby resources through which we can begin to consider, seriously, what it is that we are trying to support when we are thinking about technologies for cooperation and interaction in the workplace. This body of empirical research can also serve to delineate criteria and considerations which need to come into play if we are going successfully to evaluate, design, even deploy, new and innovative systems. Conceptual respecifications are also of some practical import. While debates concerning the user may strike one as abstract or even academic, such shifting (re)specifications have profound relevance for the shape of technologies to come, and are a critical methodological resource for those who are responsible for identifying the requirements for complex systems. Such respecifications demand a significant change in the methods and considerations which people who develop, build and deploy technology rely upon in the course of their work. In an important sense, therefore, the practical contribution of workplace studies must and should be considered long term, and will involve the whole gamut of debates, discussions and organisational politics which are inevitably associated with the influence of academic research on practical activity whatever the field.

There is, however, a growing interest in using workplace studies to more directly inform the design and deployment of new technologies. Firms increasingly recognise that a more detailed understanding of work practices, even if it is hoped that these will change, is an invaluable resource when thinking about the design and deployment of systems. In consequence there is an increasing number of projects which involve close collaboration between social and computer scientists, academics and industrialists, concerned with the design of innovative technologies. Industrial research laboratories, government and intergovernment funding bodies and innovative 'high tech' organisations, all have helped foster projects which involve the use of workplace studies to inform the design and development of new technologies. These are early days and in most cases these are demonstrator and prototype systems, but they demonstrate the richness of ethnography and its ability to influence, even drive, design and development.

Understandably there is an interest among both academics and practitioners in identifying more systematic ways in which workplace studies can inform the design, evaluation and deployment of new technologies. Many of the chapters in this book address just this problem. They are concerned with considering whether a programme of work, which is by definition open-ended, naturalistic and qualitative, can be transformed to provide a method or set of procedures which can reliably inform technology production. The chapters explore whether this is feasible, and if so, what empirical, methodological and theoretical considerations need to be identified for workplace studies to influence successfully the shape of technology. For example, there is a long-standing debate as to whether ethnography is required or just simply fieldwork, and if ethnography is required, whether by virtue of the practical constraints of software projects, it can successfully be accomplished in weeks rather than months or years. In respect to these concerns, particular tools and techniques are proposed that may be necessary to support these more applied workplace studies, and given their observations and findings, how these studies might be tailored and transformed for designers rather than fellow academics. There is also debate as to whether workplace studies can enhance our understanding of organisational change, or whether, for example, ethnographies can provide only information relevant to the current circumstances. These discussions therefore reflect debates concerning the methodological and empirical contributions of workplace studies and how these can inform practice. These are, of course, debates which have haunted the social sciences since their inception and which have certainly not been solved by others, whether social, cognitive or computer scientists.

The aim of this book therefore is to bring together a collection of workplace studies which have different substantive concerns and reflect different approaches to understanding technology and organisational conduct. It is also concerned with raising and exploring the more applied issues which arise with workplace studies and in particular the extent to which they may contribute to the design and deployment of new technologies. The book originally derived from a small conference that we held at King's College London. The conference was concerned with bringing together researchers and practitioners from various fields to present and discuss studies of work, interaction and technology. The book reflects much of the discussion and debates which arose during the conference, and we believe provides a demonstration of the contemporary issues which are informing both contemporary academic and industrial research.

We would like to thank Cambridge University Press, in particular Catherine Max and the editors of the series Learning and Doing, John Seeley Brown and Roy Pea, for their support and patience. We would also like to thank our colleagues at King's College London, especially those within the Work, Interaction and Technology Research Group for their encouragement and support, and the Economic and Social Research Council (ESRC) for providing a small grant to facilitate the conference.

1   Introduction

Paul Luff, Jon Hindmarsh and Christian Heath

In the past few years we have witnessed extraordinary pronouncements concerning the ways in which new technologies will transform the ways we work together. In both the popular press and in academic debate, an interest principally focused on extensions to existing computer networks, new forms of telecommunications and the potential of faster and cheaper systems, all have suggested that we are soon to be faced with a very different workplace. Workers will be more mobile when all the technological support they need can be provided wherever they are located and it may even be no longer necessary for individuals to travel to a particular site when they can work from home. The actual 'organisation' for which they work will become fragmented, geographically dispersed and possibly 'virtual', being transformed into a business with no physical location and little organisational structure.

Such pronouncements may seem curiously reminiscent to those familiar with the predictions associated with the microchip in the 1970s, or the motor car in the 1940s, or even earlier with the potential afforded in the nineteenth century by the telegraph, telephone and electricity (cf. Evans, 1979; Hall, 1988; Marvin, 1988). It is certainly the case that in the last few years the personal computer (PC) and electronic mail (email) have greatly transformed the way that work is accomplished in a large number of organisations. However, despite the grand intentions of proponents of novel technologies it is frequently the case that their impact is more modest. Indeed, it is not unusual for new systems once they have been introduced to be ignored, used to only a small degree of their capabilities or worse to be the cause of some great disaster. It appears that rather than radically transforming current work practices it is difficult even to achieve the less ambitious hope of supporting workplace activities, whether these are accomplished in a particular location or geographically dispersed. It appears that we need not only further technological developments to mobile devices, telecommunications and distributed computer systems but also a better understanding of the nature of workplace activities that are being intended to support, transform or replace.

1

It may seem remarkable, given the great body of work undertaken within the social and cognitive sciences concerning the use of information systems, that these do not seem to provide the resources relevant to developers of new technologies. Neither the multifarious studies of the processes surrounding the introduction of different technologies into organisations nor the detailed examination of individual activities carrying out pre-specified tasks appear to offer an account of naturally occurring workplace activities that is relevant or sufficient for developers of new technologies. Of course many of these studies have been undertaken for quite different purposes, with respect to debates within psychology, sociology and to theories of work and management. Nevertheless, even those fields with an expressed orientation to informing the design of systems through the detailed examination of individual activities with computers, like that of human–computer interaction, have had a surprising lack of influence on the development of new technologies (Carroll, 1991). Hence, more applied fields have emerged, such as requirements engineering, with a direct concern for providing practical advice and methods with respect to the needs of users.

In the light of these difficulties and a growing interest in developing technologies to support collaboration and group work, a corpus of studies has emerged that has been concerned with revealing the details of how activities are accomplished in real-world workplaces. Although many of these workplace studies have not been directly concerned with the development of any specific technology, they have begun to influence designers of novel systems, particularly of technologies to support collaborative work. They have suggested not only broad issues and topics which should be of concern to designers, but also ways of conceiving collaborative activities which can shape the development of novel technologies to support activities in the workplace. Indeed, a field has emerged which has acted as a forum of debate between developers of new technologies to support collaborative work and researchers of workplace activities: Computer Supported Cooperative Work.

In this chapter we discuss some of the background to workplace studies, both with respect to recent technological developments and to current debates within the social sciences. We begin by briefly outlining some developments in technologies aimed at supporting groups and collaborative activities. Despite their novelty, certain difficulties emerged with these systems and it became apparent that designers required a better understanding of the contexts in which these technologies were to be placed, particularly collaborative activities and social interaction in workplaces.

We then review some of the recent workplace studies that have been undertaken. Although most of this work has been related to the interests of CSCW, it is not the case that the principal motivations behind it have been towards the design of new technologies. Certainly, there is no method which transforms a study of a workplace into a set of design guidelines. Indeed, many researchers would question whether the development of such a method would be the most appropriate way for workplace studies to be relevant for design. Moreover, there are also several orientations that can be taken towards the analysis of workplace activities. Despite having a common focus on naturally occurring workplace activities, these orientations are themselves developments from a range of earlier work in the cognitive and social sciences and therefore can utilise quite different conceptions to their particular domain of study. In this chapter we outline some of the principal analytic orientations that have informed the study of collaborative activities in the workplace.

Although the implications of workplace studies are frequently considered in terms of their potential for informing the design of a new computer system, this may not be their principal contribution. Workplace studies may not only suggest requirements for specific or generic technologies, but also provide for a respecification of the conceptions that underpin various of the applied and academic fields that take technology as their focus. We review some of the many directions in which researchers have developed the outcomes of their studies of workplaces. These include not only particular exercises that seek to shape new technologies, but also those that could inform the practices of designers and software engineers. Workplace studies also appear to offer a contribution to disciplines as diverse as the study of human–computer interfaces, the social study of technology and organisational behaviour. So, although workplace studies can contribute to the design of new technologies, even suggest some radical alternative ways for computers to support collaborative work, their more significant contribution will be in reshaping the ways in which we conceive of everyday social actions and interactions in the workplace.

This chapter provides some preliminary background, nevertheless it is hoped that the contributions in this volume, through illustrative case studies, discussion of relevant conceptual issues and debates concerning the relationship of these studies to the development of new technologies, will provide a critical resource for both those interested in the analysis of social activities in the workplace and those aiming to relate this analysis to design. These two concerns are reflected in the structure of this volume, an outline of which concludes this chapter.

Background

The prevailing deployment and use of computer systems like personal workstations linked together on networks and through applications like email have led researchers to consider more advanced ways of providing support for workplace activities (e.g. Winograd, 1988; Sharples, 1993). In particular, designers have been especially concerned with extending the technology's capabilities for supporting individual activities so that computer systems can support collaborative work either when individuals are co-present or when they are remote (e.g. Stefik *et al.*, 1987; J. Olson *et al.*, 1990). Some of these innovations have directly built upon existing email capabilities, for example providing asynchronous support for individuals who are working on a common project, commenting on one another's work or writing a document together. Others have sought to provide synchronous support for several individuals working together at the same time. Some of the systems have been developed into products like Lotus Notes, but the success of more advanced designs has been harder to ascertain. For example, users appear to be ambivalent, at least, towards the kinds of technological support offered by shared drawing tools and desktop conferencing systems. Many other technologies using projection techniques, locator technologies and video and audio infra-structures have remained as prototypes (Ishii, 1990; Harper, 1992; Bly *et al.*, 1992), it being unclear whether and how they would be deployed within workplaces. Even more straightforward developments of systems for managing collaborative tasks, though requiring only a simple techni-cal infrastructure, have met with little enthusiasm and even hostility from users. Although there appear to be a wide range of possibilities for devel-oping technologies to support collaborative work, and a great number of suggestions have been proposed and prototyped, it appears to be hard to actually develop and deploy such systems in real-world settings (cf. Grudin, 1988). Those systems which have met with some success appear to be more due to happenstance than design. It may be that the difficulties associated with collaborative technologies may not be so much associated with poor design but more related to the general objectives underlying the systems, particularly with respect to how designers are considering the activities they are aiming to support.

Hence, it may be worth exploring a few of these developments in a little more detail, not only to provide an insight into work which has been undertaken within CSCW, but also to reveal how system designers have characterised the collaborative workplace activities that they aim to support. The heterogeneous range of technologies, systems and devices considered by researchers in CSCW makes it meaningless to select a 'rep-resentative' set of cases. Instead, we briefly examine three developments within CSCW that have been the focus of some debate within the field: Group Decision Support Systems (GDSS), workflow technologies and media spaces. Each of these aims to provide quite different kinds of support (both synchronous and asynchronous) to various workplace activities (both co-present and distributed).

Group Decision Support Systems are typically comprised of a range of devices within one local domain which are configured to facilitate meetings, particularly, as their name suggests, to assist the individuals to formulate 'decisions'. So in the case of an early example, COLAB, private workstations were provided for each individual in the meeting and these were linked together and also connected to a public display visible to all at the meeting (Stefik *et al.*, 1987).

Various applications aimed to facilitate the generation of suggestions within the meeting, the distribution of these to colleagues and the collaborative formulation of arguments to support the decisions that were being made. In later developments of GDSS such tools have been refined so that quite sophisticated techniques have been provided to allow members to comment on the suggestions of colleagues, to categorise 'ideas' and to rank and analyse alternatives (Vogel and Nunamaker, 1990). Although each of these tools could be used separately, their use is considered with respect to an overarching serial process through which a problem is identified, vague solutions are proposed, then clarified and analysed and finally options are ranked, voted upon and decisions are made.

Experiences with the early use of COLAB revealed some problems due to the fragmented nature of technology (Tatar *et al.*, 1991). The public and private screens and the various windows on each made it difficult to recognise which participant was making which contribution, typically entered as typewritten statements. An underlying objective of the system, common in GDSS, to ensure anonymity of the participants did not help, making it even harder to ascertain whether different contributions were being made by the same participant. It was also hard to make sense of individual contributions, particularly when references were made to other statements through the system. Although there was an intention to support decision-making by providing for natural 'conversations' through the system, the technology did not support the interactional resources participants utilise to make sense of one another's contributions, that is the sequential nature of the conduct. Even the efforts to preserve the anonymity of users, an idea that was meant to provide for greater participation, that made decisions less biased and perhaps more rational was not necessarily an advantage. It seemed to undermine the practices that participants utilise to make sense of the contributions of others and assess those contributions.

Indeed, these drawbacks with COLAB echo more general concerns with the conception of decision-making embodied within GDSS. So, for example, March (1991) contrasts the implicit assumptions underpinning such systems with observations concerning how decisions are made in organisations. He describes how 'decisions' as such, rather than prefiguring an action, are often *post-hoc* justifications for outcomes which have already arisen. March's rather ironic analysis of the work within organisations does offer an alternative to the rational and formal characterisation of decision-making by developers of GDSS systems. It also, as he suggests, leads to the possibility of considering an entirely different kind of support for 'decision-makers' – tools which focus on the presentation of decisions rather than the processes through which they are made. Hence, March (1991), even by utilising general observations of how activities are accomplished in organisational settings, provides not only a radically different conception of workplace activities, but also an entirely different direction in which to proceed for technologies being developed to support them. March's analysis suggests the ways in which even general observations of an activity may have some practical implications for system design. More importantly, it reveals how initial presumptions concerning an activity, for example that decisions are the outcomes of prior reasoning performed by groups of individuals through largely rationalistic argumentation, can be set in stark contrast with the everyday accomplishments of participants in organisational settings. Nor is the case that such observations merely present the deficiencies of everyday conduct against some ideal process, rather they reveal the 'good reasons' for such *ad-hoc*, situated and contingent practices.

Rather than supporting a real-time synchronous activity accomplished by co-present individuals, workflow technologies aim to support asynchronous collaboration between physically dispersed individuals. Moreover, they do not rely on being located in a dedicated predesigned setting, being based on more straightforward technological foundations they can be typically used on conventional personal workstations. As their name suggests these systems are designed to support the representation, dissemination and presentation of workflows – sequential relationships between activities (Winograd, 1988). Tasks which are to be accomplished by several individuals, like the preparation of a document, can be laid out, usually graphically, using the system. Then, as the workflow is accessible to all the individuals through a computer network, the workflow can be invoked. Careful preparation can allow for some flexibility to the ways in which the workflow is accomplished, nevertheless the system aims to ensure that the appropriate individuals participate in the activity at the relevant time.

Even though users could produce their own workflows with optional paths, early experiences with the technology revealed that users still found the systems too constraining (e.g. Carasik and Grantham, 1988). It being impossible to predefine all possible contingencies, there were necessarily going to be occasions when the workflows would have to be transformed once they were underway. Of course making such changes could cause problems for other users and may undermine the very reasons for using such a system. Hence it was perhaps not surprising that users would circumvent the system and use other means to collaborate and communicate between colleagues. More recent developments in workflow technologies have sought to address these problems, but their apparent inflexibility may not be so much due to the ways in which tasks may be ordered and changed but in the very ways that tasks are specified and categorised (Suchman, 1993a). The explicit definition of tasks may itself be problematic for users. It may not be straightforward to circumscribe the tasks which are relevant to users. Not only may their specification gloss critical features of the work, particularly with respect to their collaborative accomplishment, but also actually making the tasks explicit, and each individual's contribution to them, may interfere with the smooth performance of workplace activities. The pre-specification of tasks actually accomplishes quite a different activity from outlining a flow of future actions, with respect to the ongoing concerns of participants, at that moment. So, despite the good intentions of designers in making work activities more visible and manipulatable by those who undertake them, the technology might actually undermine their accomplishment. The work of the participants may thus be augmented with efforts to get the technology to work, to make the pre-specified tasks fit the moment-to-moment demands of the setting. Although aiming to develop a flexible technology that is open to redefinition by its users, designers of workflow systems may still be neglecting the ways in which workplace activities are situated and contingent. The very conception of tasks embodied within such a system appears to have been misconstrued; a stipulative and circumscribed characterisation of task actually makes it more problematic to accomplish activities through the technologies designed to support them.

Innovative communicative technologies, either in the form of desktop conferencing systems or more novel media spaces, offer the potential not only for supporting collaboration between physically dispersed individuals but also providing this in real-time (Bly *et al.*, 1992; Gaver *et al.*, 1992; Mantei *et al.*, 1991). Although such systems typically offer common access to an electronic workspace through specially designed 'shared applications', their novelty lies in the capabilities afforded by continuous access to a remote domain through both audio and video links. Through the combination and configuration of conventional audio-visual technologies, proponents of video-mediated technologies can offer systems to support collaboration that should be straightforward to operate by their users. Indeed, the more optimistic hopes for such technologies are to provide new spaces for collaboration, where informal, typically face-to-face, communication and the peripheral awareness of a remote colleague's activities can take place. Rather than refining a pre-specified task or aiming to transform the way work is accomplished, the technology should provide a resource through which collaborative activities can be seamlessly interwoven within the everyday work of the participants. However, in the new space the participants are now physically separated, in distinct offices or even in geographically dispersed sites (Abel, 1990; M. Olson and Bly, 1991). This would appear to be a straightforward deployment of audio-visual technologies to support collaborative work. Nevertheless it does not appear to have the impact its proponents would have hoped for.

Studies of the extensive use of such audio-visual infrastructures reveal that accomplishing everyday interactional activities, such as the production of gestures and their coordination with talk, may not be that straightforward through the technology (Heath and Luff, 1992b). The symmetries that underpin the accomplishment of visual conduct within interaction, that are relied on by participants in more conventional settings, are transformed through the technology. Participants are not able, in the same way, to rely on the resources they typically utilise in the production and receipt of visual conduct. This would seem to be a difficulty for proponents of such systems, particularly those who have characterised their advantages in terms of the technology's ability to provide for gaze direction, gestures and other features of 'face-to-face' interaction. These very features have been typically considered critical in providing better support for 'informal' interaction, not offered in other media, like the telephone or through the computer network.

The detailed analysis of interaction through media spaces coupled with the ambivalent results of more quantitative measures of conduct through video have led designers to rethink the focus on supporting 'informal' work. Hence, several researchers have proposed that the design focus of such technologies be redirected towards supporting the more mundane collaborative accomplishment of workplace activities, more focused on the objects used within an interaction than the remote colleague (Nardi *et al.*, 1993). Moreover, other studies of video-mediated communication have noted how participants appear to rely more on the views offered by document and object centred views, rather than those of the other. However, despite these proposals and observations, the resources offered by these technologies to support the actual accomplishment of collaborative activities are relatively undeveloped. Typically users are given some shared workspace or a document view from a separate camera, but these are provided in distinct and fragmented domains; there is little support for tying these resources to the ongoing conduct of their co-participant. It appears that by focusing on supporting informal interaction, designers have overlooked how to support more focused collaborative activities. Even advanced systems like media spaces remain largely unused in the organisations in which they have been deployed and desktop conferencing systems remain a novel, but under-utilised application. To refocus these developments, however, requires a greater understanding of the resources that individuals utilise when accomplishing work activities within interaction.

Despite the obvious differences between GDSS, workflow technologies and media spaces, they each have been designed in different ways to support collaborative activities, and in each case there appear to be profound problems integrating these technologies into the ways individuals accomplish their everyday work activities. Of course, developments in the design of CSCW systems are in their preliminary phases. Examples of these three cases are still largely prototypes or early implementations. However, it may seem surprising that technologies explicitly aiming to support collaboration, often with considerable attention being paid to how they will be used, appear to be so ill suited to the contingent, emergent and collaborative aspects of the work they aim to support. So, COLAB fragments the resources that individuals make use of in accomplishing interactions, workflow systems make explicit activities that are usually implicit and media spaces transform the conduct they are meant to support. In each of these, what appears to be a straightforward conception of a collaborative activity, a 'decision', a 'workflow' or 'informal interaction', which seems to be in need of technological support, turns out to be problematic. Activities which appear distinct, indivisible and possible to circumscribe are revealed to be emergent, complex and interwoven with others features of conduct when their accomplishment is examined in everyday organisational settings. When the complexity of collaborative work is considered it is perhaps not so surprising that examples of 'successful' CSCW products are so rare. Email is a noteworthy, and perhaps questionable, example of a CSCW product, and even groupware technologies like Lotus Notes do not appear to be used as designed or fail when introduced to support inappropriate organisational activities (Grudin, 1988; Orlikowski, 1992).

Although this may appear to be a failing of the emerging field of CSCW, it may not seem so unusual when the problems associated with the more general introduction of new technologies are taken into account. The newsworthy examples of computer failures coupled with more numerous mundane examples of unused or underused systems point to a lack in our understanding of the everyday work activities they are designed to support. This is despite considerable effort being devoted to developing methods and approaches for the design of technologies that are appropriate and easy to use. Within the field of human–computer interaction, for example, not only has there been an interest with developing an understanding of how technologies are used by individuals, but also there has been a concern for developing applied findings of relevance for design (Barnard, 1991; Card *et al.*, 1983). Researchers in this field have thus paid considerable attention to the ways in which their findings could be applied to the design of new technologies and to developing methods for supporting a more 'user centred' approach to design (Norman and Draper, 1986). These approaches have drawn on an analytic framework developed within cognitive science, accounting for the behaviour with computer systems in terms of 'mental models', 'task grammars', cognitive schemata and rules (Norman, 1983; Payne and Green, 1986). Such conceptions have informed a range of methods, typically utilising an experimental paradigm, that not only seek to provide an account of human–computer interaction, but also offer ways of evaluating and even suggesting guidelines for the design of computer systems.

Recently, HCI's orientation developed from cognitive psychology and cognitive science, focusing on the individual user, and often utilising an experimental paradigm has been called into question. Too constrained a conception of human–computer interaction appears to overlook the collaborative, social and organisational nature of how conventional technologies are used in everyday settings. Too much emphasis on the use of computers to perform circumscribed experimental tasks neglects the contingent ways in which activities are accomplished. They may also unnecessarily constrain the ways of informing the design of technologies for real-world domains. Hence, consideration has begun to focus on methods and approaches that explore the achievements of participants in naturalistic settings and in developing the ways in which computer use is conceived, particularly with respect to the social and situated nature of this conduct.

With respect to the more practical concerns of designing computer systems, a field has recently emerged that has concentrated on exploring ways of eliciting, describing and specifying user requirements for new technologies. Motivated by the practical problems associated with discovering and defining what users might need from a computer system, requirements engineering has sought to develop techniques for requirements capture, modelling and specification. Within requirements engineering there have been shifts, similar to those in HCI, towards the social. However, despite these initiatives it appears that this approach to a more systematic development of computer technologies also has its short-comings.

Although there have been a number of interesting studies within requirements engineering, the pragmatic concerns of the field have led to a rather curious amalgam of conceptions, models and approaches drawn from a range of disciplines. For example, proposed requirements methods have utilised tools and techniques that break work activities into the distinct tasks performed by individuals, that require naturalistic observation of work practices and which involve facilitators to assist with design meetings. These developments have drawn on a disparate range of work within the social sciences and elsewhere, including task analysis, cybernetics, socio-technical systems, participative approaches towards design and the analysis of group processes within social psychology. Incorporated within a method for design, the derivation and provenance of any technique can become unclear and the associated underlying conceptual assumptions can be masked. Hence, methods proposed to reveal users' requirements often draw on frameworks that are stipulative and tightly circumscribe how the activities under scrutiny are analysed. Although there may be a worthy aim to elicit the requirements of actual users often through some analysis of their current activities, the methods utilised and conceptions adopted may constrain how work activities are examined and what possibilities can be explored to support them.

In recent years, therefore, initiatives in fields associated with the development of new technologies in CSCW, HCI and requirements engineering have all involved a turn towards the social. These have been motivated by quite different concerns, whether these be the demands implied by developments in new technologies, the constraints of existing analytic frameworks or the requirements for novel approaches to the design process. Although a range of methodological orientations could be seen to be relevant to these requirements, there has been particular interest in those that are naturalistic and not stipulative, and account for the contingent and situated nature of organisational activities. However, it is apparent that these demands placed upon CSCW, HCI and requirements engineering cannot be met by a pre-existing set of tools and techniques. It requires that practitioners rethink their current conceptions of everyday work activities in order reconsider the frameworks underpinning current methods both for the analysis of conduct associated with new technologies and for the design of novel systems. The unpicking of how collaborative activities are actually accomplished in workplace settings can thus been seen as a resource for such a reconsideration. It can suggest both ways of reconceptualising key concepts in the analysis of technology-oriented activities and the design of computer systems.

The possibilities afforded by workplace studies for analysis and design have not only been informed by, but also motivated a range of naturalistic case studies of everyday workplace activities, many of which have had a particular concern with the mundane uses of artefacts and technologies in real-world settings. These empirical case studies have stood in stark contrast not only to previous studies of technologically mediated work but also to prior methods for design. They have concentrated on revealing the complexities of everyday social interaction, emphasising the relevance of particular analytic orientations for the examination of empirical materials and drawing out the implications these analyses have for the critical conceptions underpinning the study of work activities.

However, in beginning to reveal the complexity of everyday, collaborative work activities they also reveal the paucity of our current understanding of everyday technologically mediated work. So although workplace studies have been utilised to propose novel designs for technology, extensions to existing design methods and even some possibilities for new approaches to system development, perhaps their more immediate contribution is in outlining the conceptual and methodological innovations required in the social sciences to understand the ways in which artefacts and technologies are utilised in everyday workplaces.

Workplace studies

Workplace studies have arisen in the light of a number of convergent issues and concerns. First, they have been driven by a growing concern, among those in both academia and industry, with the design and deployment of advanced technologies, particularly with a recognition that problems and failures of technologies often derive from our lack of understanding of how ordinary people, in conventional organisational environments, do the things they do. Second, they have arisen in the light of the changing nature of technology, not only the shift towards complex communication systems, but also the growing ability to provide sophisticated support for collaborative activity. Again, in part, the turn towards the social has reflected the possibilities of supporting, in complex ways, people working together. In large part, however, workplace studies have been driven by a concern to develop an understanding of technology which is free from the incumbencies of certain forms of cognitive science, which takes the social and situated seriously, and which drives analytic attention towards the ways people use technologies to accomplish and coordinate their day-to-day practical activities. The practical concerns and implications of workplace studies derive from an analytic agenda, an agenda which is attempting to respecify technology with regard to human practice and social organisation.

Workplace studies have emerged from within various disciplines, including sociology, social anthropology, cognitive science and to some extent computer science. To a large extent many of these workplace studies remain relatively unknown in their original discipline(s), but have had an important impact on interdisciplinary fields such as HCI and more particularly CSCW. Indeed, major interdisciplinary colloquia and conferences such as Computer–Human Interaction (CHI), Computer Supported Cooperative Work (CSCW), and European Conference on Computer Supported Cooperative Work (E-CSCW) are increasingly dominated by papers which interweave workplace studies with more technical concerns. It is interesting to note that despite the diversity of approaches which inform workplace studies, and their wide-ranging concerns in terms of substantive domains and analytic disposition, they retain a number of common characteristics. First, they are principally concerned with the situated organisation of collaborative activities, and the ways in which tools and technologies, objects and artefacts, feature in practical action and interaction in the workplace. Second, they are overwhelmingly naturalistic, ethnographic studies, involving, to use Geertz's (1973) well-used term, 'thick description' of human conduct and cooperation in complex technological environments. Many of these environments, control rooms, newsrooms, financial institutions and the like have been characterised by Suchman (1993b) as 'centres of coordination'. Third, many workplace studies are concerned with reconsidering and re-specifying the concepts and theories which currently infuse our understanding of technology. For example, the idea of the 'user' has been reconsidered in recent years to demonstrate its embeddedness not so much in individual cognitive competencies, but rather in socially organised practice and reasoning which is inseparable from the socially organised activities in which tools and technologies are used. Parallel reconsiderations have been applied to such concepts as 'information', 'communication', 'awareness', 'cooperation' and so forth. Their concern with the contingent and situated character of practical action serves to generate a body of empirical observations and findings concerning the practices and reasoning in and through which participants accomplish and coordinate their actions and activities in the workplace. In this way, they break from the long-standing 'technicism' which Grint and Woolgar (1997), for example, argue pervades both sociological and cognitive studies of technology, and systematically attempt to examine tools and artefacts with regard to the indigenous courses of action and interaction which gives technologies their occasioned, yet determinate sense.

Within this broad set of concerns, however, there are a number of distinct approaches to practical action in the workplace. One of the most surprising developments is found not within sociology or anthropology but within cognitive science. The growing recognition of the importance of the situated and collaborative character of practical action has led to the emergence of 'distributed cognition'. While there is some debate as to the provenance of the approach, and what it actually involves, there would seem to be strong commitment to exploring the ways in which tools and technologies enable participants to develop common understandings and representations of actions and objects, and thereby facilitate cooperation and collaboration. For example Salomon (1993) suggests:

> People appear *to think in conjunction or partnership* with others and with the help of culturally provided tools and implements . . . The thinking of these individuals might be considered to entail not just 'solo' cognitive activities, but *distributed* ones. In other words, it is not just the 'person-solo' who learns, but the 'person-plus,' the whole system of interrelated factors. (Salomon, 1993: xii–xiii, original italics)

The approach has interesting parallels with symbolic interactionism, with its emphasis on the ways in which shared definitions and understandings, themselves the products of social interaction, provide the basis to practical action and collaboration within the workplace. The work of Agre (1997), Hutchins (1995), Rogers (1992) and others who, in various ways, have contributed to our understanding of distributed cognition, especially in organisational environments, also has certain similarities to an approach which developed independently in France, indeed (some suggest) foreshadowed distributed cognition. Commonly known as course-of-action analysis, a number of researchers in ergonomics in France developed an approach not dissimilar to distributed cognition but which emphasised more the ongoing coordination of workplace activities. The approach, emerging in the light of the work of Pinsky and Theureau (Pinsky, 1979; Pinsky and Theureau, 1982, 1992; Theureau, 1991, 1992), is naturalistic, and is principally concerned with explicating the use of tools and technologies from within the courses-of-action in which they are embedded. The approach preserves a commitment to the cognitive, while explicating the ways in which individuals interweave distinct courses of action, often through the assistance of tools and technologies. Like certain forms of distributed cognition, course-of-action analysis preserves the primacy of the individual, and individual cognition, but powerfully demonstrates how representations and action are assembled and disassembled through cooperation and coordination.

A number of other analytic orientations have also informed these workplace studies and begun to generate findings concerning technologically mediated collaborative activity. As suggested, symbolic interactionism, and in particular perhaps the work Strauss (Strauss *et al.*, 1964, 1985), has informed a range of empirical studies and provided a number of conceptual distinctions which have permeated discussions of the social and technical in CSCW (see e.g. Bowker and Star, 1994; Star, 1989). As in other fields, such as education and literary criticism, there has also been a growing interest in drawing on activity theory, as a methodological and conceptual framework for the analysis of workplace activities (see, e.g. Engeström and Escalante, 1996; Kuutti, 1996). Unlike other approaches used in workplace studies, it is sometimes seen as offering a solution to the vexed problem of the 'micro and macro', which even haunts CSCW, a conceptual vehicle for interweaving the fine details of interaction with the broader organisational constraints and circumstances.

However, it is perhaps ethnomethodology and conversation analysis, more than any other analytic orientation, which had the most prevailing influence on these workplace studies and more generally, social science research in CSCW. This is hardly surprising. Suchman's (1987) original critique of cognitive science and HCI drew on ethnomethodology and conversation analysis, and brought such work to the attention of an audience largely unaware of these analytic developments. They also offered a collection of analytic commitments, and a substantial body of empirical findings, which could provide a vehicle for a distinctive approach to the 'interaction' between human beings and computers within the circumstances of the workplace – an approach which placed the occasioned sense of practical action at the forefront of the analytic agenda. It is interesting to note, however, that ethnomethodology and conversation analysis do not themselves offer a unified analytic orientation to practical action and interaction, and as elsewhere, they have provided the basis to a wide diversity of workplace studies which, while all concerned in general with the collaborative production of technological informed organisational activities, reflect a complex array of interests and commitments.

If workplace studies embody a wide range of analytic orientations, they also address a diverse variety of substantive issues and domains. The substantive domains addressed in workplace studies cover a broad range of organisational settings. There is for example a growing corpus of research concerned with what Suchman (1993b) has characterised as 'centres of coordination'. These include studies of air traffic and ground control (C. Goodwin and M. Goodwin, 1996; M. Goodwin, 1990; Harper and Hughes, 1993; Hughes *et al.*, 1988; Suchman, 1993b), of emergency dispatch centres (Whalen, 1995b; Zimmerman, 1992) and the control rooms of rapid urban transport systems (Filippi and Theureau, 1993; Heath and Luff, 1992a, 1996a). In different ways such studies have examined how the members of such settings, in interaction both with each other and those outside the domain, use various tools and technologies to preserve a mutually compatible sense of constantly shifting circumstances and events, and maintain a coordinated response to disparate, and to some extent unpredictable, problems and difficulties with which they deal. There is also a growing body of studies concerned with the use and deployment of technologies in financial institutions. So for example, Harper (1998) has undertake a wide-ranging study of the use of documents in the International Monetary Fund and in a rather different vein, Jirotka and colleagues have examined collaborative work in trading rooms in the City of London (Jirotka *et al.*, 1993; Heath *et al.*, 1994–5).

This emphasis of the practicalities of cooperation, the use of documents and the management of 'normal, natural troubles' are also reflected in studies of rather different domains. So for example Button and Sharrock have undertaken projects on software engineering and examined how personnel order a complex array of concurrent and serially related activities (Button and Sharrock, 1994, 1996). Bowers and Button have examined the deployment and use of 'formal systems' such as workflow models to coordinate and make sense of activities on the shop floor in the printing industry (Bowers and Button, 1995). This interest in the deployment of both social and technical systems is also addressed in studies of the use of email in the civil service (Bowers, 1994), the introduction of information technology for customer services into high street banks (Randall *et al.*, 1995) and the use of medical systems in general medical practice (Greatbatch *et al.*, 1993; Heath and Luff, 1996b).

These and other workplace studies are all naturalistic, and involve extensive fieldwork in the respective settings. Some of the studies, especially those concerned with the interactional organisation of workplace activities, are primarily based on the analysis of video recordings, and direct attention towards the moment-by-moment, collaborative accomplishment of visual, vocal and material conduct. Among workplace studies there is also a growing body of video-based research derived from quasi-naturalistic experiments. These can range from investigations of the deployment of prototype technologies into organisations, such as research laboratories, through to short-term exercises in which subjects are requested to undertake particular tasks. Such experiments have proved invaluable for exploring the use of more advanced, experimental systems, and have helped provide insights into communication and collaboration in more conventional circumstances. So, for example, Heath and Luff (1992b), Gaver *et al.* (1993) and Dourish *et al.* (1996), among others, have undertaken a series of studies exploring interaction, sociability and work among personnel using media space technologies (computing and audio-visual infrastructures designed to support distributed collaborative working) and Bowers *et al.* (1995) and Hindmarsh *et al.*

(1998) have examined the use of virtual environments. In various ways these studies reveal how advanced technologies designed to support distributed collaborative work transform visual and vocal conduct, and can undermine the abilities of participants to establish a mutually coherent sense of objects and their respective environments. In turn these findings have begun to clarify certain practices and presuppositions found in collaborative work in co-located environments such as control centres (cf. Heath and Hindmarsh, 1997).

Despite the varied domains and issues addressed by such analyses these workplace studies share a number of analytic commitments and interests. Aside from their methodological orientation, we find a principal concern with the contingent and situated character of practical organisational conduct, and in explicating the resources on which participants themselves rely in producing and coordinating their actions and activities with each other. They also share an interest in technology, not only an applied concern in using naturalistic research to inform the design, evaluation and deployment of new tools and artefacts, but more importantly perhaps in using studies of work to reconsider the ways in which we understand the relationship between human action and objects, whether highly complex or truly simple. Indeed, perhaps the most significant contribution of these workplace studies are the ways in which they are placing tool or artefact mediated conduct at the heart of the analytic agenda, and attempting to reconceptualise technology, and in particular reveal how the use and intelligibility of objects is produced and constituted in and through social action and interaction. Finally, in various ways, such studies are providing a vehicle to question a common body of issues and concerns which underpin more traditional research concerned with technology and organisational conduct in both the cognitive and social sciences; that is that they are throwing into relief the empirical and theoretical shortcomings of studies in HCI, organisational behaviour, and CSCW, that indigenous social action can be adequately accounted for with regard to rules, plans and procedures which are insensitive to the ways in which participants themselves accomplish their conduct in particular situations and circumstances. It is their concern with the tacit, seen but unnoticed, indigenous resources which inform the production and coordination of *in situ* technologically mediated conduct which unites these workplace studies.

Implications

The growing dissatisfaction with more traditional research in HCI and cognitive science, coupled with the emergence of CSCW and the growing interest in developing systems to support collaborative work, have played an important part in the emergence of workplace studies. These academic developments have been fuelled by the problems which have arisen with the design and deployment of major technologies, reflected in press coverage of various organisational disasters (e.g. TAURUS, see T. Collins and Bicknell, 1997). These systems failures have contributed to the widespread recognition that we need to abandon the long-standing assumption that complex systems will stimulate efficient changes in work practice. Rather, there are calls to develop approaches more sensitive to the settings and situations in which new technologies are deployed.

The emergence of naturalistic studies of the workplace has begun to reveal the essentially situated and contingent character of collaboration and technology use. Such a sensitivity has been used to respecify understandings of foundational (and taken-for-granted) concepts in the areas of HCI, CSCW and even the practical world of systems design. For example, Suchman's (1987) study of photocopier use reconsidered the plan-based model of human conduct extremely prevalent within expert systems design, HCI, artificial intelligence and cognitive science. Workplace studies have similarly attempted the respecification of concepts such as 'user', 'task', 'context' and even 'collaboration' itself. As a result the findings from these studies can be seen to have made a powerful contribution to the ways in which these fields conceive of the workplace and the activities therein. They have highlighted the complexity of the everyday, tacit resources and activities that underpin collaborative work. In turn, they have provided directions for designers who attempt to envisage and develop new technologies to support (collaborative) work.

These alternate conceptions and observations of work drawn from workplace studies have begun to be utilised within the general development of workplace technologies. For example, studies in a range of domains have suggested to designers how it may be necessary to provide individuals with peripheral awareness of another's conduct. Hence, developers of a variety of collaborative technologies, including audiovisual infrastructures, collaborative virtual environments and even more asynchronous kinds of support have explored ways of providing different types of awareness and participation in their systems. Thus, findings from workplace studies are having an influence on such diverse developments as CSCW systems, ubiquitous computing, virtual reality technologies and mobile devices.

As well as generating new concepts to inform more general design concerns, workplace studies have also been used to examine particular technologies and domains. There have been numerous attempts to generate requirements for new technologies or comment on proposals for techno-logical change from a detailed understanding of the interactional produc-tion of activities in specific domains. From these naturalistic studies, it is often possible to outline key features of the work which appear relevant to the participants and which may have consequences for any future deploy-ment of technology.

For example, from a study of the work of traders in a financial dealing room, Jirotka et al. (1993) were able to comment on proposals by a tech-nology development company to introduce a new 'deal capture' system for traders. The company was considering developing a voice recognition system to overcome current problems associated with the hand-written recording of deals, where deals were recorded on paper tickets and input-ted into the computer by other personnel some time later. The proposed system aimed to 'capture' the contents of a 'deal' as it was made on the phone. Jirotka et al.'s study not only revealed some shortcomings of the developers' assumptions concerning the nature of dealing, such as the amount and nature of the activities carried out on the phone, but also highlighted the collaborative nature of financial trading – both between traders on the phone and with colleagues in the same trading room. These comments led the company to rethink its proposed development. From the analysis, Jirotka et al. were also able to propose alternative tech-nologies (e.g. digital pen-based systems) which might support the traders, suggestions that would be more sensitive to the collaborative pro-duction of the work.

Workplace studies facilitate a close look at current practices in a domain, which can usefully inform the development and introduction of new systems. This kind of sensitivity to current practices would seem crit-ical if designers are to avoid impeding staff in their everyday activities, indeed to avoid the kinds of disaster that can develop from technologies which impose an 'operational straitjacket' on workers (cf. Page et al., 1993). This is not to suggest that these studies of work merely attempt to replicate current work practices. Rather, they provide understandings of the essential user requirements from which to base thinking about the potential impact of candidate technologies. Moreover, and as mentioned above, they are also being used to inform the development of completely new, 'virtual' workplaces. Understandings of collaboration drawn from workplace studies are contributing to, and shaping the development of, advanced technologies to support distributed work, namely media spaces and collaborative virtual environments (Bowers et al., 1995, 1996; Hindmarsh et al., 1998).

In various ways then, researchers undertaking workplace studies have sought to show how their ethnographies and fieldwork reveal issues of direct relevance to any system that would be implemented for that workplace or for the general development of technologies to support collaborative work. It is inevitable, then, that practitioners have begun to consider how findings from workplace studies or the accomplishment of fieldwork can be transformed into design guidelines or 'methods' for design (e.g. Randall *et al.*, 1994); a related concern being how to present ethnographic materials and findings in such a form as to be both clear and useful to designers. The traditional 'thick descriptions' of ethnography, though revealing the important detail of workplace activities, are not amenable to the transformation into design guidelines. Indeed, such transformations are likely to gloss the very nature of the activities that the orientation makes visible. Similarly, though designers may seek ways of abstracting and generalising user requirements, methods that seek to formalise these may end up replicating the stipulative character of those approaches they are seeking to replace.

It could be that workplace studies themselves suggest ways in which system development processes could be transformed. For example, Button and Sharrock's (1994) study of software engineers reveals how the developers of a system contingently made use of design principles, methodologies and tools in their work in order to accomplish the organisational demands of the setting in which they worked. To get the work done, the engineers reversed the prescribed order of activities, producing requirements following from a design, used tools contingently for their particular purposes rather than within the confines of the methodology and were oriented to other demands of professional practices. Conventional development methods, particularly those that are highly prescriptive and force a rigid adherence to a sequential process, often overlook such organisational contingencies. In proposing any tools, techniques and methods that draw from workplace studies it may be worth considering how such tools would be utilised for the practical purposes of software designers, that resonate with their own work practices and that are sensitive to their own particular organisational demands.

The influence of these varied contributions to the broad field of CSCW and systems design can be gauged from the calls by computer scientists themselves, for their colleagues to take seriously the tacit features of human conduct (e.g. Brown and Duguid, 1994; Goguen, 1994; Moran and Anderson, 1990; Potts and Newstetter, 1997; Sommerville *et al.*, 1993b), from the growing number and strength of links between various academic computer science departments and social scientists and from the number of large industrial research laboratories that are utilising naturalistic studies of work as part of the systems development activity. This reveals another aspect of the ways in which workplace studies are described and discussed. Throughout the literature, the central concern is with the contributions that social science can make to computer science and the implications that such studies have for the design and development of new technologies. However, little is said about the importance for social science (and social scientists) of the opportunities to investigate technology use in the workplace. Indeed, workplace studies have facilitated the reassessment of a series of critical debates in the social sciences.

For example, alongside the rapid expansion of technological innovation, sociologists have increasingly become concerned with the role(s) of technology in society. Numerous approaches to the study of technology have emerged to consider how technology shapes society, how societal forces shape the development of technologies (Mackenzie and Wajcman, 1985) and how we construct the 'meaning' of technology (Woolgar, 1991). However, as Button (1993a) argues, throughout these various approaches the technology in question strangely remains epiphenomenal to the analysis. The focus tends to remain on traditional sociological concerns – class, gender, power and so forth. Workplace studies on the other hand forefront the technology and its situated intelligibility through the explication of the collaborative practices in and through which it is constituted. As Button (1993a) argues:

> technology is socially achieved in the social practices through which people recognisably and accountably orientate to technology in the course of its design, construction, development, implementation, its use, and in talking and writing about it, as these matters are accountably located in the specifics of their achievement in the local circumstances of their display. (Button, 1993a: 25)

Furthermore, the analysis of collaborative work to be found in workplace studies stands in stark contrast to current approaches to the study of work and organisations. Whereas these often examine large-scale organisational change, workplace studies turn the spotlight on the local production of work and organisation. Indeed, the very same concepts that prove of interest in CSCW, are also usefully respecified in social scientific studies of work, namely 'task', 'division of labour' and 'organisation'. In such a way, these naturalistic studies can be seen to be energising the study of work and organisations, revealing (to both CSCW *and* social science) the critical importance of investigating the tacit and interactional features of workplace activity.

Outline of book

This collection is divided into two related parts. The first includes reports of several diverse workplace studies and discussions of key conceptual and methodological issues that they raise. The second part focuses on the range of problems, issues and potential solutions that emerge when drawing implications from workplace studies for the design of technology. In each part, longer chapters and investigations are followed by shorter discussion papers. These papers focus on critical topics of concern for workplace studies and relate these to recent developments in other related fields, including CSCW, HCI and software engineering.

The first part illustrates the variety of approaches that have come to be considered as 'workplace studies'. As such they reveal how different methodological approaches, including ethnomethodology, conversation analysis and course-of-action analysis, are brought to bear upon naturalistic materials. These studies not only reveal features of the work and interaction of the participants in the particular domains in question, but also raise more general issues regarding how workplace activities are conceived within the social sciences. The shorter chapters take up particular aspects of these issues, for example the relationships workplace studies have to organisational change and development, and discuss the ways in which different methodological orientations utilise such conceptions. These discussions not only raise critical differences between different methodological orientations emerging from the social sciences, activity theory and cognitive science, but also highlight their role within such fields as CSCW.

In chapter 2 Lucy Suchman considers, through the practices surrounding document production in a law firm, different conceptions of 'knowledge' and 'routine' work. She focuses on the activities surrounding the processing of documents in corporate cases where these can number in the hundreds of thousands, and reveals the practical reasoning and situated judgements involved in coding these documents. Suchman draws upon the distinction between subjective and objective coding used to describe such work to relate these practices to recent debates concerning 'status' and 'knowledge work'.

In quite a different way Graham Button and Wes Sharrock (chapter 3) consider the organisational relevance of particular documents in the workplace. They explore the uses of a particular form, the Fault Report Form, within the work and interaction of systems engineers. In particular, their analysis reveals how, through the engineers' talk, the forms are transformed into a shape in which they can identify and possibly solve engineering problems. Button and Sharrock examine how this discussion emerges locally, turn-by-turn, an analysis which can be juxtaposed with recent attempts to prescribe more global structures to such meetings in the context of design.

Jacques Theureau and Geneviève Filippi (chapter 4) explore the activities in a setting which has been a rich domain for recent studies exploring work and interaction: the control room of a transportation system. However, as well as examining the fine-grained details of interaction among participants in the RER A Control Room of the Paris Metro, Theureau and Filippi draw on a course-of-action framework to explore longer-term co-participation. Hence, they analyse the activities of the controllers and colleagues in terms of the synchronic and diachronic organisations of the work and the relationship between the two. From this analysis Theureau and Filippi not only highlight the distinctiveness of their approach, but also draw out some implications for new technologies in the setting.

In chapter 5, Jack Whalen and Erik Vinkhuyzen focus on the detailed use of a technology in a real-world setting: an 'expert' computer system designed to support the personnel who answer calls regarding problems with the machines produced by a large corporation. Through detailed analysis of the talk of the participants and operations on the system, Whalen and Vinkhuyzen reveal the common-sense reasoning and competencies of the call-takers in using the system while they are talking on the phone. This is an analysis that is distinctive from those typically carried out within the field of human–computer interaction. Moreover, in analysing the moment-to-moment use of an expert system, Whalen and Vinkhuyzen not only discuss issues of concern to those developing such technologies within artificial intelligence and allied fields, but also reflect on distinctions regarding the conceptions of knowledge, expertise and intelligence raised by Suchman in her chapter.

Kjeld Schmidt (chapter 6) draws on such conceptual debates to highlight the contributions that workplace studies can make to CSCW. He emphasises that the critical nature of this contribution need not be in terms of specific design decisions, but rather in a far more fundamental rethinking of the conceptual foundation to CSCW. As examples, Schmidt charts the respecification of key terms such as 'goal', 'shared knowledge' and 'awareness' by a range of workplace studies.

In his discussion paper, Yrjö Engeström (chapter 7) raises a critical concern with many workplace studies – that they are unable to manage or cope with organisational change. He suggests that ethnographic studies have been rather preoccupied with observing and understanding stable orders of activity. Hence, he outlines an alternative approach drawn from activity theory and development research which focuses on the possibility of particular kinds of intervention when dealing with organisational change.

As has already been mentioned, there have been numerous exercises in which social scientists have been involved which have resulted in proposals for particular technologies to support work activities, the assessment of systems in use or the consideration of novel generic tools, devices or products. Chapters in the second part of this collection discuss some of the issues raised by the interrelationship between workplace studies and various design activities, and report some of the problems which have been found and propose initial solutions, strategies and techniques to address these problems. The problems may be practical. For example, if a workplace study is to be considered an explicit part of a design exercise then there are likely to be constraints on the length of time the study takes, there may be difficulties communicating any results to others within a multidisciplinary team and there may be a whole range of managerial problems associated with siting such an exercise within an organisational context. Although the longer chapters each focus on one of these practical issues, in doing so they raise more general concerns regarding the relationship between workplace studies and disciplines associated with the development of technology. Some of these concerns, which reflect the very different nature of the activities undertaken within social science, software engineering, research and design, are discussed in each of the discussion papers.

In chapter 8, Richard H. R. Harper draws on his extensive study of the IMF to suggest that a study based on an ethnomethodological orientation and the technological focus behind a particular design exercise may complement each other in various ways. Reflecting on his fieldwork in the IMF, Harper comments on how having a concern with the ways in which technologies could support an activity can actually help focus a workplace study, and that this can be accomplished without unduly constraining the study or moving attention away from the particular ways in which work is accomplished. He illustrates this in an examination of the activities of desk officers within the IMF and discusses how this study related to actual proposals for the deployment of technologies within the organisation.

John Hughes and his colleagues (chapter 9) explore a different practical problem concerning the relationship between social science and design. They focus on the problems of communication between ethnographers and designers within a design project, particularly on the difficulties associated with presenting detailed ethnographic materials, such as rich textual notes, semi-structured interviews, transcripts and diagrams of a work setting. To assist with this problem they propose that as well as having some framework to shape the ethnography, technologies themselves can help in the process. They propose a tool – the Designers' NotePad (DNP) – that allows information gathered through fieldwork to be flexibly managed within an ongoing design activity. They illustrate the DNP with materials drawn from a recent case study of a Lending Centre of a bank; the tool allows fieldworkers to present different viewpoints of the work, not only the physical layout but also the flows of activities and the perspectives of the participants, to others in the design process.

Whereas Harper and Hughes *et al.* explore particular issues that concern the practical difficulties of relating workplace studies to design, in chapter 10 Bob Anderson looks at the problems more generally. He considers what constrains workplace studies actually being part of everyday design processes within large organisations, particularly within corporate research and development divisions. By considering recent developments for the management of engineering projects and concerns expressed within the management literature, Anderson outlines some requirements for design methods and methodologies from the perspective of the organisation in which they could be deployed. This institutional perspective raises a great range of challenging problems for those wishing to see workplace studies being utilised within organisations. It also, as Anderson suggests, may reveal other ways in which workplace studies might inform the production of technology. It may be that by focusing on the usability of technologies and the requirements of users, researchers have neglected other areas such as the envisionment of markets and new products where workplace studies could also have a role.

This is not to say that relating the findings of workplace studies to those fields concerned with the usability of technologies and the requirements of users is straightforward. The authors of the discussion papers in this part discuss the difficulties associated with two particular fields – human–computer interaction and requirements engineering – and design more generally, to which workplace studies would seem to offer a relevant contribution. Indeed, Liam J. Bannon (chapter 11) notes that although ethnographic studies and ethnomethodological critiques have helped 'raise consciousness' to organisational and social issues within HCI, they are far from having the hoped-for impact on the conceptual underpinnings of the subject. These remain firmly within the psychological tradition on which the field was founded. Bannon suggests that this may be due to the academic and research oriented nature of the field and goes on to note some other ways in which such studies could influence design.

Marina Jirotka and Lincoln Wallen (chapter 12) discuss the potential of workplace studies to inform requirements engineering. They note that because a proposed technology will interact with or affect work practices, software engineers require an understanding of the domain as a socially ordered environment. Workplace studies of particular kinds appear to offer potential support for this activity, particularly in providing resources for warranting an analysis of requirements or a justification for a proposed technology. However, they note that the goal of the requirements engineer through the development of a technology is usually to transform a particular (or many) work setting(s). Because of this motivation, utilising workplace studies within a software engineering context requires several critical challenges to be faced, particularly with regard to how such studies can be consistent with the engineers' demands for generalisation and prediction.

In the final discussion paper, Thomas Erickson (chapter 13) also notes that the demands, constraints and motivations of social scientists differ from those of designers. He argues that particularly because of the aforementioned problems associated with time and resources within a design project that, as they stand, workplace studies are unlikely to be part of design practice. Hence, utilising an approach drawn from architecture and urban design he proposes a way of generalising workplace studies and presenting their findings. Erickson proposes presenting the findings of workplace studies in terms of pattern languages which can be easily communicated to designers and even reused if necessary. He illustrates this approach by sketching out how such a pattern language might emerge if developed from a recent field study.

As may be ascertained from the brief outlines of the chapters in this collection, workplace studies are concerned not only with a wide range of settings – included here are studies of international bureaucratic organisations, banks, control rooms, customer services, law firms and groups involved in software engineering – but also with a range of issues relating to the social organisation of the workplace activities and the ways in which we conceive of tasks, activities and the uses of technologies. Workplace studies, by focusing on the mundane details of everyday activities in natural settings, provide some novel resources for exploring some continuing themes in the sociology of work, organisational behaviour and the social sciences more generally. Despite drawing on a range of related, but distinct, analytic orientations, they suggest ways in which the uses of technology, the conceptions of skills and expertise, and the distinctions between individual and social activities can be rethought.

Part 1

Exploring the workplace

2 Making a case: 'knowledge' and 'routine' work in document production

Lucy Suchman

Introduction

> Discursive practices are used by members of a profession to shape
> events in the domains subject to their professional scrutiny. The shaping
> process creates the objects of knowledge that become the insignia of a
> profession's craft: the theories, artifacts and bodies of expertise that dis-
> tinguish it from other professions. Analysis of the methods used by
> members of a community to build and contest the events that structure
> their lifeworld contributes to the development of a practice-based
> theory of knowledge and action. (C. Goodwin, 1994: 606)

The emergence of 'information' as the dominant commodity of the late
twentieth century has brought with it an accompanying preoccupation
with 'knowledge work' as the defining form of labour. At least implicitly,
knowledge work stands always in contrast with certain other, persistent
forms of work that are taken not to involve the active production and use
of information. These latter may be either the residue of so-called
'manual' labour, or mediating processes in the operation of information
technologies that remain to be automated, still requiring human interventions but otherwise defined as routine (data input being the prototypical
case).

A starting concern of this chapter is how, in reproducing oppositions of
mental versus manual, the discourse of knowledge versus routine work
sustains old assumptions as a basis for conceptualising new relations of
work and technology. Developing an alternative to these traditional conceptualisations requires that we re-examine the basic premises about
knowledge on which they rest. One by now common-sense premise is that
professionalised forms of labour have grown up around particular bodies
of specialist knowledge, held, maintained and developed by profession
members. This premise is supported by a combination of professional
mythology and widely, albeit vaguely held assumptions about what particular forms of professional practice actually entail. Even within a particular profession, prevailing conceptualisations and available discourses

may highlight certain aspects of the practice, while rendering others invisible.

My premise in this chapter is that images of work are systematically biased to highlight judgemental, interpretive work among the professions, while obscuring the work's mundane, practical aspects. Commensurately, mundane, practical activity is foregrounded in so-called routine forms of work, while reasoning is relegated to the background. This premise is shared among a growing body of researchers interested in the analysis of forms of professional work as everyday practice, on the one hand, and on the elucidation of routine or 'invisible work' as practical reasoning, on the other.[1] Both approaches comprise steps toward the development of a richer, more nuanced and less dichotomised analysis of relations among different forms of work. This study is meant as a further contribution to that effort, through a comparison of two forms of work as, rather than sorting nicely into the two available categories of knowledge and routine, each combining elements of both. The strategy is to disrupt the received dualisms of knowledge/routine through an analysis that works across the boundary.[2]

A critical element in the reworking of traditional views on the character of knowledge is reflected in the epigraph from Goodwin above. This involves the inversion of a conceptualisation that takes knowledge as a body of propositions existing prior to, and enabling of, professional practice, to an understanding of professional knowledge as produced and reproduced through the specific practices that comprise profession members' everyday activity. Within ethnomethodological studies of work this inversion has provided fruitful directions for research (see e.g. Garfinkel, 1986; Garfinkel *et al.*, 1981; Lynch, 1993; D. E. Smith, 1993). And among the various strategies of professional knowledge production identified, practices of *coding* have received particular attention (see Garfinkel, 1967; Lynch, 1991; Wieder, 1970; Zimmerman, 1974). So, for example, Goodwin (1994) identifies practices of coding involving the transformation of 'phenomena observed in a specific setting into the objects of knowledge that animate the discourse of a profession' as central to the construction and contestation of what he names 'professional vision, which consists of socially organised ways of seeing and understanding events that are answerable to the distinctive interests of a particular social group' (C. Goodwin, 1994: 606).[3] Through coding schemes, reasoning is enlisted in the production of distinctive objects of knowledge, relevant to particular systems of activity. In this chapter I consider how objects of knowledge are differentiated not only between members of distinctive professions, but among participants within a given site of professional practice.

Cross-cutting the oppositions of mental/manual, knowledge/routine already mentioned are other, prior dualisms allied with ideologies of scientific method as the paradigmatic means of knowledge production. Of these, among the most powerful has been the distinction between 'subjective' and 'objective' ways of knowing. My interest here is in how the theme of 'subjective' versus 'objective' knowledge acts as what ethnomethodologists, following Sacks (1972), term a 'categorisation device' (see also Coulter, 1991). Such devices are among the fundamental methods by which we order the social world. In this case, moreover, the work that is being categorised by the subjective/objective opposition – that of reading and indexing documents implicated in law suits – itself involves practices of coding or categorisation, and a corresponding division of labour among lawyers and temporary workers. Specifically, distinctions among organisation members are based on the characterisation of their coding activity as either 'subjective' or 'objective'. On that distinction, in turn, rest associated differences of identity and reward.

Document production

Within the practice of law, documentary evidence provides the material grounds for the construction of legal arguments.[4] Where clients are corporations, each case includes a legally binding process known as 'document production', in which business documents (memos, correspondence, financial reports and the like), often numbering in the hundreds of thousands, are taken by a defending firm from the client organisation's files and copies are turned over to the other side. The same corpus of 'responsive' documents then provides the basis for both defence and prosecution. Lawyers on both sides are faced with the problem of locating within these very large document corpora those relatively few documents relevant to the construction of the case. To aid in that search, the set of responsive documents may be 'computerised', that is, each document is abstracted into a standard form, the abstracts are entered into a database, and the database can then be queried according to various criteria of interest to lawyers.

The 'processing' of documents from raw material into the refined product of the firm is organised hierarchically, such that as one moves 'up' in the firm one is required to handle progressively fewer and more pre-selected document sets. At the outset of a production process, the entire document corpus is reviewed by 'junior' lawyers, relatively new to the practice and to the firm. Documents identified as responsive are then coded by the lawyers in terms of their relevance (their relative degree of 'hotness') and their relation to the various substantive issues in the case.

Subsequently, the same documents are coded by temporary workers, employed within the firm's 'litigation support' department. The object of their coding activity is the creation of the database index to the entire document set. Through these practices of coding, the corpus is transformed from documents created and used in the context of multiple, heterogeneous and often unrelated activities within the client organisation into interrelated objects of knowledge relevant within the specific activity of making a case (see C. Goodwin, 1994: 606).

Subjectivity and objectivity as members' categories

The question that provides the focus of this chapter is how it is that lawyers and litigation support workers are seen, by themselves and other organisation members, to be reading the same documents in categorically different ways. For members of the firm, the difference is characterised as a distinction between 'subjective' coding, done by lawyers, and 'objective' coding, done by document coders employed within litigation support. Document production in this sense is a perspicuous site in which to look more closely at the workings of the subjective/objective distinction as a categorisation device, in that the distinction is explicitly relevant for organisation members themselves and plays a 'prominent vernacular role' in their work (Lynch, 1993: 300).

My strategy in what follows is to question the opposition of 'knowledge' and 'routine' work by considering in detail the work of subjective and objective coding, as done by lawyers and document coders respectively.[5] My approach to comparing these two forms of work is to attempt a symmetrical analysis, considering each under the thematic headings of *material practice* and *accountability*. By material practice I mean the ways in which each form of work is organised by the mundane troubles and practical resources findable in the work's materials, in this case, primarily paper documents. Accountability comprises how it is that practitioners articulate their actions as sensible and responsible, given their particular identities and organisational positionings. Together, I take these topics as referencing central aspects of what it means to do the work in a recognisably competent way.

Within this attempt at symmetry, however, I shall deliberately foreground contrasting aspects of these two forms of coding practice in my analysis. That is, in looking at the work of so-called subjective coding, asserted by organisation members to be distinguished by the interpretive judgements it requires, I shall be emphasising instead its observably mundane, practical and routine characteristics. Correspondingly, in looking at the work of objective coding, characterised by organisation

Figure 2.1 A junior lawyer with documents

members as a kind of non-judgemental reading of of documents for their
self-evident properties, I shall attempt to highlight problems of interpretation and judgement that frequently arise. My point in proceeding in this
way is not simply to invert the opposition of subjective and objective
coding, but to show the hybrid, practical and judgemental character of
both forms of work. My hope is that, having displaced the simple opposition between the practices of lawyers and document coders as one of
knowledge versus routine work, we might begin to respecify their works'
differences in new terms.

The material practice of subjective coding

Lynch (1993) proposes that

equipmental complexes can be treated . . . as matrices for human conduct that do
not simply provide places where human beings work but instead provide distinctive phenomenal fields in which organisations of 'work' are established and exhibited. (Lynch, 1993: 132)

For S, a junior lawyer at the firm, the day's work is visibly manifest as a
horizon of documents arranged around her workspace (see figure 2.1).

These are ordered within ordinary moving boxes, labelled on the outside with a range of numbers representing the first and last page within the box.[6] By their arrangement and their sequential numbering each box can be read as a course of work to be done or already completed.

Within each box, stacks of documents are encircled by rubber bands, which mark how the original documents were grouped together in the client's files (e.g. with staples, paper clips, within file folders). S uses the rubber-banded stacks as the organising unit for her work, in so far as she takes documents from the box in those groupings, sets them in front of her on her desk and works through each pile in turn. At the same time, she cannot simply maintain the groupings as they are, since the coding categories that she is using cut across the order represented by the stacks.

To get an initial sense of the material order of the work of subjective coding we can look at an exchange at the beginning of our visit with S, where we ask her to tell us about what she was in the midst of doing when we arrived. She explains:

00:12:56:14

s: I'm on a box [reading from front of box] document number, or page number, ACAD059385, that's the ending number for this box. And um [turning to the stack on her desk, leafing through pages as she talks] I've been, I'm looking right now at a set of documents that are, that look like newspaper articles about the company. This is something that the plaintiffs specifically requested from us, anything that we had in our files, newspaper articles that mentioned our company. And so I've been going through, and I would just write down [on a yellow legal pad] the first, the number of the first article that I had, and then I would go to, I would just flip through and make sure these [the documents in the stack] were all the same thing, and I've looked at them before so I know what they are, and I would just go to the last number, and the last number of this particular set is 057951 [writing down on legal pad]. And I'd actually write this down, the set [hand gesture indicating a span] the bracket, because these are all belonging in the same category. And then I'd say it's 18, 'cause category 18 is [reading from master code list] 'articles and press, press releases or analysts' reports'.

ls: And at this point you don't really actually care what these articles are about, you just need to know that they are about the firm.

s: Right. If they're labelled with white [Post-its™], I would also give them a 1, 2, 3 coding as well.

ls: Okay, because you did go through them before, and if as you went through that time you'd seen one that you actually thought was substantively relevant

s: Exactly

ls: You would flag it.

s: And so for example if I [takes top document from stack and examines it, enacting what she would do] let's say that this one were labelled already with a white tag then I would say, Oh, okay I have to look at it now and I have to decide where on the stratum of hot I think that this belongs. Well, it's interesting but

it's not really relevant, you know, so I'd just give it a 3 and I'd put it in my third
category over here as 3, next to the document [number].

LS: Okay, so this pile, this upside down pile [on the desk] you've been through.

S: Right.

S's work relies in part on her ability to recognise conventional document
formats, enabling her to code an entire stack of documents simply by
looking at the first page, then looking through to make sure there are no
other document types within the stack. Her work is often, then, simply a
matter of scanning a stack to determine whether all of the documents
within it are 'of a kind'. This assessment is informed by a prior review of the
documents, during which S and other junior lawyers decided which of all
of the documents taken from the client's files were 'responsive' and would
need to be turned over to the opposing firm. During that review the documents were also marked by S with coloured Post-its™ to indicate various
aspects of their status (e.g. 'hot', non-responsive, confidential), then sent
to another group of workers, called case assistants, who remove the non-
responsive documents from the set. The responsive documents are then
returned to S for coding. This means that her inspection of the documents
is now being done as a second time through: a familiarity that informs her
seeing. The Post-its™ at this point serve as markers for work postponed,
highlighting a document in order that it should stand out during coding as
a document to which S needs to pay closer attention.[7] Put another way, the
Post-it™ identifies the document as a member of the category 'hot', while
deferring for later the question of just what its relevance is to the case:

00:39:15:15

S: [takes large stack from box, removes rubber band] These are financial statements [flipping through] they look like for the entire year, they're not particularly hot [writes first and last page numbers down on pad, replaces rubber
band, puts face down on top of completed stacks, stands up and takes all of
remaining stacks out of the box]. Sometimes the entire folder will be exactly
the same [looking through stacks]. Is this the same issue? Okay, this one [top
stack] looks slightly different, so I'll look at it. This looks like, it says here on
the front 'restructuring notes', there was a big reorganisation of the company,
which they've asked for information about, and this entire folder does look
like it deals with the organisational restructuring of the company [writing].
So that's category 14. And this [single document] looks like it's labelled hot.
And it's number 2 because it's just something that I know we're gonna need,
it's got [showing organisation chart] where everyone sits, but it doesn't really
matter that much, we'll just have to use it later on. Again, organisational
structure [writing down numbers, takes up next stack]. Then this whole
folder looks like [flipping through] historical sales information.

Subjective coding, in sum, makes use of and makes possible (a) strategies
for the efficient manipulation of documents as stacks that are 'the same'

for present purposes (e.g. all newspaper articles), (b) the appearance of documents as conventional types (e.g. financial reports, organisation charts), which are identified, in turn, as categorically relevant or not to the interests of the case and (c) assessments of the significance of specific documents (e.g. a particular financial report found in the files of a particular organisation member, or a particular organisation chart). Which of these assessments comes into play depends in part on the point in the course of the production process where the work gets done. At the point of subjective coding, most document stacks are simply categorised as a whole. So at this point the relevant features of the documents for S are largely categorical, and are distinctions that can be seen at a glance.

Accountability in subjective coding

S's coding work is guided by a master list of codes or 'issue list' (see figure 2.2). The list of issue codes is developed by S and her co-workers in discussion with more senior lawyers on the case, and then serves as a standardised scheme to be used in subjective coding. The default relevance coding for documents in the set is a '3', indicating that while the documents are responsive (that is, within a time period specified by the court, taken from an implicated organisation members' files, within a category explicitly requested, and so on) and need to be turned over to the opposing side, they are judged irrelevant to the issues of the case. Documents coded either '2' or '1' (those flagged by a white Post-it™ during review) are assessed during coding either as 'relevant, but not hot' or 'hot document' respectively.

An identifying mark of S's coding practice is her positioning of herself as author of, and therefore responsible for, the coding scheme that guides her actions. This includes deciding that a category is good enough, reassessing previous assignments, creating new categories, and taking responsibility for the adequacy of the categorisation scheme itself. S's assignment of documents to categories of relevance, including what constitutes adequate categorisation, is informed by what she knows about the case and about the document corpus:

00:35:35:02
S: It's a very subjective determination at that point. Um, you know what belongs in a 1 and what belongs in 2. I just, I mean, I know the case and I know that this [indicating document in her hand] is the kind of thing that's interesting to have, but it's not going to make or break either our case or the other side's case. I mean another person could look at it and make a different determination.
JB: How long have you been involved with this case?

ISSUE LIST
(as of 6/5/92)

```
1.    Inventory levels
2.    Sales and financial forecasts
      2.1  Historical Reports of Sales
      2.2  Forecasted Sales
      2.3  Budgets
3.    Resignation (Green)
4.    Insiders purchase/sales of stock; motives for sales by
      individual defendants during the class period.
5.    Decreasing profit margins
6.    External guidance to street; analyst contacts
7.    Internal forecasts: shortfall in revenues
8.    Accounts Receivable, Collections
9.    Management; internal dissention or criticism of management
      policies, actions or decisions
10.   Backlog
11.   Shipments/Revenue Recognition
12.   Pricing/Discounting
13.   Distributors
14.   Company reorganization split into 5 business groups
15.   Information Letter #14
16.   Canada
17.   Other Asia
18.   Articles in press, Press Releases, Analysts Reports
19.   Stock repurchase
20.   Accounting controls
```

Key Document Information

```
1.    Hot document
2.    Relevant but not hot
3.    Not relevant
```

Figure 2.2 The issue list

S: Since the very beginning. And it was filed back in February. I mean I've actu-
     ally, I'm probably the only person who's been in every aspect of the case other
     than B [a senior attorney]. Um, you know like every telephone call with the
     other side, every court appearance, everything, you know I've gone to the
     client's and all their meetings and stuff like that. And I'm in charge of the pro-
     duction, so I've been doing most of it.

While the master code sheet acts as a set of instructions for S, then, it is
read in relation to her own participation both in its development and in a
range of other interactions with clients and co-workers. This positioning
of herself in relation to the coding scheme and the developing case stands
in contrast with the work of objective coding, wherein documents are
coded onto a standard form created by authorities other than the coders
themselves, who have in turn no direct interaction with the actors and
events of the case (see C. Goodwin, 1994: 609).

Figure 2.3 Working with documents

The material practice of objective coding

T is a document coder at the firm, employed as a temporary worker within the firm's in-house litigation support department. At the time of our visit with T he had been at the firm for about three and a half months, and had worked on five or six cases. T told us that he has a bachelor of arts degree in psychology, and has worked previously as an admissions counsellor and manager of a retail sporting goods store.

T's work involves a series of translations from the documents themselves to fields on a standard form (see figures 2.3 and 2.4). Like S, T's work is organised by boxes of documents. But unlike lawyers doing subjective coding, who can assign a single code to multiple documents, document coders must actually treat each document separately, assigning a separate code sheet to each document. Coding documents individually requires in turn designating what in each stack is to be treated as a single document. This is not as obvious a judgement as it may at first seem, as documents when they come to the document coders do not wear their identities on their sleeves. Rather, as for the lawyers, they come in the form of cardboard boxes full of paper.

DUPDOC TABLE:

DUPLICATE OF: _ _ _ _ _ _ _ _   -   _ _ _ _ _ _ _ _ _

DOC TABLE:

Beg Bates: _ _ _ _ _ _ _ _   End Bates: _ _ _ _ _ _ _ _ _

Estimated : [ ]   Date: ___ - ___ - ___   Worth: 1   2   3   N

Doc. Type:_____   Source: _____

File Title:_ ☐ _____ ☐ EST

Date Prod: - -   Attached To: _____

DOCFLDS TABLE:

Redacted: Y   N

ISSUES TABLE:

Description: (Issue 1)_____

_____

_____

_____

_____

_____

_____

☐ MARGINALIA:

ISSUES:

____ ____ ____ ____ ____ ____ ____

NAMES TABLE:

Name: [ ]	Name: [ ]
Role: A R M C S PA PR	Role: A R M C S PA PR
[ ]	[ ]
Role: A R M C S PA PR	Role: A R M C S PA PR
[ ] [	[ ]
Role: A R M C S PA PR	Role: A R M C S PA PR

Figure 2.4 A standard form

Coders are aware of the practicalities of handling documents during their removal from client files, photocopying, document review and subjective coding, at which time staples and clips are removed and replaced, but not always reliably in their original groupings. Moreover, the original attachments even if maintained represent the status of documents taken from a client's files, which does not necessarily correspond to the interests of lawyers. In so far as objective coding is done for the purpose of creating a database index to the documents for use by the latter, their interests must be considered in the designation of document boundaries. Accordingly, T makes the assessment of document boundaries based on a reading both of the documents and of their appearance in the context of a history which he knows to include their previous and prospective reading by the lawyers:

00:37:20:14

T: [referring to a document in front of him] This one's a judgement call. It could stand on its own, but the things that are after it are exhibits to it. And it discusses the exhibits. So I'm gonna code them all together. And in addition they've been clipped together, which to me is an indication that the lawyer has done this, and that the lawyer thinks it's one document . . . they [the exhibits] could stand on their own, but I think it would be, the description would be much less clear as to what they were. By putting them with the memo it just makes the whole thing more clear.

The set of documents has a more local history for T as well within the context of his own work, such that his orientation is not only to the document that is immediately in front of him but also to a prospective and retrospective field made up of all of the documents on which he is currently working. That field includes both problems to be solved and potential resources for their resolution. So like S's use of white Post-its™ to flag 'hot documents' during review, T uses a Post-it™ as a visible marker of a problem in a specific document, making it possible to relocate that document if the solution to the problem should appear in a document encountered later on. For example, one of the most important aspects of any document from the point of view of its potential relevance to a case is the occurrence of proper names, including document authors, recipients and any persons, companies or products mentioned in the text. Every name that appears in a document is entered on to the code sheet by document coders, along with a designation of the 'role' of the name within the document (author, recipient, mention and so on):

00:22:31:08

T: In this case [an agreement, with signatures at the bottom] I don't know what this name is, so I can't capture it as a signatory. What I would usually do is just take a Post-it™, and [takes one and attaches to page] put a note on it, at least so that I know that I didn't know what this was. And if I happen to come across it somewhere where it's signed and it's typed or printed below, then I'll go back and enter it on here [the code sheet].

Coders cannot literally code every appearance of a name in a given document, however. Most simply, they need to consolidate multiple appearances of a name into one code. Over time, coders become familiar with the actors in the case and bring that knowledge to bear. For example, a document may contain only a first name, in which case the name is included by the coder in the document description, rather than in the names table:

00:13:53:11

JB: If you just have a first name you put it in the description of the document? This person is mentioned, but

T: Right, because if we put it in the names table there's not really any way that we can accurately search for it. 'Cause if it's for instance Dave, it's not really that helpful. It might mean something in a description, you know, like it might say, like there might be marginalia, a handwritten note from Dave to Bob or something like that. And it might be clear then. And in that case, if I happen to know who those people are, I would put them down here [in the names field] and use the little 'L' for likely mention, or likely recipient, or whatever.

Similarly, creating a coherent and usable names database involves ongoing work of normalising across multiple designations for the same referent, for example B. Jones, Bob Jones, Robert Jones may all refer to a single person. Coders are given specific instructions about how variants should be reconciled and how names should be entered. At the same time, they are expected to exercise ordinary judgements in an open-ended horizon of ways, for example recognising from context when Bob and Robert refer to the same person. Similarly, coders need to know that Martin Marietta is a company rather than a person, UNIX™ is an operating system rather than a company, and DEC in the context of the Silicon Valley refers to Digital Equipment Corporation, not to December.

Accountability in objective coding

At the outset of our visit, I asked T to say a bit about the case on which he was working at the time. I expected a response in terms of the size of the case, how long it had been going on, the number of boxes of documents to be coded, and the like. Instead, T offered a summary of the legal issues in the case:

00:01:01:05

T: It's basically like any other securities case. The stockholders are saying that [company] withheld information about problems with the company that would have affected the price of the stock. So they're saying that uh, they didn't know that they should unload their stock, basically. The issues, some of the big issues in this case are issues dealing with [name of product], which is one of their most famous toys. And that seems to be quite a big issue. Issues with shipping the product, problems with returns and broken merchandise, and things like that. Another product was late, they had some kinds of production problems with it.

In contrast with S, T's knowledge of the case comes not from direct engagement with clients and lawyers but in part from an initial briefing provided by his supervisor, in part through inferences gleaned indirectly from the documents and in discussions with other coders working on the case. Moreover, deciding the issues of the case to which a document relates is not T's responsibility, his task being simply to transfer the issue codes provided by the lawyer from the latter's notes to the assigned field on the coding sheet. Along with the transcription of these 'subjective' codes, however, T is faced with the task of finding terms in which to construct an 'objective' description for each document. As for S, those terms are tied in part to a conventional typology of documents such that some are describable simply by their type (e.g. financial reports for a specific time period) while others actually require a description in terms of their specific content (e.g. letters). At it turns out, the document description is a field that makes evident the contested character of the subjective/objective distinction within the firm.

Document description as a contested field

From the point of view of lawyers with whom we spoke, the document description is of limited usefulness in so far as it is not indexed directly to the issues of the case. In this respect, lawyers seem to question the very possibility of an 'objective' description of the documents that could have any value.[8] At the same time, they hold the province of 'subjective' coding to themselves, precluding the document coders from creating the kind of connections to issues that would make the document description more useful. While document coders maintain the possibility and usefulness of creating objective document descriptions, in constructing such descriptions they are required simultaneously to demonstrate the neutral, disinterested character of their texts and to project the lawyers as their prospective readers, attempting to shape the descriptions with their specific interests in mind.

This controversy suggests the paradox inherent in the notion of an 'objective' document description, and of the subjective/objective distinction that underwrites it. To be the work of document coders, the lawyers maintain that the description must be constructed in terms not informed by the issues of the case and not presupposing what they might be. Somehow coders manage to find terms of description that meet the requirement that the description be independent of the case at hand. But that same requirement renders their descriptions of uncertain value from the lawyers' point of view. This dilemma is a kind of inversion of the problematic identified by Garfinkel (1967) in the case of clinic records, where records created with the practical interests of medical work in mind were found inadequate as a resource for the 'objective', actuarial analysis of clinical demographics. Both cases point to the intractable difficulties encountered in attempts to create a universally applicable logic of categorisation.

Subjectivity and objectivity as organisational positionings and orders of accountability

A central concern of studies of work has been to show the mutual constitution of knowledges and artefacts in practice. Within science studies in particular, the investigation of scientific practice is motivated not only by interests in the specificities of that particular form of work as one among others, but also by a sense that science, and other high-status knowledges, are emblematic of classic epistemological claims. If science can be shown to be embodied and enacted, then the case can be strengthened for displacement of a universal, mentalist epistemology by consideration of knowledges as specifically situated discursive and material practices. At the same time, having challenged the premise of science as independent from the mundane considerations that characterise other forms of practical activity, science studies can begin to develop an account of the identifying character of specific forms of scientific practice on other grounds.

A corollary of the restoration of the mundane to scientific practice has been a re-examination of the premise that scientific achievements are the accomplishments of some few 'great men', in favour of recognition of the essential work of 'invisible technicians' (Shapin, 1989). This brings to science and technology studies as well a concern with distributions, or reproductions of differential identity and associated reward, within specific divisions of labour (Law, 1991).

Consistent with these efforts, the goal of this analysis has been to displace the a priori, oppositional characterisation of the work of lawyers and document coders as 'knowledge' and 'routine' respectively. Instead, knowledge as practical reasoning and routine as ways of ordering familiar materials and activities are co-present and rely upon each other in every form of working practice. As for the subjective/objective distinction, a closer consideration of practices of document coding suggests that that distinction orders not so much ways of knowing or acts of reasoning as it does identities, actors and distributions of material and symbolic reward among them. In the place of the subjective/objective opposition we can begin to identify terms of difference given by actors' different relations to the materials of their work, maintained in turn through their different positionings within the network of others and forms of social interaction that constitute the firm and the practice of law.

Moreover, the case of document coding underscores a deep equivocation in the workings of the subjective/objective opposition. In the context of the sciences, objective knowledge is clearly the preferred element of the pair, set in privileged comparison with things known only through experience, interpretation or judgement. In so far as judgement is involved, so is unreliability. Reliability is achieved in the natural sciences not so much, or not only, by superior forms of reasoning as by knowing objects or methods: established technologies and techniques that encode and ensure the validity of knowledge produced. In the case of document coding, in contrast, subjective knowledge is the province of lawyers and is set in privileged comparison with mere objective features of a document, taken to be readable directly from it. Knowing subjects are required for subjective knowledge production but not for objective coding, where in this case objective means objectified/self-evident and therefore not in need of interpretation (see Hekman, 1990: chapter 3).

Law (1991: 7) has suggested that heterogeneity as a topic for social studies is about how similarities and differences are constructed and sustained, and the social and material arrangements that hold things together or keep them apart. In this chapter I have offered a preliminary account of how certain knowledges are (re)produced and maintained as different across members of a particular organisation, in relation to an associated working division of labour. Central to this differentiation are discursive devices for characterising the work to be done and who should do it, which rest in turn on systematic practices of interaction and separation that bring certain actors into contact with each other and with activities central to the organisation (interactions of lawyers with clients and with other lawyers), while keeping others (document coders) on the periphery. My point in this analysis is not to argue that, in so far as both lawyers' and document coders' work involves them in a combination of mundane and judgemental activities, there is no difference between them. Nor do I want to suggest that document coders, if brought more directly into the activity of making a case, would become indistinguishable from their colleagues who are lawyers. Rather, I want to suggest that simple oppositions of knowledge and routine work are more ideological than descriptive, and act rather to obscure works' actual demands than to clarify them. As an alternative, I have tried to show similarities as well as differences among the work of lawyers and document coders, and how the maintenance of differences between them rests not only on differences in their backgrounds of experience and expertise, but also on specific organisational discourses and working orders. In so far as that is the case, an organisation interested in identifying more effective working orders might do well to abandon simple distinctions in favour of an appreciation of the specific requirements and possibilities that the work, and the heterogeneity of organisation members, actually present.

Acknowledgements

The ideas and materials that form the basis for this chapter were developed through close collaboration with my colleagues on the Work-Oriented Design Project, in particular Jeanette Blomberg and Randy Trigg. Randy Trigg worked with me on articulating the specific observations regarding the work of subjective and objective coding on which the analysis offered here depends.

NOTES

1 On professional/scientific work as practical activity see, for example, Button (1993b); Clarke and Fujimura (1992); Engeström and Middleton (1996); C. Goodwin (1995); C. Goodwin and M. H. Goodwin, (1996). On invisible work as knowledge see Barley and Orr (1997); Clement (1993); Lave (1988); Star (1991); Suchman (1995, 1996b); Suchman and Jordan (1988).

2 Disrupting dualisms is a well-established feminist and post-structuralist practice. For an example with respect to work and technology see Robertson (1997).

3 As Goodwin points out, the characterisation of diverse activities across disparate settings as forms of coding, as a way of drawing attention to observable regularities among them, is an instance of the self-same practice as that described (C. Goodwin 1994: 607).

4 The account that follows is based on a study of a large law firm conducted by myself and my colleagues in the Work Practice and Technology research group at Xerox PARC. I am deeply indebted in particular to my colleagues Jeanette Blomberg and Randy Trigg. (For more on that project and many of the issues discussed here, see Blomberg *et al.*, 1996, 1997; Suchman, 1996b.)

5 The materials on which my argument is based comprise videotaped sessions of work by a junior lawyer, here called S, and a document coder, called T. In both cases Jeanette Blomberg and I were present by prior arrangement with S and T, and requested that they proceed with the work they were in the midst of when we arrived, talking to us about it as they went along.

6 At the outset of the document production process other workers, called case assistants, affix a unique identification number (sometimes called a 'Bates number' in reference to the stamp machine traditionally used for the purpose) to each page of every document, with documents themselves marked as a range, e.g. XYZ112345–XYZ112350.

7 See C. Goodwin (1994) for a discussion of highlighting as a common practice in the structuring of complex perceptual fields.

8 This despite the fact that when introduced as evidence in the case, the documents will again assume their 'objective' status. See C. Goodwin (1994: 616) on the valuation of this sense of objective, taken as unbiased or impartial, in the practice of law.

3   Design by problem-solving

Graham Button and Wes Sharrock

Introduction

Over the course of a number of investigations we have examined aspects of the organisation of engineering work under the rubric of ethnomethodology's programme of 'studies of work' (Garfinkel, 1986). Our investigations were initially undertaken with the purpose of contributing to an understanding of the design process through the close observation of design and development work under 'industrial' conditions, rather than, as was more usually the case with studies of design, located in contrived experimental settings (cf. Button and Sharrock, 1994, 1996, 1998; Sharrock and Button, 1997). The close observation of the day-to-day work of design in large organisational conditions could enhance the awareness of conditions and contingencies that would be part of the design process in complex arrangements of work. They could thus provide informational input to the circumstances under which tools to support design would be used and the practical requirements with which such tools would need to be articulated. These studies also have cogency for the area of Computer Supported Cooperative Work (CSCW). One of its concerns is the development of systems that will support large and complex ventures in coordinated work and the 'industrial' (hardware and software) design and development project is an example of a sizeable and complicated exercise in coordinated work.

Ethnomethodology's programme of work was itself developed as a corrective to the tendency of sociological studies titled as 'studies of work' to attend to almost everything that goes on in the workplace, except the work being done there. Our studies have, therefore, been primarily centred upon that work, and upon the way in which participants organise their work in an attempt to ensure that it gets done, contending with the problems of delivering a product as much in accord with the project's objectives and specifications as is feasible, as close to the required delivery date as is possible, and as near to budgetary targets as can be managed. Two interests have driven our studies. First, the ways in which engineering

46

work is done so as to display its organisationally accountable character, and second, the ways in which engineers attend to what Harold Garfinkel has called 'the practical question par excellence: What to do next?' (Garfinkel, 1967:12). In this chapter we continue our investigations and further develop our concerns by examining one prominent feature of engineering work in organisations, which displays an orientation to Garfinkel's question, the problem-solving character of engineering work.

The audio and audio-visual materials we examine are taken from a 'design setting' (a 'sunrise meeting')[1] of the representatives of the different modules involved in the design and development of a photocopier being undertaken by a leading international company. We use them to provide a sequential anatomy of a problem and a candidate solution that were developed in the course of the meeting. We are thus interested in understanding the organisation of the activities we examine by explicating their combinatorial logic. Our previous investigations have been sociologically motivated, and were not undertaken with any intention that they should lead directly to design recommendations but would provide more 'realistic' information about design practice to those reflecting on the design process. In this latter respect, although our prime interest in this chapter, which is in how the engineering problem and solution we examine are organised, resides in our sociological preoccupation with how participants display to one another the ordered and organisational character of their activities, we should note that the setting and the type of materials we address are ones that others who are interested in understanding design in order to directly both improve and support it have previously examined (G. Olson et al., 1992, 1996).

Olson et al. have suggested that in order to support 'group work' with both new methods and technology it is necessary to have a detailed understanding of what is done in the context of a group, usually in the context of a meeting of the group. Further, the 'group work' that has been extensively studied has taken the form of design meetings within design and development organisations. In addition, it has been proposed that the participants' problem-solving activities should be highlighted and that this reveals the extent to which the activities undertaken during the course of the meeting are sequentially organised and how, consequently, the meeting is sequentially structured. This suggests to these authors that the design meetings they study have an existing structure to them which must be borne in mind in the development of design tools that attempt to impart a structure to design meetings, such as 'design rationale' (cf. Moran and Carroll, 1996).

Our examination, in this chapter, of the sequential anatomy of a problem and candidate solution found within the course of a design meeting may, consequently, appear to be treading a well-worn path. However, Olson *et al.* place a stress upon the fact that the object of their study is not so much the work of design but the organisation of design meetings, and in their conclusion they emphasise the relevance of their study for other types of meetings such as policy meetings and negotiations. We, however, are less concerned with the fact that the problem and the candidate solution we examine is occurring in a meeting and are more concerned with the way in which it is organised so as to display an orientation to aspects of the work of engineering. Certainly, a meeting was going on when we made our recordings, and we draw a contrast between the organisation of the problem and the solution that we examine with the way in which problems and solutions may be ordered in other types of speech exchange such as conversation. However, this is not a contrast between talk-in-interaction that can be characterised as conversation and talk-in-interaction that can be characterised as a meeting. Rather, it is a contrast that is intended to highlight the character of engineering problems and solutions, and is done in the interest of drawing out the ways in which engineers orient to the ordered properties of their work activities. In the example of the problem and the candidate solution we examine, it will be seen that the participants pay little attention to the fact that they are pursuing their work in what can be characterised as a meeting. In none of the extracts do they build in an orientation to this characterisation of their activities through reference to such matters as 'items of business', 'a chair', 'an agenda' and the like. This is not to say that they do not do so at some junctures but that in their problem-solving activities we examine they orient to making the problem tractable to an engineering solution, an orientation that they also display in other settings that would not lend themselves to the ready characterisation of a meeting (Sharrock and Button, 1997). We are not saying that studying meetings is somehow problematic, we are merely trying to emphasise that although on the face of it we might be seen to be contributing to a body of work which studies design meetings, we, rather, view ourselves as contributing to a body of studies that are concerned with the ordered properties of work.

Our main reason for undertaking this present study is thus to understand, in part, how the participants are displaying to one another the ordered properties of design work in the meeting. We are aware, however, of the fact that in the various examinations undertaken by Olson *et al.*, the structuring of the activities and meeting is viewed as consequential for the development of design support tools, particularly design rationale (cf. G. Olson *et al.*, 1992). Their argument is that through their investigations it becomes possible to see that meetings have an existing structure to them, and consequently the design of tools such as design rationale to support design meetings by structuring them should be re-examined: 'Our data suggest that these discussions are already structured; there is, across meetings, a very regular pattern within the episodes of design discussion . . . It is not immediately clear if there is a need for further structuring of the activity' (G. Olson *et al.*, 1992: 370).

Our interest in the work of design and development that occurs in these meetings may, however, lead to a different emphasis with respect to initiatives such as design rationale. The 'structure' of the problem and solution we examine is one which the participants orient to in terms of an ordered property of their work, and thus the 'structure' of the meeting has much to do with how the participants go about their work of engineering in visible and recognisable ways. These ways are not immutable, they are the product of engineers trying different ways of organising their work. They need to, as we shall examine, turn temporally organised problems into causally textured problems and develop solutions, the effectiveness of which can be measured. Our understanding of design rationale is that it is a tool to support an aspect of design work, the practical problem of making decisions in methodical and recorded ways, not so much a tool to support meetings (MacLean *et al.*, 1996). In this respect the fact that design meetings 'already have a structure' is not itself a barrier to design rationale, as if, so to speak, it was not a natural structure and the structure evidenced by the meetings was.

We are neither champions nor detractors of design rationale. We merely note that from the materials we have gleaned from meetings of designing engineers that the ordered properties of their actions and interactions are often accountable to the work of engineering, for example, trying to figure out engineering solutions to the problematic operation of machines. Inasmuch as design rationale is intended to support that work it hardly matters if it provides for different ways of organising the work to get it done, to those ways that previously existed, if indeed it requires those to be changed.

The materials we use are taken from a routine daily sunrise meeting on an engineering project (known as 'Thames') which marked the beginning of the official working day, starting at 8.30 a.m. These sunrise meetings were being held in the fourth year of a project which involved some two hundred people and was scheduled to last five years. The project was directed towards the production of a distributed digital printer, and was at the stage at which the design and development was well advanced with the first machines emerging from the production lines and being put through various tests.

The sunrise meeting's major business was to review and respond to the results from a major, on-site test operation. This operation involved running print jobs on the machines in ways which were meant to simulate the actual use of such printers, in respect of the types of paper, amounts of toner and so forth. This was done with the expectation that it would reveal remaining faults with the design, and would permit redesign of machine features until the design would be in a stable configuration. That is, that the machines with that design set-up would perform up to certain standards of reliability, such as specified frequency of breakdowns, length of print cartridge life and so on. The machines were test operated by a labour force of casual workers, who were required to run the machines according to a set of instructions and to record the faults which occurred. These faults were to be recorded on the Fault Report Forms (FRFs, one of which is exhibited in figure 3.1)[2] along with the observations of a repair technician who would be called in to fix any problems that, under the test rules, the machine operators could not fix for themselves.

The completed Fault Report Forms were collected (with a lunchtime cut-off) each day from the test operators and handed over to the project's data analyst, who would enter much of the information pertaining to the conditions and character of the form into the computer. A digest version of this information would be printed out for the engineers attending the following day's sunrise meeting (with each of the recognised subgroups in the project team being required to send a representative). The data analyst would bring copies of the digests to the meeting, along with the original Fault Report Forms. He would distribute copies of the digest, and when the meeting's business came to the point of reviewing the Fault Report Forms, would read out the information on the report pertaining to the nature of the fault that had occurred, and whatever action had been taken.

The FRF contained a good deal of information about the conditions under which a particular fault occurs, identifying *inter alia* the machine's number; the humidity and temperature conditions; which image from the array of images provided for test use was being printed from; and whether the operation involved one-sided or two-sided printing. From the point of view of reading out the FRFs, however, the main matter to be read out was the information falling under the headings of 'Reason for call' and 'Service actions'. The former provided for the recording of the circumstances of the reported fault, and any actions taken by the test operator to overcome the fault. The latter provided for reports about the fault as encountered and dealt with by the repair technician who would be summoned if the measures allowed (under test rules). These FRFs were read out one by one, and the reading out of each one (by the data analyst) was the occasion for other engineers to comment on the nature of the problem revealed in the report.

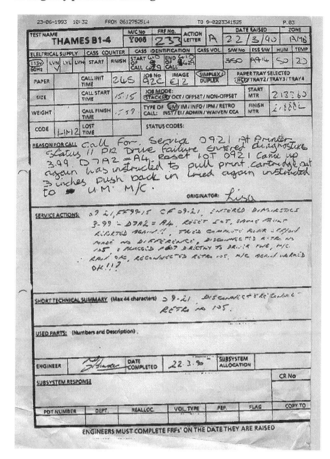

Figure 3.1 A Fault Report Form

We consider how the participants in the meeting we are concerned with display themselves to be facing the practical problem of working out from a Fault Report Form just what the problematic operating of the machine consists of as an engineering conundrum. The FRF does not provide a description of problematic operating that is accountable to engineering practice. That is, the problematic operating as described in the FRF is not immediately tractable to an engineering solution. However, as an engineering conundrum engineering practice can be brought to bear in its resolution and the problematic operating can be made accountable to engineering practice.

In other words, the test operator's written report of a malfunction raises for the engineers the question of whether this malfunction exhibits a remaining deficiency in machine design. From the description provided in the FRF and from their general familiarity with the project's work and problems the engineers must attempt to figure out at least a candidate cause for the malfunction and determine if this requires corrective action on their part.

Part of what constitutes engineering work is thus the quest for the cause of the problematic operation in order to bring to bear their engineering knowledge in the determination of a solution. The problem that the engineers face is that the information contained in the FRF does not necessarily exhibit the causal texture of the malfunction it describes. In order to provide such a causal texture the participants to the meeting engage in a transformation process through which the FRF is turned from a document that is, in engineering terms, a flat history of events into a document that is textured with engineering relevancies. Accomplishing this transformation is, in part, the work of engineering and the way in which this transformation is accomplished displays an engineering orientation, for the translation consists of turning a temporally organised history of events into a causally textured account of the events.[3] What is interesting for our purposes here is that this transformation is organised interactionally through the sequential practice of reading out the record in order to read into the record. What is read out is a temporally organised sequential history of the various states that the machine entered and which were reported as operation faults and the responses of the operators. What is read into the record is a causal efficacy of events. Transforming the Fault Report Form from a history of events into a causal texture provides the opportunities for the engineers to work out what to do next in the light of the reported problematic operations. What to do next is oriented to the solution of the problematic operation in as much as it provides for next steps to be taken by the engineers.

We shall build our explication by first examining what the participants display as constituting a possible solution to a problematic. We shall describe how this involves the decision to take a particular next step. We then examine how that possible solution is itself provided for by a prior activity and how it is ordered with respect to 'a next step proposal'. We go on to notice, however, that as a next step proposal this occasioning activity is not offered as the problematic. Thus, unlike conversation, for example, the candidate solution is distanced from the problem. We consider the structure of the delivery of the problematic in this respect. It is offered as a 'reading out' of the history of a problem. Delivered in this way it does not provide next steps, rather it provides the opportunity for participants to 'read in' the cause of a problem.[4] The reading in of a cause then provides the occasion for proposing next steps to be taken, and it is this, as we have seen, that provides the occasion for the formulation of a candidate solution, taking next steps. Thus the solution is distanced from the problem by a series of sequentially ordered turns at talk that provide the opportunity to produce a candidate solution, an opportunity not itself provided for by the reading out of the problem.

Finding out what to do next as an engineering solution

The examination of the transcript in the line-by-line way we employ in the following analysis relies upon the techniques developed in the area of 'conversation analysis', most particularly in the work of Harvey Sacks (1992). This form of analysis is directed to understanding how activities are organised in and through talk. As such, it constrains us to ask about the ways in which the engineers talk their way towards a solution to their engineering problem. How, through listening to and commenting on the details read out from the FRF they can begin to say what the cause of the problem might be. In this case, we describe the way in which the engineers attempt to reconstruct from the description in the FRF what 'really happened' on the occasion of the fault's occurrence. We find, in the first instance, that they cannot track the sequence of things that happened and were done in the test operations and that they consequently seek to clarify which events occurred in what order as a means of clarifying relations of consequence between them.

To begin our analysis we describe the shape that engineering solutions take in this setting. One prominent feature can be revealed with a short comparison with ordinary conversation. Within conversation, solutions, like answers, are located with respect to prior activities. Thus as answers follow questions, so too do solutions follow problems and are regularly positioned in the adjacent turn to a problem. The mechanism through which these two activities are thus ordered in relationship to one another has been extensively described as 'adjacency pairs' (Schegloff and Sacks, 1973). Adjacency pairs display the following ordered properties of combinatorial tolerances:

(1) two utterance length, (2) adjacent positioning of component utterances, (3) different speakers producing each utterance, (4) relative ordering of parts (i.e. first pair parts proceed second pair parts [problems proceed solutions]), and (5) discriminative relations (i.e. the pair type of which a first pair type part is a member is relevant to the selection among second pair parts). (Schegloff and Sacks, 1973, in Turner, 1974: 238)

Within the following extract taken from the meeting, and contrary to one of the features of problems and solutions as adjacency pairs in conversation, the formulated solution is, however, distanced from the statement of the problematic. (The transcript symbols are explained in the appendix, p. 66.)

(1a) [Sunrise: 15/6/90]

```
46   ➡ A:  Oka::y so they had on eleven 0 nine from which
47          they reset. (1.5) They were told still to clear the
48          jam so they did:: (.) the machine entered 0 four 0 one
49          but the ESS did eleven 0 nine. (1.5) The observations ar::e
50          from stacker group disc angle was thir- thirty de::grees::
51          which is software category five:: failed to reach home
52          (.) during initialisation (.) no paper in the path:: the IOT
53          went (.) directly from ready to print to eleven 0 nine
54          call for service. (.) First job after the ESS (.)
55          software was reloaded. (2.0) Conclu::sion category zero
56          (.) IOT tries to reinitialise disc and failed. (0.5) Not after
57          reset press (    ) category one.
                                 .
                                 .
                                 .
176  ➡ P:  Yeah (.) prhaps you ought to look at the logs
177          as well an just get ah (.) little sequence
178          of events put together Stewart.
179     S:  Yeah. I'll ask Kevin to look at it.
180     P:  So you you'll handle the whole thi::ng.=
181     S:  Yeah
182     P:  *Right*
```

A statement of the problematic functioning of the machine initiates talk on the problems that it reveals, and the possible solution provides for the closure of talk on the problems. We can note, however, from the line numbering that the two are distanced from one another by numerous turns at talk. Thus a statement of the problematic operation of the machine begins at line 46 but the beginning of a possible solution can be located at line 176. In line 46, A initiates talk on the problematic, notice how the 'okay' in the turn initial position segments the upcoming talk, and, as we detail below, how in line 182, P closes talk on the item. Thus the formulation of a possible solution which is looking at the logs and getting together a little sequence is distanced from the statement of the problematic which is the stacker group failed to reach home.

Consequently, a first question we shall address is whether this distancing of a solution from the problem is a systematic feature of the organisation of problems and solutions within these types of design and development meetings. If it is, a second question will be asked, which is how it is that participants move from the problem to the solution. It is in answering these questions that we can begin to unpack some of the work of the engineers in this meeting.

To start to address these questions we can examine the possible solution and closure of talk on the problematic in more detail. The solution provides for some of the ensuing day's work and takes the form of providing for some next steps to be engaged in outside of the meeting. It is organised into two related sequences of talk that are oriented to closing down talk on a Fault Report Form item. That is, the closure of an item is done in providing for what to do next and the closure is itself made up of particular and identifiable actions that display an orientation to the business-at-hand. One sequence that is involved in providing for the ensuing day's work is assigning responsibility and the other is proposing the next step. We can observe this in more detail by working through the extract.

(1b) [Sunrise: 15/6/90]

```
176      P:  Yeah (.) prhaps you ought to look at the logs
177          as well an just get ah (.) little sequence
178          of events put together Stewart.
179   ➤  S:  Yeah. I'll ask Kevin to look at it.
180   ➤  P:  So you you'll handle the whole thi::ng=
181   ➤  S:  =Yeah
182   ➤  P:  *Right*
```

Closure of talk on the item on the Fault Report Form is organised over the course of three turns at talk. First, the assignment of responsibility (line 180, P: So you'll handle the whole thi::ng.). Second, the acceptance of the responsibility (line 181, S: =Yeah.). Third, an acknowledgement that responsibility has been accepted (line 182, P: *Right*). Thus some next work is provided for in the assignment of responsibility and its acceptance which organises the closure of a particular item on the report.

However, we can further observe that the way in which this closure is organised displays that it has been occasioned by some prior activities. That is, the provision of some activities to be engaged in and which will make up part of the day's work displays itself to be orderly positioned in terms of the course of the meeting. In this respect, notice that the assignment of responsibility in line 180 is done in terms of a summary of an outcome. With 'So' occupying the turn initial position and tying in the turn to the prior talk by marking that it is dependent on, originates in, that prior talk, and 'the whole thing' standing on behalf of, or a formulation of, something agreed. Thus the way in which the closure of the item is organised displays that it has been occasioned by some prior activity.

This prior activity is an agreed course of action to be taken. This is organised in two turns of talk. First, a next step proposal which proposes some next step to be taken (lines 176–8, P: Yeah (.) prhaps you ought to look at the logs as well an just get ah (.) little sequence of events put together Stewart.). Second, a claimed agreement to a next step proposal (line 179, S: Yeah . . .) which is upgraded into a demonstrated agreement in the proposal as to how the next step will be taken, a next step enabler (line 179, S: . . . I'll ask Kevin to look at it.). Thus, it is upon the agreement as to a course of action to be taken that the initiation of the closure of the item is undertaken. In this respect we can see in these two sequences of talk 'an agreed course of action' and the 'closure of the item' provide, in part, for what some next steps will be.

Inasmuch as the participants to this meeting orient to the closure of current talk on the problematic they display what can constitute a possible solution to a problematic organised in working out an agreed course of action to be undertaken. In other words a possible engineering solution is organised in providing for a course of action involving next steps to be engaged in, where here that consists of proposing some work to be undertaken following the meeting.

Having described the shape that a possible solution can take, we can now turn to the shape that the statement of the problematic takes. As we do so we need to remember that the question we are attempting to answer is whether there is any systematic reason for distancing the possible solution from the statement of the problematic.

Reading out the report form

A decisive feature of the statement of the problematic is that it is made in 'reading out the report form'. Reading out the form is organised as reading out a sequence of events that occurred and activities performed by the machine. We want to emphasise one feature of reading out the form which is that in reading out the form the events are given a 'temporal order'. In this reading, as we detail below, the reader audibly glosses the details on the form, partially reformulating these in ways which highlight the stepwise sequence of events in the report. Thus reading out involves the selection of certain activities from the day's operation that stand as possible problems, and activities that were undertaken in response to those, and also relating those events to other events, and activities to other activities and other events through a temporally ordered sequential structure.[5] We can see this if we examine the following fragments:

(1c) [Sunrise: 15/6/90]
```
46  ➡  A:  Oka::y so they had on eleven 0 nine from which
47          they reset. (1.5) They were told still to clear the
48          jam so they did:: (.) the machine entered 0 four 0 one
49          but the ESS did eleven 0 nine. (1.5) The observations ar::e
50          from stacker group disc angle was thir- thirty de::grees::
51          which is software category five:: failed to reach home
```

52   (.) during initialisation (.) no paper in the path:: the IOT
53   went (.) directly from ready to print to eleven 0 nine
54   call for service. (.) First job after the ESS (.)
55   software was reloaded. (2.0) Conclu::sion category zero
56   (.) IOT tries to reinitialise disc and failed. (0.5) Not after
57   reset press ( ) category one.

(2) [Sunrise: 15/6/90]
27   A: Paper jam on the IOT   ESS still said eleven 0 ni::ne.
28   (1.5)
29   A: They then clear the imaginary jam. (.) The machine
30   wahrhmed up the:n gave a four 0 one. (1.0) An' the ESS
31   still sa:id eleven 0 nine.

Reading out from the form involves reading out a sequential list of events. In the first example this involves: having an eleven 0 nine; resetting; clearing the jam; having the machine entered 0 four 0 one; the ESS doing eleven 0 nine; observing that the stacker group disc angle was thirty degrees and failed to reach home; that there was no paper in the path; that the IOT went from ready to print to call for service; that the IOT tried to reinitialise disc and failed. In the second example this involves: having a paper jam on the IOT; having the ESS saying eleven 0 nine; clearing the imaginary jam; having the machine warm up; getting a four 0 one; having the ESS say eleven 0 nine.

However, while it is possible to observe that reading out the form entails reading out a sequential ordering of events, it is also possible to observe that order is constructed in a particular way. That is, there is a particular mechanism at work in the production of the sequential order. In this respect notice that the events are connected to one another in a particular way. Thus in the second example notice in line 27 the use of 'still' to connect the paper jam and the ESS saying eleven 0 nine (A: Paper jam on the IOT ESS still said eleven 0 ni::ne . . .). Also note the use of 'then' in line 29 to connect the ESS still saying eleven 0 nine and clearing the imaginary paper jam (A: . . . ESS still said eleven 0 ni::ne. (1.5) They then clear the imaginary jam . . .). There is another use of 'then' in line 30 to connect warming up and giving a four 0 one (A: . . . The machine wahrhmed up the:n gave a four 0 one . . .). And again 'still' is used in line 31 to connect giving a four 0 one and the machine saying eleven 0 nine (A: . . . gave a four 0 one. (1.0) An' the ESS still sa:id eleven 0 nine). In the first example some of the events are similarly connected. First, notice in line 46 the use of 'from' to connect having an eleven 0 nine and resetting (A: . . . they had on eleven 0 nine from which they reset.). Second, in line 47 'still' to connect resetting and being told to clear the jam, (A: . . . they reset. (1.5) They were told still to clear the jam. . .).

While this way of connecting events organises them into a sequence of events, it is also possible to see that they account for the sequence having a particular ordering mechanism. They account for the sequence of events as having been produced over time. That is, they give a temporal order to the organisation of the sequence of events that are read out from the Fault Report Form. This is particularly evidenced in example 1c where A uses temporal descriptions 'during', 'went directly', 'first' and 'after' in connecting the events in reading out the observations. Thus reading out from the form is organised as reading out a history of the events for the connection between the events is accounted for in time.

Within ordinary conversation it can be readily found that following a statement of a problematic, possible solutions are offered. However, we have described how, within the meeting we are examining, that the possible solution to the problematic operation of the machine is not positioned adjacent to the statement of the problematic functioning but is distanced from it. Thus, rather than a possible solution being offered in the next turn to the statement of the problematics, as we might expect in conversation, that turn is occupied by another activity. This activity is one of 'reading into the record'. That is, the activity of reading out from the record is followed by the activity of reading into the record. In order to see if there is a systematic relationship between reading out the record and reading into the record, that is, whether reading out the record systematically provides for reading into the record, we will turn to building up a description of reading into the record.

Reading into the record

Following A's reading out from the record, F reads into the record:

(1d) [Sunrise: 15/6/90]

```
46   ➡  A:  Oka::y so they had on eleven 0 nine from which
47            they reset. (1.5) They were told still to clear the
48            jam so they did:: (.) the machine entered 0 four 0 one
49            but the ESS did eleven 0 nine. (1.5) The observations ar::e
50            from stacker group disc angle was thir- thirty de::grees::
51            which is software category five:: failed to reach home
52            (.) during initialisation (.) no paper in the path:: the IOT
53            went (.) directly from ready to print to eleven 0 nine
54            call for service. (.) First job after the ESS (.)
55            software was reloaded. (2.0) Conclu::sion category zero
56            (.) IOT tries to reinitialise disc and failed. (0.5) Not after
57            reset press ( ) category one.
58            (2.5)
```

59   F: It must have been out of position and jus tried t⌈o refit its⌉elf
60   ():   ⌊H h r m ⌋
61   (): Hr⌈m
62   F: ⌊And probably couldn't get home.

In lines 59–62 F is reading in a possible cause for the stacker group disc not having reached home which furnishes an account for the machine's problematic operation. In order to bring out a number of features of the activity of reading in, we can briefly contrast how it is organised with how reading out is organised. First, reading out from the record involves reading out the events that occurred as 'the facts'. That is, the Fault Report Form is treated as a factual record of events. On the other hand, reading into the record involves conjecture. For example, notice the conjectural status of F's description that it could not get home which is achieved in line 62 with his use of 'probably' (F: And probably couldn't get home). Second, although we do not want to say that reading out from the record cannot be challenged, it is our observation that it is not challenged, on the other hand, reading into the record is designed to be refutable. We can see this in the following extract.

(3) [Sunrise: 15/6/90]
112   A: . . . the machine rewarmed and then gave a 0 four 0 one.
113   (1.0) On the IOT the ESS was still at eleven 0 nine.
114   P: It's a question whether the four 0 one Jack wz (.) havin
115   attempted to start or reques⌈ted to start.
116   J: ⌊No ⌈::
117   A: ⌊No the next next FRF
118   specifically sez that the 0 four 0 on::e (.) wz one sheet
119   into the job.

Here in lines 112–13 A is in the process of reading out the record, following which P in lines 114–15 reads into the record that there might be an ambiguity, whether it was one thing or another, an attempt or a request to restart. Again this is conjecturally marked (line 114, P: It's a question whether. . .). However, both J in line 116 and A in lines 117–19 refute his reading in. Reading into the record is designed to be refutable for while reading out is presented as a statement of the facts, as a factual record, reading in is done conjecturally and thus provides the opportunity for refutation in a way that reading out does not. Refuting the factual record is not provided for by reading out the record whereas refuting a reading into the record is provided for by the conjectural status that is designed into the reading into the record. This is not to say that the factual record cannot be refuted but that it is not organised to receive this activity; refuting here would require different resources to refuting reading in.

Third, reading out the record gives a flat temporal organisation of a sequence of events whereas reading into the record involves imputing a causal efficacy to the events. We can begin to get at what is involved here if we examine the continuation of the refutation in the example above.

(3a) [Sunrise: 15/6/90]

```
116    J:                              ⌊No  ⌈::
117    A:                                   ⌊No the next next FRF
118         specifically sez that the 0 four 0 on::e (.) wz one sheet
119         into the job.
120    P:  That's wh⌈at
121    A:            ⌊With one copy out.
122    P:  Thats what I was confused by (.) wz the
123 ➤  L:  *No it doesn't say that at all to in my view,
124    P:  The second one does=
125    A:  The second one does.
```

In line 123 L is not questioning the events read out of the report, rather he is questioning what the events read out could be read as (L: *No it doesn't say that at all to in my view). That is, he is distinguishing between the events as a temporally organised sequence of events from what having those events occur in that way could be said to mean. Consequently we can now see that what F in fragment 1d was doing when he was reading into the record (line 59, F: It must have been out of position and jus tried to refit itself) was reading in a particular explanation of the events. This explanation is an account of the problematic operation of the machine. Thus he is reading in an antecedent event that if it had occurred would provide for the stacker being out of alignment. The antecedent event that is read in is given the status of a causal event. Thus reading out the record does not describe the stacker as out of position and trying to refit itself. Reading this possibility into the record provides an account of what caused the problematic event that has been read out, what the temporally organised events could mean.

Fourth, reading in is done selectively. That is, reading into the record features aspects of reading out the record. For example, in fragment 1d, following A's reading out the record F's reading into the record features a particular event selected from a number of other events that are read out in the reading out of the record. In this respect reading in gives a texture to the events featured in the reading out by raising some above others, in the example we have just been looking at, raising one event above the others. However, a feature of the activity of reading into the record that we have described above is that a causal antecedent to the event is read in. Thus in reading into the record a causal antecedent and in texturing the events of the reading out, a causal texture is being given to the events that have been read out.

Thus reading into the record is distinguishable from reading out the record. Reading out the record is to read out a temporally ordered sequence of factually occurring events, while reading into the record is to read into those facts conjectures as to what could have caused the events read out to have occurred. As conjectures they can provide for refutation. Reading into the record thus transforms a flat ordering of the sequence of events recorded in the record into a causally textured account of the problematic operation of the machine.

The work of transformation is particularly transparent in the following piece.

(4a) [Sunrise: 15/6/90]

92	F:	When does it actually say it indicated the 0 four 0 one
93		(.) ( ).
94		(0.2)
95	A:	Right let's try goin through. It starts of:: with:: an
96		eleven 0 nine.
97	F:	Right.

In line 95, in response to F's query in lines 92–3, A proposes that they go through the sequential history bit-by-bit. He then reads out one event, preserving its temporal location within the structure of events (line 95 A: . . . It starts . . .) and thus marking this event as the first event. Following this, F in line 97 checks off that event, 'Right.' Checking off in this way passes up an opportunity to talk to that event and in so doing it also marks that they can proceed to the next event. This then provides the opportunity for A to read out what will be heard as the next event, which may also be checked off, and which may also then provide for reading out the next event.

(4b) [Sunrise: 15/6/90]

92	F:	When does it actually say it indicated the 0 four 0 one
93		(.) ( ).
94		(0.2)
95	A:	Right let's try goin through. It starts of:: with:: an
96		eleven 0 nine.
97	F:	Right.
98	A:	Reset.
99	F:	Right.
100	A:	Paper ja::m on IOT. ESS still sez eleven 0 nine.

Reading out the events bit-by-bit involves reading out the sequential history of the events and locating their place within the temporal organisation of that sequence in such a way that the event can be checked off which then provides for moving on to the next event to be read out. These sequences are thus chained together and organise reading out the events bit-by-bit.

Reading out the record bit-by-bit is, however, designed to attend to features of reading into the record. We have described how reading into the record is done selectively, and how it gives a texture to the events. Reading out the record bit-by-bit is attentive to this feature because it provides the opportunity for participants to select an event to address. Thus while reading out an item allows it to be checked and the next one moved on to, it also provides the opportunity for the event to be selected for talk on and thus featured. Thus as reading out the events progresses in the extract above, a place is reached at which an event is selected for further explanation:

(4c) [Sunrise: 15/6/90]

92	F:	When does it actually say it indicated the 0 four 0 one
93		(.) ( ).
94		(0.2)
95	A:	Right let's try goin through. It starts of:: with:: an
96		eleven 0 nine.
97	F:	Right.
98	A:	Reset.
99	F:	Right.
100	A:	Paper ja::m on IOT. ESS still sez eleven 0 nine.
101	F:	Paper jam on IOT.
102		(1.3)
103	A:	Clear imaginary paper jam.
104	F:	*Right*.
105	A:	Machine warmed up. Then 0 four 0 onne:: (1.8)
106		ESS still eleven 0 nine.
107 ➡	P:	There's no mention of a code for that paper jam is
108 ➡		there.
109	J:	No:: (.) for one thing=and the other (.) had they actually
110		(0.8) requested another job down from say had we
111		actually cycled up IOT to get the 0 four one or requested one.

In this regard, in line 107 P is able to use the slot following the reading out of one event to query an issue with respect to the previous event read out in line 103. That is, although A's reading out in line 103 of 'Clear imaginary paper jam' is checked off by F in the following turn, line 104, P is able to return and focus upon the event by querying that there was no mention of a code for the paper jam. This query is confirmed by J in line 109 and a further event is latched on to it (lines 109–11 J: . . . and the other (.) had they actually (0.8) requested another job down from say had we actually cycled up IOT to get the 0 four one or requested one.).

Thus reading out the record bit-by-bit provides for the events read out to be checked or queried. In querying an event it is highlighted and providing for the query to be answered provides for further talk on the event. It is organised to invite reading into the record and can be used when reading in has not been done so as to produce a causal texture to the account. Going through the Fault Report Form in this fashion slows down reading out the record. This enables the participants to go through each event frame by frame, as it were, looking for a feature of the event that would allow them to begin to attribute a cause to the faulty operation of the machine.

So we are saying that reading out the record systematically provides for reading into the record. Reading out the record is to read out a sequence of events that are organised according to a temporal order, while reading into the record involves a transformation of that temporal order into a causal texture.

Causal efficacy and next steps

The transformation of the record from a flat temporal history of events into a causally textured account provides the occasion whereby the participants can talk to the cause of the problematic operation of the machine. Talking to the cause of the problem enables them to propose courses of action to deal with the problem. Thus in example 4c above, reading out the events from the form bit-by-bit provides the occasion for P, in line 107, to observe that 'There's no mention of a code for that paper jam' and for J to question whether or not the operators had 'actually cycled up IOT to get the 0 four one or requested one'. That is, the participants are able to read into the report events not stated in the reading out of the report that may furnish resources that may be used to explain the problematic operation of the machine.

With resources in hand that may be used to furnish an explanation, participants are able to propose courses of action that can be undertaken with respect to the problematics contained in the reading out of the report. Thus in the following extract (5) it is possible to see that in line 140, P is able to propose a course of action that they may engage in. (P: We::ll there's:: a couple of things we should do there we should go an' see what 0 seven A three sez when you look in the proper place.) This follows a statement concerning the 0 four 0 one and preserves the query concerning the paper jam (line 138, A: It gave no:: 0 four 0 one.).

(5) [Sunrise: 15/6/90]
138   A: It gave no:: 0 four 0 one.
139   (3.4)

```
140    P:  We::ll there's:: a couple of things we should do
141        there we should go an' see what 0 seven A three
142        sez when you look in the proper place.
143    S:  Uhm
144    P:  An' we should see if there wz er:: a paper jam
145        code,
```

We began by describing how a possible engineering solution is organised in providing for a course of action involving next steps to be engaged in. We have also described how the statement of the problematic operation of the machine does not provide for the production of these sorts of next steps but rather provides the opportunity for reading into the report. We can now see, however, that reading into the report can be preserved in the proposal for next activities to be engaged in. That is, it is the activity of reading into the report that furnishes resources through which a course of action involving next steps to be engaged in can be proposed. Reading into the report can be used to organise a possible solution.

We posed the analytic questions: are there systematic reasons for distancing possible solutions from the statement of the problematic and if so are there any methodic ways in which the participants move from the statement of the problematics to the solution? We are now in a position to answer these questions.

First, the possible solution is distanced from the statement of the problematic by talk that is initiated by reading into the report or by talk that is designed to provide for reading into the report. There are two related issues here with respect to this first question. First, reading out the report systematically provides for reading into the report, for reading out the report describes undifferentiated problematic events to be explained. Reading into the report in the manner in which we have described provides a texture to the events described in reading out the report and furnishes candidate explanations or initiates talk on candidate explanations. Second, it is reading into the report that provides for the possibility of formulating next activities to be engaged in which we have described as being part of the organisation of solutions here. Thus reading out the report provides for an activity that can in turn lead to solution relevant activities to the problematic. Reading into the report is an occasioned activity. It does not occur without first being preceded by reading out the report and inasmuch as reading out the report is looking for a possible solution that only reading in can provide, reading in is systematically provided for by reading out. In this respect, the fact that next steps to be engaged in as engineering solutions are distanced from the statement of the problematics they are aimed at is a systematic feature of the way that these problems and solutions are organised. This organisation consists of the constitution of problematic events in reading out the report form, and the constitution of next steps to be taken as possible solutions. Thus not only is there a systematic reason in terms of the sequential organisation of 'problems and solutions' within these sorts of setting, for distancing 'the problem' from 'the solution' there are also methodic ways of working towards 'the solution' from 'the problem'.

Conclusion: step-by-step, turn-by-turn

We have examined a single brief episode of problem solving within a large engineering project involving many individuals and taking several years. We do not, however, imagine that we have exhausted the things that could cogently be said about it. We have examined some of the ways in which the engineers address and transform some problematic materials into a shape in which they can identify and possibly solve an engineering problem, but have said little about the social occasion, or setting, within which this takes place.

The episode involves problem-solving, and in that respect this instance reflects and implements the policies of the organisation within which it occurs. The projects in which engineers participate are organised as a succession of problem-solving operations. The decomposition of design work in this way is a technique for managing the scale and complexity of design problems, of turning these into a series of small, even 'bite-sized' problems which can be handled singly, and by a small proportion of the project's team. The problem-solving operations are not merely sequenced, but are designed to provide the project's work with a step-by-step structure, with the ordering of problems being placed within a series which progresses the work towards the delivery of a finished product. This step-by-step arrangement often structures the work into a hierarchy of phases. Thus, the problem-solving operation we have examined is only one in the series that makes up this day's sunrise meeting, while the sunrise meeting in its turn is only one of a daily series which are being conducted in the 'testing' phase of the project's organisation.

The organisation prescribed the conduct of work by way of identifying and solving a multiplicity of small problems, but the implementation of the step-by-step policy is something which, on its actual occasions, must be realised on a turn-by-turn basis. In this chapter, we have been examining some of the methodic ways in which, through distributed turns at talk, the turn-by-turn organisation of the talk, the project's engineers locally realise the step-by-step policy of design by problem-solving.

Appendix: transcript symbols

[	Utterances or parts of utterances linked by left hand bracket begin simultaneously.
=	Equals sign links together utterances or parts of utterances that run together.
(0.4)	Timed interval within or between utterances.
(.)	Full stop in parentheses indicates an interval of less than a tenth of a second.
____	Underlined utterances or parts of utterances are discernibly stressed.
::	Colons indicate stress.
.	Full stop denotes a stopping fall in intonation.
,	A comma indicates a continuing intonation.
*	The asterisk symbol marks quietly spoken words.
↑↓	Arrows pointing upwards or downwards indicate a marked rising or falling shift in intonation.

Acknowledgements

We are grateful to the participants concerned and to Bob Anderson, Christian Heath, Jon Hindmarsh and Paul Luff for comments on previous drafts of this chapter.

NOTES

1 So-called because they are held at the beginning of every working day.
2 This FRF is not the one that we consider in the main body of the text. The FRFs are highly confidential and we were not allowed to retain copies of active ones, including the one that figures in our analysis.
3 The transformation of 'flat' narrative reports into causal diagnoses is of course likely to feature in other occupational settings, such as those of social work where, for example, case reports are transformed into evidence of social problems. We are not suggesting that in so doing, in this example, social workers are engineers or that engineers are social workers because the accomplishment of some of their work activities is done through the use of similar interactional devices. It is, after all, not just the engineering and science that are concerned with causal textures. What does, however, differentiate one from the other, engineering from social work for example, is the terms in which the causality is accountable and the form in which the causal determination must be cast. In the engineering case, it is those of machine operations and problems.
4 There are two aspects to 'reading out'. The first is the practical interactional fact that only one person in the meeting possesses a copy of the form, which contains the detailed operator and technician reports. The data analyst therefore reads these out so that everyone else in the meeting can be aware of these

details. The second aspect of 'reading out' is that it places on the table, so to speak, the sequential order of the events involved in the fault's manifestation and correction. This narrative thus provides the material they must work with in order to impute a causal texture to the reported events.

5 The section of the form that is read out concerns the two sections identified as 'Reason for call' and 'Service actions' (see sample FRF in figure 3.1).

4 Analysing cooperative work in an urban traffic control room for the design of a coordination support system

Jacques Theureau and Geneviève Filippi

Introduction

The investigations which we shall present here form part of a research programme whose objective is the design of computer systems in terms of support systems for users. This research programme was initiated in 1979 (after two decisive studies, one about nurses' activity, the other about human–computer interaction and data coding) by an investigation aimed at designing a system for a data collecting and coding station (Pinsky, 1979; Pinsky and Theureau, 1982). Since then, it has been developed in various work situations: offices, hospitals and other services, control of sequential and continuous industrial processes, air and urban traffic control, agriculture and fishery. Such a design involves helping the users to understand the situation and take action themselves, including the search for information, and relieving the users as much as possible (within technical and economic limitations) of the details of data supply and action, in so far as these are unnecessary for an understanding of the situation. The computer system is thus considered as an element of the support system among others, like documentation, training, organisation and other sources of information on the situation here and now.

This design approach is an alternative to the design in terms of cognitive prosthesis which emerged at the beginning of computerisation and is still dominant (see Woods and Roth, 1988, for its criticism). A computer system designed as a cognitive prosthesis is supposed to concentrate the intelligence of experts (hence the commercial name 'expert systems' for the most sophisticated of these systems). Ideally, the role of the user is that of a cognitive invalid: to provide data for the system in so far as the latter is unable to acquire them in other ways (within technical and economic limitations); to understand the instructions of the system and to act accordingly, in so far as the latter cannot act alone (within technical and economic limitations). Such systems generally reveal they have not attained the desired ideal by also allocating another role to the users: to manage on their own when the system fails. Hence a contradiction which can entail a heavy price to pay, for both the actors and the quality and quantity of the production: on the one hand, if the users thus accept to lose, under ordinary circumstances, their decision-making powers and the means to implement them, they play the role of a cognitive invalid at the high risk to become one; on the other hand, they are called upon to play the role of a super-expert in certain isolated circumstances.

Designing support systems for users in specific situations is not an easy task. It requires a creative and future oriented synthesis of three kinds of analysis:

1 analysis of the global activity of specific users, having a specific culture, in the situations that are concerned, non-computerised or comprising an unsatisfactory computer assistance (for the definition of what must be assisted by computer);

2 analysis of the global activity of assistance supplied to the user by other more competent users in these situations (for the inspiration provided for the design of computer support through the knowledge of human assistance);

3 analysis of the global activity of users in other situations with a more satisfactory computer support (in order to define the computer support using the highest technical possibilities).

Therefore, this research programme has been essentially concerned by the theoretical notions and methods which are needed to make these three kinds of analysis in the current constraints of design processes, with sufficient accuracy and validity for the design of support systems (see Theureau, 1992; Theureau et al., 1994). We are concerned here by the first kind of analysis in presenting a recent study which highlights the relations between this research programme and others.

The RER A line control room

This investigation was part of a wider research programme which linked the analysis of public announcements to the analysis of traffic control in order to guide the modernisation of the different technical and organisational components of the complete chain of traffic supervision, starting from the control room and ending up with the passenger.[1] It concerned the control room of the RER A line which was, at the time of the study, undergoing important changes.[2] First, computerisation was progressing: it concerned the rolling-stock follow-up, new functions of signalling and automatic calculation of train delays at each station. Second, the control room was moving to a larger room because of the extension of the line

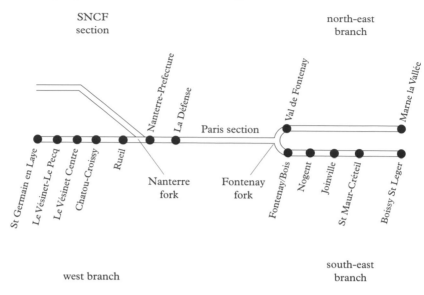

Figure 4.1 The RER A line

towards Disneyland Paris, which was the occasion to modify its general layout. With 70,000 passengers per hour at rush hours, the RER A line has one of the highest traffic densities in suburban rail transportation in the world. Its operation is made fairly complex because of two forks at both ends of the line, its connection with the French railway company (SNCF) and the use of two different kinds of rolling-stock incompatible with one another (see figure 4.1).

Every train is identified by a name which indicates its route (such as ZHAN 07 or NAGA 12). Once the train movement has been completed upon arrival at the terminus, this name and the corresponding route and sequence change (for instance, RUDY 12 becomes ZHAN 23, the name of the return route of RUDY 12).

The equipment installed in the control room was not designed as an integral system. It has been extended on a piecemeal basis, in line with traffic growth. It consists of communication facilities (telephone and radio), a fixed-line diagram giving real-time information on traffic, computer terminals displaying the same sort of information, but with more details and on several computer images, along with various working documents (timing graph, empty coaching-stock (ECS) diagrams, train-crew rosters and so on). Traffic control is a collective exercise involving a dozen or so operating staff located in the control room, consisting of a team of

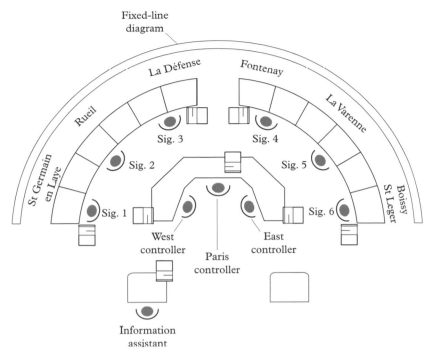

Figure 4.2 The RER A line control room

three controllers, each responsible for one of three geographical sectors of the line (western sector, Paris sector, eastern sector) each assisted by two signalmen and an information assistant and also, in the event of a major incident, the line manager (figure 4.2).

Signalmen identify the trains, check the times at which trains enter their sectors and notify the controllers of any delays. They supervise stock movements and issue instructions concerning ECS movements, all of which are logged. They also check the timetables displayed in the stations, which they alter when necessary. Controllers supervise these various functions, take decisions affecting traffic control with regard to supervision of drivers and keep an eye on stock workings, to ensure that units get back into the depot for maintenance and repairs. One of their main responsibilities is to return traffic to normal after an incident (fairly serious incidents are quite commonplace during rush hours, but passengers are hardly ever aware that anything has happened). What we have here, therefore, is a work situation in which teamwork is regarded as essential, something which is reflected in the importance both of verbal communication and body language between the various staff in the control room and of contact made over the telephone or the radio with people outside, such as drivers, station masters, depot managers and the emergency services.

The RER A line control room as a collective organisation of multiple courses of action

Let us consider the system constituted by the RER control room, its actors included. It is fairly complex: it involves many different components, which are linked in many different ways. Besides, many of these components cannot be observed directly. Most of the physiological processes can be observed only in the laboratory, and can be analysed only with very simple tasks and environments. But this complexity is not the main difficulty. It can be overcome by finding a level of the system which could be analysed in the natural situation. The main difficulty is that this system involves autonomous systems. The system formed by each actor and the environment (including the other actors) is autonomous. This autonomy is, according to the cognitive paradigm known as 'constructivist' or 'enaction' paradigm, initiated by Maturana and Varela (1980) in biology, a fundamental characteristic of human actors, and more generally of living systems. It is the capacity of such an actor or living system to exist as a unit and to make a relevant and significant, while not predefined in advance, world to emerge (Bourgine and Varela, 1992; Varela, 1980; Varela *et al.*, 1991). The important consequence of this autonomy is that, at a given moment, an actor interacts with a situation to which the emergence and relevance of the actor's internal structure has itself contributed. This internal structure is a product of the actor's physiological and neuro-physiological constitution, personal history up to that moment and interactions with the immediately preceding situation. Therefore, neither spatial or temporal boundaries nor content of this situation can be determined a priori. They depend on the actor and on the personal history, and vary with the actor's interactions with the immediately preceding situation. Evidently, in the case of the control room, a part of the personal histories of its actors is shared and constitutes a common history. Therefore also, these boundaries and content cannot be determined by an observer alone. This determination needs to be made from the point of view of the actor's internal structure. A correlated difficulty is that the system formed by each actor and the environment (including the other actors) is open. It changes from day to day, not only because of the interactions which occur inside itself, but also because of the interactions of the actor with other situations: other work situations, the characteristics of which can be very different from the former difficulty, and the situations of the actor's different practices of leisure, household and so on. The control room, with its multiple actors, is a multiply open system.

Although requiring a detailed methodology, the simplest and most natural way to deal with the autonomy and openness of the system formed by each actor and the environment, that is to include the point of view of the actor's internal structure, is to reduce the study of the actor's activity to the study of what we call the course of action: the activity of one specific actor, actively involved in a specific situation, belonging to a specific culture, which is pre-reflexive, or, otherwise stated, which is significant for him **or** her, or can be shown, related and commented on by **the actor** at any moment to an observer-interlocutor, under favourable conditions for observation and interlocution.

The aim of the study of a course of action is to understand its intrinsic organisation and its extrinsic constraints and effects in the state of the actors, their situation and culture. The description of the intrinsic organisation of the course of action articulates two complementary descriptions: a description of its global dynamics, characterising the units of the course of action and the relations of sequencing and embedding between these units; a description of its local dynamics, characterising the underlying structure of the elementary units. These units include in various ways actions and communications, but also other elements: interpretations, feelings, changes in focus, perceptive, proprioceptive and mnemonic judgements, commitments of the actor to the situation and the use of past experience in the present course of action. All these elements, including the less public ones, belong to the actor's interactions with the situation. However, we must take due note of the fact that this notion of interaction differs from the usual notion of interaction, which is defined from the point of view of an observer of the actor and of the physical and social environment, as human–human, human–machine or human–environment interaction, and not from the point of view of the actor.

A given course of action is collective, yet from the standpoint of a particular actor it is both social and individual, like the activity in Vygotsky's (1962, 1978) approach and in Engeström (1987). To deal more thoroughly with this collective aspect, as was necessary in this RER control room study, we had to study the collective organisation of multiple courses of action: the synchronic and diachronic relations between the intrinsic organisations of the courses of action of the different actors of the control room, and their constraints and effects in the state of the actors, their situation and culture.

Data on the courses of action in the control room

As a first stage, we carried out an analysis of the courses of action of the various staff members in the control room: controllers, signalmen and information assistants. The purpose of that stage was to clearly follow the course of action of each person concerning the traffic control, while seeking to understand what the actions of the other colleagues mean to this person. Doing so facilitated the cooperation of the actors to the study, by showing them that this study was aimed, not only at improving the performance – which is evidently collective – but also at supporting the activity of each individual. We could then consider collective action as such, as several individual courses of action which take place synchronically, so as to see how they are linked to each other to constitute a coordinated collective activity. It is this analysis of the collective organisation of multiple courses of action, which we realised as a second stage.

The choice of data to be collected was induced by this interest in the cooperation between officials in the course of their traffic control activity. But it was also induced by the possibilities offered by the work situation. It was by considering these possibilities that we decided to observe moderately disrupted situations, that is all the usual incidents that occur nearly every day at rush hours (inopportune use of emergency brakes, delayed trains and so on), rather than to focus on major incidents. These major incidents are fortunately rare, and their study, with a few exceptions, can be made only a posteriori. Also, as they imply very heavy individual responsibilities which the persons involved must account for to their superiors, we took the engagement to stop the data collection in case of their occurrence in our presence. This choice therefore depended just as much on methodological criteria as on criteria linked to the social organisation of work.

The data collected covered continuous observations of the behaviour of action and communication of diverse chief controllers and signal assistants in the control room which consisted of recordings (by tape recorder and video camera), completed by notes on the events taken into account by each actor and the actions of the others when related to the actor's course of action; different kinds of instigated verbalisations from the actors, in particular those arising in self-confrontation interviews (the operator is shown a video recording of his behaviour and he is asked to comment on very specific aspects of this behaviour). The purpose of such a self-confrontation interview is not only to obtain a description of the actor's activity and situation from his own point of view, but also to probe more deeply into the problems encountered by the actor.

During the first stage, with a view to analysing the courses of action of each individual, we made several observations, with a camera focused on a controller and a microphone in the middle of the team of controllers. Likewise, during the second stage, in order to perceive the synchronic linkage between individual activities, we collected systematic data on two kinds of subsets of cooperation: three controllers belonging to the same team who are constantly coordinating their actions in order to control the line's total traffic; a traffic controller and the signalmen of his geographical sector, who have to work together concerning their part of the line. These observations were made with two video cameras and two tape recorders. The duration of the observations was about three or four hours, corresponding to the rush hours and their preparation, that is to say, roughly from 6.30 a.m. to 10 a.m. and 3.30 p.m. to 7 p.m. The choice of these observation periods corresponds to the times during which the common incidents which we wished to study were likely to occur.

Analysis into significant units of the courses of action in the control room

The theoretical framework, which we have coined as 'semio-logical', makes it possible to describe courses of action in general structural terms, expressing underlying regularities. It allows, on the one hand, such a description of the global dynamics of the courses of action, and on the other hand, such a description of their local dynamics. It also links these two descriptions. Here we limit our analysis of the collective organisation of the courses of action to the analysis of its global dynamics. More precisely, we shall deal with its local dynamics only in a narrative way using the framework given by the analysis of its global dynamics. Then, of this semio-logical framework, we present only the two general hypotheses which were considered in this particular study, the ones which concern the global dynamics of the courses of action of the different actors and the relations between these global dynamics. The first hypothesis is that the units of courses of action are significant units for the actor (or actors) which are classified by more abstract structures, significant structures of different ranks; a significant unit, and also the significant structure which classifies it, expresses a coherence through time between the ranges of the possibilities open for the actor at every moment of the time span of this unit. Consistent with this first hypothesis, a given course of action is composed of a stratified set of significant units and this composition gives depth to the range of possibilities for the actor at every moment. The second hypothesis is that the actors in the control room share significant units, at certain ranks. In other words, they share parts of the ranges of the possibilities open for each one at every moment. This sharing is the key to their coordination.

The analysis of data in significant units for a controller (or signalman) provides a particular description of the incidental situations observed. It is a matter of dividing the continuous development of the course of action of this controller (or signalman) into significant units by replying to the question: 'What is this about, from the point of view of the controller (or signalman)?' By naming each of these units, an account is built up which gives meaning to the rough data. This analysis clarifies the temporal organisation of the actions and events and provides elements on their sequencing. Thus, the intricacy of significant units, that is the interruption of significant units by other significant units, reflects the fact that several preoccupations are handled simultaneously by the controller (or signalman).

The significant units at a given moment can be separate for the different actors of a subset of cooperation. But they can also overlap on all ranks or on certain of these ranks. Along with the second hypothesis above, such overlappings witness that these actors share parts of their ranges of possibilities. This sharing is more or less developed depending on the ranks where the overlappings take place.

After showing, through an example incident, the characteristics of the synchronic collective organisation of the courses of actions in the subsets of cooperation, we shall make more precise, through the example of another incident, the diachronic collective organisation of the courses actions and its relations with the synchronic one. We finally present the directions for the design of a support system for coordination which this analysis allows us to formulate.

Significant units and the synchronic collective organisation of the courses of action in the control room

Let us, for example, present the following extract from the handling of an incident, which has been observed during the second stage of the study (figure 4.3).[3] This incident and its handling can be described using also the rest of the transcript and the self-confrontation interviews.

NAGA 12, a train running in the direction of Boissy St Leger, breaks down at the exit of Joinville's station, stopping all trains eastbound. As soon as the east controller, in charge of the Joinville sector, understands there is a breakdown concerning platform 1, he directs the next train, RUDY 12, on to platform A, letting it wait in the station. The solution viewed by the controller is to ask NAGA 12 to go back 100 metres in order to free the station exit point (see figure 4.4).

This solution allows trains following behind to pass NAGA 12 by platform A. It stems from a very precise knowledge of the configuration of the platforms and tracks at Joinville, and also of the possibilities of movement often left to the train in case of such a breakdown. But it may fail and its implementation is rather difficult because the controller cannot communicate directly with the NAGA 12 driver, who is busy trying to repair his train and is therefore not in the front cabin: the controller has to pass on his message to the RUDY 12 driver, who has stopped along the other platform.

Considering the uncertainty of a rapid outcome of this solution, the controller launches another solution which is more costly in so far as it requires trains to run on the opposite track. But, eventually, the NAGA 12 driver succeeds in reversing his train and the controller is able to cancel the second solution. Once the core of the problem (i.e. NAGA 12 blocking the Joinville station) is solved, the controller has to deal with the other problems resulting from this disruption such as using RUDY 12 to ensure the rest of NAGA 12's journey up to Boissy St Leger, and also finding replacement trains and standby drivers for the return journey of these two trains.

The implementation of a decision is gradual and shifted in time, that is to say that the handling of the incident is dependent upon the time needed to manoeuvre the trains as well as the possibility of communicating with the drivers. In the mean time many other problems have cropped up and some have already been solved. The relatively long time – about twenty minutes – needed to sort out the breakdown makes it very difficult to turn back once a decision is launched. Consequences of the decision must, therefore, be evaluated in advance. Furthermore, this type of relatively long processing time leads to overlapping problems to be solved: other incidents are tied with that of the NAGA 12 breakdown and must be handled simultaneously.

The analysis of the handling of the incident also reflects the importance of colleagues for each controller's activity. A high number of persons involved in an incident (drivers, station masters, signal assistants and other controllers) have to be informed. This creates an additional difficulty for planning the actions of the controller, for he must ensure that everyone has completely understood what it is about and what has to be done. The way we have presented the extract of the transcript in figure 4.3 already shows in its centre part of the collective synchronic organisation of the courses of action in the subset of cooperation formed by the west (CR W) and east (CR E) controllers. The left part of the figure concerns CR W and the right part his colleague CR E. A central column is created when they are involved in the same, usually collective, communications.

S	Action of CR W	Communications of CR W	Communications of CR E		Actions of CR E	S
			CR E → train	OK, your colleague who is trying to solve the partial blocking, if you see him on the platform, ask him to call before going on	Hangs up the radio-telephone	1
1	Turned toward TCO (East branch)	CR E → others CR W CR P CR E CR P → CR E CR E CR W CR P → CR W CR E CR P		And, I will try to make him drive back a little… … with rear gear No, with rear gear, you… And, where can I get through? But, yes, a transit action It's a TGS! But, no, he is right, it doesn't get through, even with a transit action Why does it not get through? Because, I don't know… how much he is on the point Oh, … he isn't on the other point zone.		2
1	Looks at TCO and its East branch		Sig. → CR E CR E → train	I think that he is speaking now. Yes, the train which is in Joinville, platform 1, it's you… who calls me up?	Picks up the radio-telephone	1

Sig. → CR E	You cannot… it is diverted up there	CR E → train	Yes, the train who just called up, I listen	
CR W	xxx in case of partial blocking of the brakes, we have it in the ass	train	who is on platform 2 at Joinville. It's to tell you that there is one carriage and a half out of the platform, and that he is inquiring. You will not easily contact him.	
		CR E → train	OK, I thank you. We will try to contact him anyway, because if he drives back a little toward the platform, we will be able to make the other trains get through	
		train	OK, listen, he is on the platform, the colleague who is on the platform, xx to tell him, but he is gone…	
		CR E → train	OK, thank you	Hangs up
				3
		Man. → CR E	Did you contact La Varenne?	
		CR E	There is nobody there	
		Man.	There is nobody there	
		CR E	There is nobody there	

Figure 4.3 An extract from the transcription of data about the courses of action of CR W and CR E during the handling of the breakdown of NAGA 12 in Joinville

Joinville station

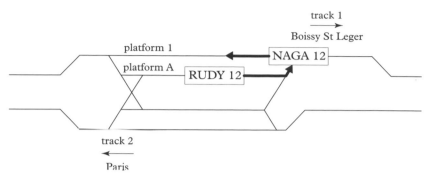

Figure 4.4 NAGA 12 blocking Joinville station

The analysis of this extract of the transcript makes this collective synchronic organisation of the courses of action more precise (figure 4.5).

The significant units resulting from this analysis belong to three ranks, namely story, theme and sequence. The analysis shows that the shared sequences, though named identically at the lower rank, are named differently on the higher ranks. For example, the sequence 1 of CR W and the sequence 2 of CR E correspond to a discussion with CR P: CR E informs the two other controllers about his intention to ask the driver of NAGA 12 to drive back 100 metres, in order to free the end point of the station that this train blocks, and they collectively evaluate the idea. For CR E, this discussion makes him immediately prepare his action, which will consist in beginning to undertake this first solution by asking the driver to try to drive back.

This analysis into significant units for the different subsets of cooperation constitutes a frame for different findings concerning the collective organisation of courses of action. Various forms of cooperation emerge during such disrupted situations. Relative to a story like the breakdown of NAGA 12, the different significant units for a given actor can be classified into four categories: he is responsible; he is co-responsible; he follows up in the background; or he is busy with other stories and ignores it. While a controller solves the core of an important incident, the other controllers and signalmen often carry out secondary jobs to help their colleague, such as holding back, in a station, the trains following behind a defective train to avoid jamming them under a tunnel; or informing station masters of a breakdown; or searching for a line manager to go into the field. They also participate in the background to the solving of an incident by giving advice to their colleague in charge of it and by showing him aspects of the

Course of action of CR W			Course of action of CR E		
Story	Theme	Sequence	Story	Theme	Sequence
BREAKDOWN OF NAGA 12			BREAKDOWN OF NAGA 12	NAGA 12 blocking Joinville: undertakes a first solution	1 Tries to give the message to NAGA 12 through RUDY 12
	CR E's problem: NAGA 12 stopped in Joinville	1 Discussion with colleagues to find a solution to prevent NAGA 12 blocking the traffic		(to back NAGA 12 100 metres)	2 Discussion with colleagues concerning the position of NAGA 12 at the station exit point to determine the feasibility of the solution
					1 Asks RUDY 12 to tell NAGA 12 to try to drive back out of the station exit point
				Provision of extra drivers	3 Man asks if La Varenne station master knows about NAGA 12

Figure 4.5 Analysis in significant units of the extract of the transcript presented in figure 4.3

problem he may have overlooked. In this sense, they play a role of guardians of the smooth handling of an incident. When the controller's attention is focused on a specific problem, the intervention of others makes it possible to 'de-focus' on the general context when this is necessary. Or else, when a breakdown occurs at rush hours, the urgent nature of the situation immediately generates an implicit sharing of the work: the controller concerned by the core of the incident tries to solve it with the driver, while the other controllers handle the upstream and downstream traffic. Finally, they anticipate the repercussions of the incident and of the actions performed to handle it in their own sector, as can be shown by an extract from the transcript and self-confrontation interview presented in figure 4.6.

However, when the general situation in the control room is too disturbed because of the accumulation of incidents, everybody tends to focus on his own problem solving, and nobody can play the role of collective guardian any more. The result is often a lack of coordination in the passing of information towards colleagues outside the control room.

Significant units and the diachronic collective organisation of the courses of action in the control room

To characterise also the diachronic collective organisation and its relation to the synchronic one, we shall take another example, an incident which proved to be a repercussion of the breakdown of NAGA 12 in Joinville, which has been submitted to the same kind of analysis into significant units. About an hour after the stopping of NAGA 12 in Joinville station, that is quite a long time after this incident had been settled by the east controller, a problem appears concerning track 2 at the other end of the line: one of his signalmen reports to the west controller that three ZHANs (return journey of the RUDYs) and three XILOs (return journey of the NAGAs) are following each other without their usual spacing. The consequences are important for passengers because the XILOs stop in all stations up to Le Pecq whereas the ZHANs are semi-fast to St Germain en Laye. From the self-confrontation interviews of the controllers, it appears that the origin of this erroneous sequence of trains is an error of the signalman in charge of the Fontenay fork (see figure 4.1). The many manipulations of trains made by the east controller to make up for lost time after the breakdown of NAGA 12, and in particular the change of decision concerning ZHAN 23 (the return journey of RUDY 12) which had first been cancelled and eventually had been reintroduced, confused this signalman.

The west controller is immediately able to connect together this sequence of three ZHANs and three XILOs with the breakdown of

s		Actions and communications of CRW
21	CRW → ALL	But, it's the NAGA 12, we must find this guy of the NAGA 12, am I right?
		CRW looks at the timing graph and follows with his finger NAGA 12 working.
		CRW uses his second hand to follow another train working.
22	CRW → CRE	Hi, Jean Louis, why don't you get the XILO 25 out now so that it could be taken out again at Rueil?
	CRE → CRW	No, wait a minute, we will do even better. The train which is at the platform here
	CRW → CRE	Yes
	CRE → CRW	(whistles) without travellers, and it makes ZHAN 23 working.

Observer: You look at your timing graph?

CRW: Yes, I don't know the development of the incident. I know that there is one. I see that Jean Louis handles it OK. So, I am sure that he will get new trains from the Boissy depot… but when there an incident, we don't know if there won't be another one. Then, I pay attention to the situation: I look at Jean Louis's action. And I tell to myself: 'If it goes wrong, maybe I will have to be prepared'. And I have already called up the Rueil station master about the incident.

Observer: What do you prepare?

CRW: I try to anticipate the evolution of the incident as it is now. Do I have train crews available? Do I have rolling-stock elements available? Then I call up the station master. The answers are 'yes' and I can wait for events.

Figure 4.6 An extract from the transcript and self-confrontation interview

84		*Looks at the fixed-line diagram between Joinville and Rueil.*
	CRW	What's this bloody hell! Well Jean Louis [CR E's name] wasn't that good!

Figure 4.7 An extract from the continuation of the transcript

NAGA 12 which happened an hour earlier (figure 4.7). It is a consequence of the synchronic articulation of his course of action with the course of action of the east controller. In particular, he had kept up with its management by the east controller, in particular when the latter had found a replacement train for ZHAN 23, which consequently was running behind schedule. Thus, the synchronic organisation of the courses of action during the core of the handling of the breakdown of NAGA 12 and its repercussions contributes to the diagnosis of the incidents which follow.

But, this synchronic organisation has not enabled the controllers and the signalmen to manage all the repercussions. Apart from the numerous manipulations of trains already considered, there are three more reasons for that: first, there is a coexistence of two logics in the sharing of the handling of an incident, which, in certain cases, can be contradictory; second, the handling of the breakdown of NAGA 12 and of its repercussions has taken place in a multi-disrupted situation; third, the shared feeling of success after the good conclusion of the breakdown of NAGA 12 in Joinville. Let us consider the two first reasons more thoroughly.

The first logic, which corresponds to the prescribed allocation of roles, is *geographic*: each controller manages the disruptions occurring in his own sector, even though the sectors' borders are loose and giving a hand is a tacit rule. The second logic, which follows the dynamics of train movement, can be called *historic*: it postulates tacitly that the person who starts handling a disruption is responsible for it during its entire course, because he knows all the surrounding circumstances and the consequences of his own decisions. The coexistence of these two logics is implicit to the coordination of the controller's action, the choice of one or another depends on how each person is involved in the situation: a controller may make way for his colleagues depending on their receptiveness at the moment and on the fact that they have participated in the background to the beginning of the incident's solving. In the case of the repercussion of the breakdown of NAGA 12, the signal assistant who mixed up the trains is in charge of the Fontenay fork, which is at the border of the eastern and Paris sectors. Following the geographical logic, both controllers were liable to supervise what was happening at the junction. But, at that time, the Paris controller happened to be dealing with another incident on his sector and had not paid attention to the details of the arrangement made by his colleague in relation to the NAGA 12 return journey. The east controller was busy evacuating the defective NAGA 12 out of Joinville station and he did not consider there could be a problem for the signalmen to follow up the return route of the trains.

In fact, the handling of the breakdown of NAGA 12 has taken place in a multi-disrupted situation. Three important incidents have kept the officials busy: the breakdown of NAGA 12, handled principally by CR E but which has been followed more or less by everybody; the breakdown of OLAF 12, which has been handled by the cooperation between CR W and CR P, and also the ZHAN 27 stuck in Auber station, handled principally by CR P. To these important incidents, we must add many small or medium-scale incidents, such as an alarm concerning the electric power supply of the tracks, the non-display of the ZHANs in Rueil station, the presence of passengers on the tracks in the direction of Joinville station, and the bad succession of ZHAN and XILO we have already described. From this evidence, it is clear that multi-disrupted situations, when controllers and signal assistants are busy with several incidents at the same time, affect functioning of the group because neither of the two logics can be efficiently followed.

The definition of a coordination support system

Such an analysis of the courses of actions of the different officials and of their collective organisation orients the reflection concerning the modernisation of the traffic regulation apparatus toward the design of a coordination support system (see Winograd and Flores, 1986). The proposals for the design of tools supporting coordination we put forward after this analysis were along three complementary directions: developing the current computer support; improving the fixed-line diagram and the spatial design of the control room; and improving the tools for communication. We shall briefly present these directions and stress one of the proposals along the first direction, which stems directly from the examples we presented above, while the others stem also from the analysis of other disrupted situations.

Three directions for design

The first direction is developing the current computer support. Different proposals have been made, with a decreasing order of importance. One of the proposals along this first direction concerns the synchronical/diachronical and chronological aspects of the traffic which we shall present further in more detail. A second proposal concerns the display of the reordering of the trains. At present, when an agent updates the computer, these actions are not visible enough for the other agents. A simple solution would be to display the number of a reordered train with a different colour, so that an agent who has not followed the actions during the handling of an incident is immediately informed about the resultant modifications. A third proposal concerns computer support to the supervision of drivers. One of the imperative criteria when handling an incident is to respect the schedule of the drivers. To enforce this criterion when the mission of a train is changed, the controllers aim at restoring, as rapidly as possible, the tie between drivers and missions. They use standby drivers and replace the drivers as soon as they reach the station where their mission begins. Therefore, the controllers must know which drivers are tied to which trains. At present, they write down the drivers' numbers on the timing graph, but it is difficult to find on this graph the different missions of a given driver, because the relationship between drivers and trains is unstable. Hence, when there is a change concerning this relationship, the controllers are obliged to consult the train-crew roster. In order to harmonise the multiple sources of information used when handling an incident, we proposed to make the drivers appear on the computer display, in two different modes: for each train, the train-crew which is really assigned; and for each train-crew, the succession of its trains. The final proposal is for computer support to estimate the number of passengers. When handling an incident, the controllers try to transport the maximum of passengers, at the risk of penalising the passengers, less important in number, who are at the end of the line, or who go in the opposite direction to the main flow. But they work blindly. An apparatus detecting the approximate number of passengers in certain key stations would allow them to refine their decisions.

The second direction is improving the fixed-line diagram and the spatial design of the control room. The analysis of the collective organisation of the courses of action in the control room shows that there is a necessity for mutual visibility, mutual listening and for a common referent. The proposals along this direction concern the interior design of the control room and also improving the fixed-line diagram. Against the present international tendency to exclude fixed-line diagrams and to rely on computer terminals, the fixed-line diagram must be kept and improved. All agents can see at a glance the state of traffic, which is scattered in the different images displayed on computer terminals. When

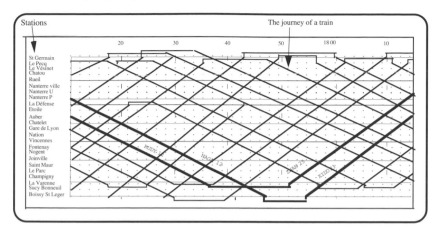

Figure 4.8 A page from the timing graph

positioning their body in the direction they are looking at, they make visible for everybody the focus of their attention.

The third complementary direction is improving the communicative tools. Many proposals stem from the analysis. The first is to improve the quality of the present system, which is responsible for many communication failures, some of which have dramatic consequences. To facilitate the communication by the radio-telephone and prevent confusion, the agents need also an automatic display of the name of the train the driver of which is calling. To facilitate the multiple communications which occur between the driver, the station master of the station where the driver is assigned and the controller, a multi-communication device would be useful.

Computer support concerning the synchronical/diachronical and chronological aspects

The proposal we present in more detail is a device that enhances the present computer system. It is aimed at supporting the individual handling of an incident, and also the cooperative supervision of train movements.

We have first to consider more precisely the present means of handling an incident. The three main devices of permanent use, the fixed-line diagram, the computer images and the timing graph, are different maps representing the same territory, the RER A line. The timing graph is a reference document indicating the routes and sequences of the trains (figure 4.8). Its graphic presentation makes it possible to follow a given train (Where does it come from? What was its previous route? Where does it go? What will be its future route?). It also allows a comparison between several trains. Compared to the fixed-line diagram, or to the computer images, the timing graph is not a representation of what is going on here and now. It is the basis on which controllers continually refer, as a tool to evaluate the present situation. In this sense, it is a map of the 'normal' situation, from which amendments can be made on the route and sequence of a train. When perturbations occur, information given by the computer system is meaningful only with reference to any discrepancies with the normal situation seen on the timing graph. However, it is not easy to draw a correlation between these two information sources, because they do not relate to the same level of information. On one hand, the graphic is about the dynamics of the normal traffic, as a whole. It is a very rich tool, which shows several aspects of the traffic. The first is the diachronical aspect: each train has its past and future route. The second is the synchronical aspect: at a given time, the location of all the trains is defined. What the controllers are actually interested in is a combination of the synchronical and diachronical aspects: on a given portion of the line, there is a set of trains going in the same direction but having different routes. By considering this set of trains, it is possible to replace a defective train by another train with a similar route. The last aspect is the chronological aspect: at a given location, one has all the trains passing from the beginning of the day. On the other hand, the computer images give, in real time, a precise view of all trains at a given moment, or in other words, of only one aspect, the synchronical one, through a succession of snapshots.

This design proposal is optimising the current computer system for the follow-up of train movements which should give the historical background of all the trains by providing equivalent information to those of the timing graph, but applied to the real running of trains. Hence, this dynamic tool would hold concurrently the synchronical/diachronical and the chronological aspect of train movements which is now lacking. When the computer system is updated, this tool would also support the coordination of actions between the staff by rendering the amendments made on trains more visible than they currently are. For instance, a changed route should be displayed one way or the other on the terminals so that any member of the staff knows immediately of modifications of the traffic even if he or she is unaware of the details of the handling of the incident.

Discussion

The empirical and practical results presented in the sections above give an idea of the fecundity of the constructivist or enaction paradigm and of its methodological consequences in the terms of the course-of-action approach. This course-of-action approach is part of the French-language ergonomics tradition which, contrary to other 'human factors' and 'ergonomics' traditions, has – since Ombredane and Faverge (1955) at least – considered that ergonomics development and design absolutely requires analysis of the activity of operators in real work settings. It is also part of a larger international research trend which includes the interactionist approach of work situations and the socially distributed cognition approach.

For example, along the interactionist approach, the studies of Goodwin and Goodwin (1996) Suchman (1996a) and describing communications in an airline operations room, or Heath and Luff's (1991) study of coordination in London Underground control rooms, stress the construction of context by the partners and the importance of verbal and body language in the coordination between individuals. These investigations, systematising the use of video recordings as a methodological principle, explore the way that participants show one another the meaning of what they are doing or saying. Yet, emphasising the role of communication as if the whole of cognition was included in the communicative interaction itself may lead, in some cases, to neglect the fact that individuals interact all along their courses of action in order to attain the specific objectives constrained by the work environment. This may explain why most of these investigations tend to focus only on relatively short periods of interaction (about five minutes), leaving aside the global dynamics of longer and more complex incidents.

The socially distributed cognition approach consists in considering the group, rather than individuals, as the unit of analysis, that is to say, as a functional cultural unit. Thus, to describe how the crew of a large ship fixes its position, or how pilots manage the take-off of an aircraft, Hutchins (1995) traces the movement of information through the joint cognitive system composed of the team and technical artefacts. The notion of 'distributed cognition' he proposes offers a promising approach to study large groups, but it deliberately does not cope with individuals participating in the collective activity.

If course-of-action analysis can be characterised as the implementation of what can be called a 'situated methodological individualism', then these last two approaches can be characterised as implementing a 'situated methodological sociologism or collectivism'. By going through the analysis of the courses of action before addressing that of the collective activity, one takes account of certain phenomena that are difficult to appreciate by means of these two approaches. In summary, by considering the pre-reflexive aspect of the actor's activity, that is the actor's course of action: (1) one specifies the links that public communication and action have with private emotions and interpretations; (2) one looks for more than simply the current definitions of 'tacit', 'implicit' or 'non-propositional' to characterise the competence of the actors; (3) one can thus be more certain of the relevance to the actor's internal structure of the description given of the activity and the situation; (4) one can express recommendations concerning both the individual situations and the collective situation. In the example of Metro traffic control, to understand what is happening it is especially important to know how the activity and the competencies of each of the actors (signalman Sig., controller CR W, controller CR E and the signalman of the Fontenay fork) are constructed. In addition, the work situation of each of them has specific features that must be taken into account in the design recommendations.

However, the constructivist or enaction paradigm does not exclude the possibility of studying collective activity directly, that is without going through study of individual activity. If agents are autonomous, collectivities or even cultures can be autonomous. A study of the collective construction of the activity can give rise to theoretical objects and data collecting and analysing methods which are more parsimonious than the ones of the study of courses of action. These theoretical objects and data collecting and analysing methods sacrifice phenomena of the individual construction of the activity – or at least some of them – to acquire easier access to its collective construction. Let us add here that the study of the collective organisation of multiple courses of action developed in the study presented above is based on an interpretation, obviously in connection with the constructivist and enaction paradigm, both on what was learnt in previous research on courses of action and on research carried out in accordance with these two other sorts of approaches.

Were we to leave things there, the interactionist studies and studies of socially distributed cognition would simply appear to be more parsimonious and therefore faster approaches that are more limited than studies of the collective organisation of multiple courses of action, but which are sufficient in certain cases and for certain aspects of the activities. But they are much more than that. In fact, as Heath and Luff (1991) point out, these interactionist studies and studies of socially distributed cognition also consider relatively subtle phenomena of spoken and body-language interactions which are not appreciated by the study of the collective organisation of the courses of action, due to the limits of the pre-reflexive phenomena appreciated through self-confrontation interviews. If the description and explanation of these pre-reflexive phenomena allow us to produce and validate theoretical notions which go beyond them, they are nevertheless limited by them. Evidently, these limits can be overcome using notions produced through the other approaches.

In all, we feel that in the current scientific context of abandonment of the 'computer image of mind' (or paradigm of 'man as an information-processing system'), with human methodological individualism, in favour of a concept of cognition as embodied, situated, cultivated and implacably individual and collective, the course-of-action analysis, the interactionistic approach, and the approach of socially distributed cognition, in conjunction with other resembling approaches which it is not our purpose to list here, are currently building the various facets of what could be called cognitive anthropology or empirical praxeology and the methodology for the corresponding technical and organisational design. This methodology could be coined activity-centred-system-design, as it makes more precise and operationalises the user-centred-system-design proposed by Norman and Draper (1986).

NOTES

1 M. Grosjean and I. Joseph, with a more ethnomethodological background, studied other aspects of this work setting. Different theoretical and methodological discussions took place with them and also with Heath and his colleagues, who have been developing a similar research in the London Underground (see Heath and Luff, 1991). Refer to Filippi (1994) for more details.

2 The RER (Réseau Express Régional) is a high-speed suburban branch of the Paris Metro.

3 In figure 4.3, CR W, CR E and CR P are the three chief controllers, respectively in charge of the western sector, the eastern sector and the Paris sector of the line. 'Sig.' is a signal assistant. 'Man.' is the manager of the control room. 'TCO' is the fixed-line diagram.

5 Expert systems in (inter)action: diagnosing document machine problems over the telephone

Jack Whalen and Erik Vinkhuyzen

Introduction

Computer system developers often speak of the 'coupling' of human intelligence with machine power in a single, interactive system that substantially enhances performance. But achieving this objective is not primarily a matter of deciding how to allocate functions between the machine components and the human elements, as much of the literature on human factors in expert and automated systems would have us believe. Without denying that this allocation problem has some heuristic relevance, the most important and vexing issue facing developers is how to build effective tools that take the fundamental *differences* between human action and machine operation into account.

Although several studies of human–machine interaction have demonstrated the significance of these differences for effective expert system design and deployment (e.g. Suchman, 1987; Hartland, 1993; Whalen, 1995a), and both cognitive science and the artificial intelligence (AI) research underpinning expert system design have been subjected to far-ranging criticism for their views on human action (Coulter, 1983, 1989; Winograd and Flores, 1986; H. Collins, 1990; Dreyfus, 1992; Button *et al.*, 1995; Hutchins, 1995; Clancey, 1997), most artificial intelligence practitioners have continued to assume that machines can do, or can in principle be designed to do, what humans do.[1] Accordingly, they remain focused on the allocation problem, and have been intrigued about the possibilities for designing expert applications that contain most, if not all, of the knowledge required to perform a task or solve a problem, with the 'knowledgeability' of the user confined largely to data entry and information retrieval procedures.

In this chapter, we report on an expert system built on these premises. We do not concern ourselves with the *technical* achievements of the system itself; instead, we examine the common-sense reasoning and competencies that ordinary users bring to bear in utilising the system (see Luff and Heath, 1993). By way of this analysis, we identify some of the

problems that arise when an 'allocation of expertise' commitment –
without any serious recognition of the distinct capacities and practices of
human users or, especially, the requisite manner of their engagement with
such artefacts – drives the design of expert systems and their deployment
in the workplace. We also identify some of the problems that result from
an inadequate understanding of the social context in which a system is
going to be used. We argue that expert system design should be founded
upon the demonstrably indispensable aptitude and competence of users,
and more responsive to the socially organised features of their activities.
Such a system would be less an expert system than a system for experts, a
tool designed to support and complement rather than thoroughly replicate or replace the knowledge, communally organised work practices and
problem-solving strategies of its users.[2]

Data and setting

The materials upon which our analysis is based consist of ethnographic
observations and video recordings of naturally occurring expert system
use in a large corporation's customer support telephone centre.[3] This
corporation, henceforth 'MMR Corporation', designs and manufactures
document machines – copiers, printers, fax machines and multipurpose
products that combine these document-processing functions. MMR has
a service organisation that installs, maintains and repairs these machines
at customer sites. When customers need to report a problem with their
machine and request service, they telephone the company's support
centres. These calls are answered by Customer Service and Support
Representatives (CSSRs), who are then responsible for processing these
requests and dispatching service technicians. CSSRs accomplish this task
by entering information about the customer (notably the serial number of
their machine) into a computer, which allows them to create a job ticket
for the appropriate group of service technicians. In particularly urgent
cases, a technician can be paged by the CSSR directly.

In the customer support centre, CSSRs are seated at individual desks
that support a computer monitor, keyboard and mouse. Their desks are
located in a large, open work area, with only waist-high barriers between
desks or groups of desks. Each representative wears a telephone headset
that is connected to a small phone console. CSSRs use this console to sign
on and off the central telephone system. When a representative is signed
on, customer calls are automatically directed towards a free (available)
representative: they do not pick up the phone or select which incoming
call to answer. Each CSSR handles between 120 and 200 phone calls per
shift. They are generally expected by management to handle as many calls

as possible, which may in turn limit what they can do in any particular call.

We observed and listened in to conversations between CSSRs and customers for two months before recording approximately thirty-six hours of work activity, involving twelve different CSSRs at two centres. Our recorded data include the phone conversation between CSSRs and customers, the CSSRs' actions on their computer screens, and interactions between these CSSRs and their colleagues in the center. These data were augmented by several months of additional, periodic ethnography at one of our two centres. We also held several discussions with system developers concerning their design intentions. Finally, we talked with several MMR managers about their views on telephone customer support operations and the corporation's technology strategy.

These data and methods allow us to analyse a particular situated activity system – a customer service and support telephone centre – in its interactional, socio-technical and organisational dimensions; respectively, the encounters between customers and CSSRs on the telephone, the expert system used by CSSRs during those encounters and their work practices around that technology, and the corporation's policies and practices that shape both the work of CSSRs and the design of their expert system. To examine the history of a particular set of actions in this complex social/organisational/technical matrix, one must use several different, complementary types of data: audio-visual recordings of CSSRs at work and on the phone with customers, video records of their interactions with the expert system during those telephone conversations, and fieldnotes collected through traditional observational methods and informant interviews. Our analytic approach thus combines ethnography with conversation analysis, bringing together our field observations with analyses of many customer calls collected in two settings. Our treatment of the data presented here is weighted somewhat toward the ethnographic; it includes the largely ethnographic use of transcript materials, although we present a limited conversation-analytic treatment of several examples (similar to the analytic strategy adopted by Whalen and Zimmerman, 1998).

MMR and call-centre technology: 'reducing dependency on people knowledge and skills'

Beginning with the early days of MMR's customer support organisation, CSSRs have, on occasion, been able to assist customers with their machine problems, thus eliminating the need in those cases for a service visit. A few CSSRs formerly worked as technicians, and are able to draw on that prior knowledge and experience to diagnose and fix problems. Others learned about copier operation and problem-solving by reading company technical materials, observing the functioning of copiers located in the customer support facility, and – most commonly – talking about copiers and service problems with knowledgeable CSSRs and especially technicians, who until recently (i.e. before the introduction of automated notification) had to phone the customer support centres to report on the outcome of their service calls and receive information about pending requests.

It is important to note in this regard that MMR did not provide its CSSRs with any formal training on copier operation. However, to aid the telephone representatives in fixing problems over the phone, the company did supply them with a relatively simple computerised help system, Customer Call Assistance (CCA), which offered possible solutions to common copier problems such as paper jams and defective copies. To use CCA, representatives would access the help screen for the type of problem being reported. Problem identification and diagnosis was dependent primarily on the CSSR's judgement or expertise – however acquired – and, drawing on that knowledge, their adroit questioning of the customer. The system was useful only in so far as it could be used to help CSSRs evaluate the situation and then suggest solutions once they had identified the problem. Still, telephone solves were relatively rare, and most calls for service involved nothing more than the creation of a job ticket.

MMR's decision to develop the expert system described in this chapter was based on several factors. The company wanted to reduce service costs, and there were significant savings associated with solving machine problems over the phone and avoiding service visits (e.g. a telephone solve rate of only 3–4 per cent could save several million dollars per year). In addition, customers would then receive quicker service (the time between requesting service and the arrival of a technician on site was sometimes eight hours or more), which would reduce machine downtime and improve customer satisfaction.

Although MMR recognised that effective use of a help system like CCA to achieve these telephone fixes required some understanding of both copier operation and common service problems, they were reluctant to invest in training or other support for CSSRs that would increase their knowledge. Instead, they believed that 'reducing dependency on people knowledge and skills through expert and artificial intelligence systems', as one company manager put it, offered the best approach. From this view, an expert system would embody the knowledge lacking in most CSSRs, and thus *automate* problem diagnosis. Of course, because this system would have to be used while on the phone with customers and few of those customers would have expert knowledge about copier or printing system operation, MMR's approach would necessarily entail – in the words of one system developer – 'the blind leading the blind'.

Finally, the company had recently launched several products that relied extensively on software for their operation. Determining whether a problem with machine operation was hardware or software based (independent of whether it could be fixed over the phone) was now a crucial first step in the service process for these products, since service technicians were trained only to fix hardware problems. Software problems required software analysts for resolution, and analysts did not travel to customer sites but rather assisted customers over the phone. If a service technician was dispatched on a problem that turned out to be software rather than hardware in origin, the cost from wasted resources, delayed problem resolution, and customer dissatisfaction was considerable.

Initially, MMR attempted to address this problem by asking customers to call a special phone number for software problems, which connected them directly to software analysts. They soon discovered that customers could not always be counted on to make a correct problem-type diagnosis. Consequently, the analysts were receiving many calls that involved hardware problems, and the customer support centres were processing requests for service for problems that turned out, after a visit from a technician, to be software in nature. An expert system that would allow CSSRs to determine the general problem type – and, if no easy solution were possible at that stage, would at least ensure proper routeing to either a service technician or software analyst – appeared to offer a solution.

In developing their system, MMR turned to a particular approach to building intelligent artefacts, 'Case-Based Reasoning', and to a software package called CasePoint (™Inference Corporation) that utilises this approach. In the next section, we briefly describe this approach and the technical functioning of the system that was actually deployed in the customer support centres.

Case-Based Reasoning as implemented at MMR

Case-Based Reasoning is founded on the idea that people tend to solve problems by storing information about situations they have encountered in the past in their memories, and when they are confronted with a new problem, searching their memory for similar situations or 'cases' to solve those problems. That is, people make sense of problems by finding the closest cases in memory, comparing and contrasting the problem with these cases, making inferences based on those comparisons – and asking

CASE118:	"[118] CQ Streaks on copy - Place a service call"
Description:	"streaky, like watercolors, undefined edges transparency "
Questions:	**Question 78** "<What type of problem is it?>" A: "Copy quality" Eliminate case if question answer differs **Question 58** "What type of copy quality problem are you having?" "This question is establishing the category of copy quality problem the customer is having." A: "Streaks" Eliminate case if question answer differs **Question 67** "Are the streaks/lines in the same place on every page?" "If the streaks are not in the same place on every page, this could be a different problem." A: "No" Eliminate case if question answer differs
Actions:	**Action 1** "Place a service call."

Figure 5.1 CasePoint showing details of a case for a copier

questions when enough inferences cannot be made or when they need more information – to find the best case, adapt the solution associated with the best case for the current problem and thus solve it (see, e.g. Kolodner, 1993). The CasePoint software used to create MMR's expert system is designed to work in this way, combining automated decision-making with known solutions to previous problems.[4]

We do not wish to take up the issue of Case-Based Reasoning as an approach to AI; rather, we shall describe how CasePoint, which is a very flexible software package, was adapted and customised by MMR. Following this condensed account, we shall then be in a position to consider the issues that CSSRs faced when using this system during phone conversations with customers, and the practical reasoning that they employed to deal with such issues.

At MMR, the system is designed to take the problem description entered by the CSSR – who is expected to type in a 'full description' (as MMR's CasePoint user manual puts it) of what the customer says the problem is, using the customer's own words whenever possible – and conduct a search of its files to find the same or similar cases. Each case in the CasePoint system consists of a title (for example, 'Jams in area 6'), a description, some question–answer pairs and an action. Figure 5.1 shows an actual case for a colour copier (there are close to 500 cases for this particular machine).

Observe that the description of the case consists of a series of keywords and short descriptions, which are used by the matching search algorithm described below. The question–answer pairs are designed such that if the answers specified in a case are given, further evidence is added to the case; if other answers are given, the case is eliminated. The action is a brief explanation or description of the remedy for the case. There are three types of actions. The first is to place a service call, which indicates that the problem has not been solved and that repair by a technician is necessary. The case shown in figure 5.1 lists this as the applicable action. The second possible action is to escalate (transfer the call) to an analyst, which indicates that the problem is with the software rather than the hardware of the machine. The third type of action is an activity the customer can perform – clean the glass, reset the machine, turn the machine off and on, clear a jam, and such like – to fix the problem.

The search algorithm used by MMR in their adaptation of CasePoint is character matching. The system first removes 'noise' from the problem description text string entered by the CSSR (for example, deleting punctuation as well as suffixes like 'ing', and connective words like 'or' and 'of'). It then breaks the remaining text up into trigrams (three-character fragments), and these trigrams are compared to trigrams in the text of each stored case description and case title. Points are awarded for matches and the best matching cases are listed along with questions associated with those cases.

The system can also use certain abbreviations and keywords, like 'jam' or 'CQ' (for copy quality), to immediately bring up on the screen a basic, initial question relevant to that specific problem category, such as **What type of copy quality problem are you having?** (Note that CQ is part of the title for the case shown in figure 5.1 because this case is for a copy quality problem, 'streaks on copy'.) In addition, most machines have a small LCD screen that displays information about the machine's status or operation to users, including 'fault codes' that appear when the machine is not functioning properly (sensors within the machine trigger the codes). Most fault codes have several possible causes, however, so these codes tend to work much like the abbreviations just mentioned, narrowing down the search to certain cases or problem-classes, but rarely establishing, without additional information obtained through questioning, the precise fault or cause.[5]

The CSSR is expected to ask the CasePoint questions of the customer just as they are displayed on the computer screen, asking each question in turn and then inputting the answer. Each answer leads to more points being awarded to some cases and the elimination of others, as the system progressively narrows down the search. For instance, in the case shown as figure 5.1, 'Case 118: Streaks on Copy', there are three questions listed. These questions may also be associated with other cases (usually cases of the same general type, such as 'copy quality'), which is why each question has a distinct number. If, as a result of the character-matching procedure performed on the problem description text, Case 118 was one of the 'best matching' candidate cases, then – as we noted above – the answer to Question 58, **What type of copy quality problem are you having?**, would determine if it remained a candidate (and had more points than before Question 58 was answered) or was eliminated. That is, the selection of any answer but 'streaks' would eliminate this case, while the answer of 'streaks' would add points for Case 118. If this same question were also associated with another candidate case, the selection of a different answer, such as 'lines' or 'blotches', would add points to that case while eliminating this one. Conversely, the selection of 'streaks' would eliminate that other case. When a case has been awarded a specified number of points, it is the 'winning' case and CasePoint will indicate the pertinent action (i.e. place a service call, transfer the customer to an analyst, or instruct the customer to perform certain actions to try to fix the problem).

This sketch of CasePoint's operation has been necessarily formal and abstract. We now move to an analysis of the significance of its rules and structure for the work of CSSRs, and the problems they face when using CasePoint while engaged in conversation with a customer who has phoned to request service on their machine.

Data analysis

We shall begin with the following transcript to introduce some noteworthy features of the work of CSSRs and several of the more critical issues involved with their use of CasePoint. (For an explanation of the transcript symbols see the appendix on p. 66.)

[Call 1] 95.04.26 WC JR screen/18:55

```
1    CSSR:   MMR Cust:omer Support this is Jimmy, how can
2            I ↑he:lp you.
3    CUST:   Yeah machine number:: zero five y ( ) zero one
4            four (.) six=six two
5            (1.3)
6    CSSR:   Thank you one moment while I bring up your
7            information
8    CUST:   Uh ke?
9            (2.0)
```

```
10   CSSR:   I show Smith's?
11   CUST:   Tha↑::t's me
12   CSSR:   Okay and your name please?
13   CUST:   Mike Hammer-
14   CSSR:   >Still at< uh eight five six
15           (.)
16   CUST:   ⌈Yeah
17   CSSR:   ⌊Nine six three eight
18   CUST:   Yip
19   CSSR:   What fault code are you getting Mike=
20   CUST:   =I::m not gettin' one (.) uhhm it's (0.7) leavin'
21           lines looks like somethin' >scrapin' the paper<
22           'cause >its goin all the way to the e:dge of the
23           pa::ge<
24           (1.5)
25   CUST:   L-L:esley just called me about another problem
26           and she cancelled the >first service call 'cause
27           it was< okay
28   CSSR:   °Uhuh°
29   CUST:   But ↑now I got an↑other problem >let her< know heh
30   CSSR:   Okay with this line
31           (4.0)
32           and how often does this uh::
33           (0.4)
34           (defect or)⌈occur          ⌉
35   CUST:            ⌊>every copy<⌋
36           (0.3)
37   CSSR:   Every copy
38   CUST:   Mmhuh
39   CSSR:   Alright
40           (1.3 )
41           good clean originals?
42   CUST:   Yep
43   CSSR:   O:kay
44           (4.0)
45   CSSR:   An' nothin' on the glass? You've checked that?
46   CUST:   na⌈no no
47   CSSR:     ⌊Okay
48           (2.5)
49   CUST:   Na' it's it's I've seen it do this before an'
50           it's it's somethin' scra:pin' in there I believe
51   CSSR:   Okay
52   CUST:   'Cause it's goin' to the f- full edge of the
53           paper which (0.6) you know didn't copy it all
54           the way to the edge=
55   CSSR:                      =Okay=
56   CUST:                           =so there's somethin'
57           scrapin' as it goes through
```

58	CSSR:	Do you need the log number
59	CUST:	Nope
60		(4.0)
61	CSSR:	Just verify your address an- five six seven
62		four east eighty se:cond street is what I have
63	CUST:	That's it?
64	CSSR:	'kay totally down would you say?
65	CUST:	O:::::h >pretty much< so unless the bad
66		qual(heh heh heh)ity.
67	CSSR:	Okay I'll let them know you're down and have the
68		technician contact you with an estimated time.
69	CUST:	Okay th⌈-
70	CSSR:	⌊Have a nice day
71	CUST:	Thank you
72	CSSR:	Bye Mike
73	CUST:	Bye-bye

While our principal interest is in the use of CasePoint to diagnose the machine problem it will be useful to first take note, although only an abbreviated discussion is possible here, of the conversational work (and the concurrent work by the CSSR on the computer) that precedes the initiation of that activity. In this call, the caller states, in response to the CSSR's 'how can I help you?' opening query, his machine's serial number (lines 3–4). MMR requires that number in order to retrieve essential information from their customer database – a job ticket cannot be created without it – and the customer is in this sense short-cutting the opening of the call, intending through that action to prompt the CSSR to immediately retrieve the information. That is to say, in response to the customary 'how may I help you?' question, most customers begin with an account of why they are calling, typically in the form of a direct request for a service visit or a story about some problem with their machine, and then are asked for their serial number.

Using the serial number to 'bring that information up' (lines 6–7), the CSSR is provided with a 'Customer Information Screen' listing the company name, address, phone number and contact person (shown in screen 5.1, with all these information fields blanked out) which the CSSR is then expected (indeed, required by MMR policy) to verify – thus the exchange that takes place over lines 10–18.

The verification sequence completed, the CSSR, using this same screen, is now in a position to start creating a job ticket by obtaining a description of the machine problem, which is also a potential first step toward problem diagnosis and the launching of CasePoint (launching the program is accomplished by selecting the 'Casebase' button on the Customer Information Screen).

```
┌──────────────────────────────────────────────────────────────┐
│ ▭                  Customer Information Screen                 │
│  ┌──────────┐ ┌────────┐ ┌──────────────────┐ ┌─┐  ┌────────┐ │
│  │ Hist 13  │ │ Msg 31 │ │                  │ │±│  │ Done   │ │
│  └──────────┘ └────────┘ └──────────────────┘ └─┘  └────────┘ │
│ ┌Customer Info─────────────────────────────────────────────┐ │
│ │ Custome ┌──────────────┐  ┌──────────────┐               │ │
│ │ Contact ┌──────────────┐  Contact ┌──────────────┐       │ │
│ └──────────────────────────────────────────────────────────┘ │
│ ┌Product Info┐                                                │
│ │ Serial ┌──────────┐  Product: ┌──────────────────┐ ┌─┐     │
│ │              Transfers use Speed Dial 11          └─┘     │
│ │  Pending                              ○ History           │
│ │                                       ◉ Pending           │
│ ┌Contract Info─────────────────────────────────────────────┐ │
│ │ Contract: ┌────────┐                                      │ │
│ │ Shift:    ┌────────┐                                      │ │
│ │ Spec Bill ┌──────────────┐    Contract    Y              │ │
│ │           └──────────────┘   ┌Options┐ ┌Contract┐        │ │
│ │ Problem ┌──────────────┐  Employee ┌────────┐            │ │
│ └──────────────────────────────────────────────────────────┘ │
│  ┌────────┐ ┌─────┐ ┌───────┐ ┌──────┐ ┌────────┐            │
│  │Casebase│ │ CCA │ │SVC 01 │ │ ICSS │ │ SOLVED │            │
│  └────────┘ └─────┘ └───────┘ └──────┘ └────────┘            │
└──────────────────────────────────────────────────────────────┘
```

Screen 5.1

Entering a problem description

Before considering the difficult issues involved with initiating and, especially, sustaining the kind of diagnostic interrogation necessary for using CasePoint (in Call 1, this interrogative activity takes place over lines 30–47, with the CSSR then indicating that a service technician will be dispatched) we need to examine the practical issues CSSRs must address when entering that problem description into their computer.

For CasePoint, the problem description is especially important, not only because it determines the first, best matching case and therefore the first question, but because this description remains constant throughout the CSSR's interaction with the system (unless the CSSR wants to essentially start over in CasePoint by entering a new description, an action we observed only once during our several months of data collection). Most crucial for our interests, the problem description entry is an activity over which the expert system cannot exert its expertise – it is forced to rely on the CSSR's input. The system developers were convinced that CasePoint would work best if CSSRs would record what the customer said, and did not attempt to analyse or independently rework that account or report to any significant degree (since there was no plan to ensure CSSRs developed enough expertise to make such judgements and interpretations).

That is in part the reason for the developers' use of the character-matching search procedure described above, which has the advantage of being able to parse *any* problem description, regardless of the spelling of the words used by the CSSR, and will interpret utter gibberish just as readily as syntactically proper English sentences. From this view, even if the system could not fully control the CSSR's problem description input, it would *not* have to depend on a CSSR *understanding*, at any significant level of expertise, the customer's description of a problem; they would simply have to record it. The developers believed that this feature would give CasePoint exceptional 'ease of use'. As the MMR user guide states:

A traditional data-base requires a knowledgeable user who can set up queries in a format understood by the software and appropriate to the fields of the stored records. Field names and desired values must be entered correctly. With [CasePoint] the initial search uses *unconstrained natural language*, and the words don't even have to be spelled right! Then the software generates the queries and poses them to the user, instead of the other way around. The expert knowledge resides in the program, not the user. (original emphasis)

But is such 'blind' entry – with the CSSR acting only as a simple conduit for the passing of information between the customer and CasePoint – a reasonable expectation? We shall address this question by first considering what the CSSR does in Call 1, both interactionally with the customer and on his computer.

In that call, following the completion of the verification activity, the CSSR asks the customer, 'What fault code are you getting Mike.' Recall that fault codes are produced by the machine's sensors, and that entering a fault code in the problem description field has the advantage of bringing up only the cases associated with that code, rather than those selected by a character matching search. The ability to use fault codes in the problem description field was included in CasePoint by MMR developers from the very beginning, because it allowed the system to focus immediately on the relevant cases and questions, and was not dependent on CSSRs or customers understanding anything about, or having to interpret, machine functioning, symptoms and the like. CSSRs are thus encouraged to use fault codes whenever possible. However, CSSRs also are motivated to use fault codes whenever they can obtain one – in Call 1 the CSSR asks *just* for that, rather than for some narrative account of a problem – and their reasons are not only those the developers had in mind.

The fact that a fault code entry provides a reliable, presumably objective (no human interpretation or description of machine trouble needed) short-cut to the most applicable cases and questions, based as it is on the machine's self-report, is certainly very important. For many CSSRs, however, this is as much a corrective for quirks in CasePoint's search algorithm as it is a remedy for their own lack of expertise. Soon after CasePoint was deployed, CSSRs discovered that its text parsing and matching search procedure – a procedure that had been briefly explained to them by trainers responsible for instruction on system use – could lead to questions that seemed to have little relation to the words they had typed, producing what they took to be spurious matches. Even with minimal knowledge of MMR's machines, they believed that some questions did not make sense or were confusing, given what they had entered – and had been trying to convey through that entry. Accordingly, they wanted some control over CasePoint, some way to direct its actions so they could better understand the results, and recognised that using a fault code offered this kind of opportunity.

This raises a serious point. CSSRs, or any users of any expert system, unavoidably have to work at making sense of what that system is doing and why. After all, they are *interacting* with the system, not simply 'using' it. Related to this point, the use of abbreviations like CQ, which we noted above, was added to CasePoint by the developers in response to these same complaints and user requirements. At the very least, CSSRs argued, the use of an abbreviation like CQ, if it was matched to only that set of cases (copy quality problems), would give them control over the first question that was presented to them in a way the text parsing procedure did not (leaving aside for the moment the problem of whether their knowledge was sufficient to make a correct decision about the problem type, and thus the appropriate abbreviation to use).

It turns out that in Call 1, however, the customer explains that the machine is not displaying any code. This is often the situation: no fault code is available and, like in this call, the customer provides instead a brief account of the problem. In Call 1, this account includes 'it's leaving lines' and 'looks like something scraping the paper 'cause it's going all the way to the edge of the page'. Offered this account, the CSSR types, in the appropriate field on their Customer Information screen the following problem description: **cq lines across print**.

We can make several observations about this entry. It begins with the **cq** abbreviation, indicating an assessment of the problem as being in the 'copy quality' category, and adds some limited detail. This detail, **lines across print**, uses but one word from the caller's account, **lines**. The remainder, **across print**, is a summary reworking of part of that account (**across** perhaps used as a synopsis for 'all the way to the edge of the page' and **print** a way of referring to the copy 'printed' or produced by the machine). The CSSR's description does not include anything from the customer's suggestion concerning the possible cause of the lines: 'something scraping the paper'.

Plainly, this is not anything like a near-literal transcription of the customer's words or a 'complete statement' of everything reported. Certainly, the CSSR is exercising a good deal of judgement and interpretation in assembling a relatively concise – and categorised (**cq**) – description. Whether that judgement is correct, or thoroughly misguided – the reference to 'scraping' could suggest a part that is out of position, and while that may leave 'lines' and thus affect the 'quality' of the copies, it may not have much to do with the kind of 'lines' that result from common copy quality adjustment problems – is beside the point. Rather, these observations suggest that various sorts of judgements and interpretations may be routinely employed, and are indeed *required*, to determine the correct or relevant information, or what term to use – or, more generally, to ascertain what should even count as 'information' – in the problem description field out of all the possibilities.

To continue with this line of analysis, consider the issue of how to even describe what the customer is seeing on the copies, whether 'lines' as a symptom is in fact a correct word to use, given the possible differences between 'lines' that are 'scrapes' and those that are produced by some other kind of machine trouble. In writing CasePoint's cases (the descriptions and titles), the system developers were continually confronted by this problem of what is the correct or best way to describe some event in the machine or some visible result of the machine's copying or printing activity, with that event or result now defined as a 'symptom', so that certain words or groups of words, as equivalents of symptoms, will be matched with the correct case for that kind of trouble when entered in the problem description field.

An enormously complicating factor for this problem, of course, is that the CSSR, the CasePoint user who will be typing the descriptive words into the system, has no visual access to the customer's site and thus no visual access to machine events or results. This means that the CSSR has to rely entirely on what the customer says, thus setting up an interesting correspondence difficulty. Is a 'streak' for one person a 'line' or a 'stripe' or a 'band' for others? Or is a 'blotch' also describable as a 'smear' or should it be a 'spot'? And so on. Related to this, since any choice between these various possibilities may result in a match with certain cases and no match with others, there is the added difficulty of understanding the possible significance for determining a machine trouble of choosing one word over another. For example, the various troubles that might cause 'lines' may be different from those that cause 'streaks', and the troubles that cause completely 'blank' copies may be different from those that cause 'deletions', where only portions of the copies are blank. Finally, there is the significance of that choice for CasePoint's actions, for what it will then do in terms of diagnostic analysis, since the expert system is a mediating device between a machine and textual descriptions of that machine's behaviour.

Consider some alternatives to what the CSSR did in Call 1. Should, or could, the CSSR have typed the *entire* account that was provided by the customer, which contained mostly diagnosis or analysis (looks like something scraping the paper) and descriptive remarks that were being marshalled to justify that diagnosis ('cause it's going all the way to the edge of the page), with little in it that could be defined strictly as 'description' (leaving lines)? That would make for a very long problem description text, and would include words that were organised for purposes – analysis and diagnosis – not anticipated by the CasePoint developers in their expectations for entry of the customer's *description* of machine *symptoms*. Or, given the proposed causal relationship, in that account, of the 'scraping' and the 'lines', should the CSSR have focused on the customer's 'scraping' conclusion rather than the 'lines' symptom (defined by him as indicating copy quality trouble) in his problem description entry? But does not that then require an analysis by the CSSR of the validity of the customer's hypotheses, of what was truly important in that story, and of the 'real meaning' of the customer's words? And isn't that precisely what the CSSR tried to do, albeit by ignoring the customer's diagnosis and reaching a different conclusion of the problem's nature (and possibly a different understanding of the words used to describe it)?

In our several months of observations and in our recorded data, customers regularly provided accounts, stories, candidate analyses, or complaints about their machine and its problems that varied in detail and form, and CSSRs were thus routinely faced with a situation similar to that of the CSSR in Call 1. And they regularly engaged in a similar action: selecting and sometimes revising or restating, out of an account or story, certain features to include as problem description text, with the common aim appearing to be assembling a concise or summary description (rather than a complete statement of everything the customer mentioned).

Consider in this regard the following call extracts.

[Call 2] 95.07.12.CSSC MY1
```
CSSR:   Hi  [( ) this is Mandy at MMR
CUST:       [Hi
CUST:   ah yes hi, I=uh (.)I'd ah wha I just make a
        copy and ah see this ah (.) horizontal dark
        strip (.) o- on the page and ah (.) wondered
```

if what needs to be done or if (.) if I can
handle it=ah (.) to fix it.

In Call 2, the CSSR types only the word **lines** in the problem description field. This does not capture all the possible information the customer has supplied, and it reworks the customer's own descriptive remarks. Presumably, **lines** is the CSSR's interpretation of 'strip'. There could well be a difference between the two; for example, a 'strip' may be thicker in width than a 'line' (the correspondence difficulty once again). The customer also mentions that the strip was horizontal and dark. Neither piece of information is included in the problem description.

[Call 3] 95.07.13 CSSC JS12

CSSR: o:kay and what kinda problems=ye havin?
CUST: uhm it's putting a big black streak along the
       top of eleven by seventeen paper
CSSR: black streak (the) to:p?
CUST: uhhuh?

In Call 3, the CSSR types **black streaks** as his problem description text, but does not include anything from the customer's explanation that these streaks occur on a certain type of paper and along the top of the paper.

[Call 4] 95.04.26 WC JR15

CSSR: What's the fault code or problem that you're
       having?
CUST: u:h problem is <u>scra</u>tches outboard
       (2.0)
CSSR: scratches outboard?
CUST: right (0.4) and this is after a new <u>mat</u>- (0.8)
       photoreceptor put on (.) and: the scratches I got
       out- I have outboard <u>now</u> are different then the
       reason for changin' the (.) photoreceptor

Finally, in Call 4, the customer has produced a rather extended story about his trouble. Listening to the story, the CSSR types **cq scratches outboard new pr belt**. The **cq** indicates that he has interpreted this particular trouble as a copy quality problem; **pr belt** is short for photoreceptor belt, which the customer mentions that he has recently changed (thus the reference to **new**). Although the trouble in this case could turn out *not* to be a copy quality problem, the CSSR has clearly analysed the customer's story in a certain way rather than typed everything or even nearly everything the customer said.

The issues involved with making use of the customer's account or story to assemble a problem description text become even more complex when information is provided over several turns at different points in the call, as in the following example.

[Call 5] 95.07.12 CSSC MY37

```
   CSSR:  what's the problem with it?
➤  CUST:  blurry blurry blurry
   CSSR:  blurry⌈blurry
   CUST:         ⌊blurry blurry blurry
   CSSR:  okay, hav- you have you tried anything to see
          if you might (.) be able to
   CUST:  yeah, I've tried to sh:ift it around you know
          the uhm (.) takin' it out and shifted the powder
          around (the uh )
   CSSR:  Okay, lemme see if there is anything I might
          might suggest for ya. (.) before I get the ca:ll
          in
   CUST:  Okay
          (2.0)
➤  CUST:  and my copies are coming out very light.
```

The customer offers 'blurry blurry blurry' as the problem. The CSSR types **blurry copies** in the problem description field and has started navigating through CasePoint, with the search procedure having already listed a first question, when the customer adds 'and my copies are coming out very light'. This is a potentially important remark, and raises, once again, the issue of what the correct or best descriptive word(s) should be for what the customer sees, for the visible characteristics of the copies produced by the possibly malfunctioning machine. That is, are the copies 'blurry' or 'light' or both (the customer does say 'and . . . very light'), and what are the implications (if any) for the expert system's operation, for choosing one word over the other or including both words?

In this instance, though, the CSSR does not do anything with this added information. This is not in any way surprising. Although customers sometimes offer, after their initial account, additional information that they consider possibly relevant to the problem, recall that no additional text can be added to the problem description field that can then be used by the system without first resetting CasePoint and starting over. As we stated earlier, in virtually every instance like this that we observed, the CSSR acted similarly, ignoring (at least with respect to entering anything in CasePoint) the additional information and continuing, as is the case here with **blurry copies**, with the expert system operating upon (and having knowledge of) only the initial description.

This extract illustrates another shortcoming of MMR's expert system: it is awkward to adapt it to new information. The system is built with the idea that the initial problem description adequately represents the problem. CasePoint is designed to gather additional information along the way, but that information is supposed to be elicited only through answers to the case-related questions that it poses. Further, this can only prune the tree of possible cases selected by the initial character-matching procedure that was performed on the problem field text.

Plainly, problems cannot always be discretely described or have their basic characteristics readily determined through a single 'What kind of problem are you having?' query. Rather, their important features or symptoms may only gradually become evident, emerging over time through a more extended exchange of talk, and the understanding of how to describe the problem may even change radically as new information becomes available. But incorporating this much more realistic approach to problem description and assessment into CasePoint would call for users with the expertise to delve into the customer's initial account, using their knowledge to evaluate what was potentially important, what descriptive words needed elaboration or clarification, and what the implications were of describing a problem in a certain way when attempting a diagnosis. As we have emphasised, the system was designed with a very different 'user model'. In that model, the CSSR is expected to be more or less 'blind', functioning as an information conduit between customers and the system, which is why any analytic or diagnostic questioning is supposed to be driven solely by CasePoint's expertise.

To reiterate, our data demonstrate that CSSRs regularly engage in some kind of analytic, sense-making work concerning the customer's account, generally assembling a relatively concise problem description by selecting (and in some cases reworking) only some portions of that account. Their efforts at conciseness (and categorisation) appear to be a practical solution to the interpretive work in which they necessarily have to engage, the time constraints they operate under (recall they are expected to handle at least 120 calls each shift), their knowledge (however limited) of document machines, and their conscientious desire to gain some control over CasePoint's actions (particularly the first question it will then ask). In short, these efforts are responsive to the exigencies of their natural environment. CSSRs do not function solely as a transmission belt for information during their concurrent interactions with customers and the CasePoint system – any more than customers act only as a transmission belt for information between their document machine and the CSSR. While most CSSRs and customers lack expert knowledge about document machines, they are both unavoidably faced with interpretive tasks related to assembling a description about a machine's operation, the nature of its problems, what might count as a 'symptom' of a 'problem', what the 'best' descriptive word might be to describe a particular kind of machine trouble or a particular characteristic of the copies the machine is producing, and the like. Moreover, as we suggested above,

CSSRs have to also consider, as they try to assemble their textual description, the quirks and other attributes of the CasePoint search procedure that will be performed on that text. That is, they naturally anticipate and try to assert, through what they type, at least some control over what the system will do next (for example, using abbreviations like CQ to direct that search).

The MMR developers, by disregarding or seeking to exclude this essential interpretive or analytic work in their model of system use, by assuming that all expertise or analysis could reside in the system and that users would – and could – remain 'blind' and engage the system largely as information conduits, created a situation where the users, despite MMR's intentions, are regularly and necessarily engaged in various kinds of analyses but are denied full access to knowledge that would make such analysis more effective, accurate, and reliable.

Interrogating the customer

Because the problem description text is the only basis for CasePoint's search for 'best cases' and pertinent questions to ask customers, the difficulties associated with making sense of the customer's account (despite what is usually a dearth of knowledge about document machines), with entering a text that is somehow representative of that account, and with the procedures performed on the CSSR's entries or choices can all carry forward into the diagnostic questioning, as the following call illustrates.

[Call 6] 95.04.26 WC JR screen/VTR 13:40

      CSSR: What's the fault code or problem with the machine?

➡   CUST: It's leaving like blotches on the pages.
           (0.9)
      CUST: He's supposed to come back out and he said it was
           <u>run</u>nable but it- now it's to the point it's- we
           can't even <u>run</u> it and >we've got these huge orders
           and we h- need somebody out here to fix it like
           A S A P.<
           (3.5)
      CSSR: 'kay.
           (8.0)

➡   CSSR: Like a blurred ima:ge
      CUST: [Uh huh]
      CSSR: [Are   ] you usin' film projector
      CUST: No.
      CSSR: °oh okay.°
           (1.3)

CSSR: Is the stock being used with the rec- with the
       recommended specifications?
       (1.2)
CUST: Far as I know.
CSSR: Oka::y.

In this call, the customer describes the problem as 'it's leaving like blotches on the pages' and follows that description with a story about what their regular MMR service technician previously said about their machine's functionality and the crisis the current problem has created for their business. The CSSR types **CQ blotches/mach dwn/asap** as the problem description, a concise summary of both the customer's description and her story, which includes a judgement about the relevant problem category. The text also reveals that CSSR is planning on paging the MMR technician directly, which means the technician will see this problem description text displayed on his alphanumeric pager. The **mach**[ine] **d**[o]**wn asap** portion is oriented to that fact; that is, it is intended to alert him about the urgency of the customer's situation. Our interest is in the **CQ blotches** portion, and in the questions that entry induces in CasePoint.

The first CasePoint screen that comes up on the CSSR's computer, shown as screen 5.2, is generated by the **CQ** abbreviation and includes a **What type of copy quality problem are you having?** window that lists all the admissible copy quality symptoms. The CSSR must select one of the items from this list as his answer to that question. This is *always* the situation in CasePoint: the answer to a question from the system must be chosen from an enumerated set of candidates, even if the set consists only of **yes, no** and **not answered**. Note that the eleven choices listed in the window shown on screen 5.2 represent only the first part of the total list, which is alphabetically ordered and contains nineteen choices in all.

Observe that **blotches** is not on this list – it is not available as an answer. Thus, even when CSSRs record a customer's description in a fairly literal manner, they may still have to deal with a situation where interpretive 'translations' and other work on that description will be necessary. One choice on the list that could have selected in a situation like this is the last of the nineteen items, **Other (marks, spots, lines, faded, etc.)**. While 'blotches' is not provided as an example for the **Other** category, 'spots' is. But the CSSR makes a different choice, selecting **Blurred image or text** from the list. Observe that he also says, 'Like a blurred image'. This utterance, in the way it is delivered, does not really have the sound of a question from the CSSR to the customer, asking for confirmation of his choice; it is uttered after the choice has already been made in CasePoint and there is no upward, questioning intonation. Instead, it has

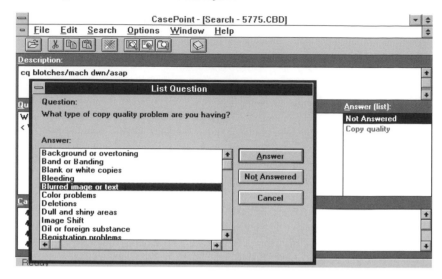

Screen 5.2

the sound of 'thinking out loud'. Moreover, although its status as an action is ambiguous enough for the customer to respond with an answer, 'uh huh', the CSSR has not left a slot for that answer, but rather overlaps it with another question. That query – 'Are you using the film projector?' – is not directed at pursuing the issue of how to translate 'blotches' into a listed CasePoint symptom term (by, for example, seeking a more detailed account of what the customer means by a 'blotch', and whether what she sees could also be described as a 'spot'). Rather, this query is based on CasePoint's algorithmic analysis of the CSSR's **Blurred image or text** selection. As a result of that choice, CasePoint has now brought up the 'film projector' question on the CSSR's computer screen (see screen 5.3) as the question he should now ask the customer. Actually, this particular question is the first on a list of six questions; the ordering of questions on that list reflects the ranking of cases by CasePoint at that point in the diagnosis, and questions may be removed from the list with new questions replacing them as CSSRs select answers to questions and CasePoint uses those answers to award points to different cases and eliminate others. CSSRs are expected to answer the question that is first or 'top' on the list at each step in the diagnostic process.[6]

This question about using the film projector – some copiers can be used with projectors, also known as mirror units – is from a case that deals with troubles induced by the use of such devices, where blurry copies can result from not positioning the mirror unit correctly on the glass (see the

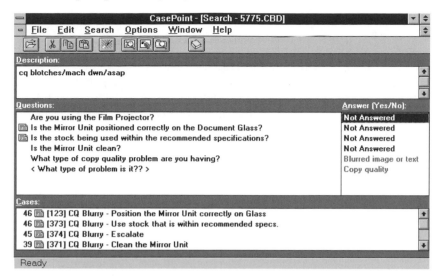

Screen 5.3

ordered list of candidate best cases under the 'Cases' heading at the
bottom of the CSSR's screen in screen 5.3, where the current number of
points awarded for each case, along with the case number, title and
action, are all noted). Although the customer has made no mention of a
mirror unit or film projector, and the report about 'blotches' hints at a
different direction in terms of the nature of the problem, none of this is
available as a resource to CasePoint. That is to say, CasePoint has had no
access to or knowledge of the customer's 'blotches' account. Indeed, it
faces severe restrictions on its access to the evidential resources, like the
customer's account, which are readily available to the CSSR (see especially Suchman, 1987). Its diagnostic, case-matching analysis is therefore
limited to the only information it does have available, the answer of
Blurred image or text.

In this sense, CasePoint is in a position somewhat similar to that of the
CSSR, who has only the words of the customer to use when trying to make
sense of a remote machine's behaviour. There is one crucial difference
between these two situations, however. The CSSR can use the *potentially*
rich resources afforded by natural language and conversational interaction
to explore and clarify, to achieve a mutual, reasonably clear understanding
of the problem, and these quintessentially human resources (and capacities) are not available to any expert system. Of course, in order to take full
advantage of such resources, the CSSR would have to know enough about
document machines to anticipate possible difficulties with categorising a

machine problem in a certain manner (as 'blurry image', for example), or to immediately grasp the important clarifying and probing questions to ask when presented with a particular account of machine behaviour. It strikes us as rather ironic that MMR's technology strategy vests all document machine expertise in software that is restricted by its very nature from access to the most powerful resources available for achieving a mutual understanding of the machine problem – understanding that is plainly a prerequisite for correct diagnosis – and withholds expertise from software users, the CSSRs, who do have such access but then, because of that withholding, cannot make much use of it.

In these circumstances, the outcome will often be like that described by Suchman (1987: 170) in her analysis of expert help systems for users of copiers, and like that observed in Call 6. In this call, the CSSR takes an action – the selection of **Blurred image or text** as an equivalent symptom for 'blotches' – that is probably faulted, which none the less satisfies the requirements of the system design under a different but still compatible interpretation. That is, an answer has been chosen from the proffered list, which satisfies CasePoint's requirement for a listed answer but under a different 'substantive' interpretation (that a blurry image is equivalent to blotches) than the one CasePoint presumes would be the basis for such a choice. Still, the CSSR's choice is 'formally' compatible. As a result, the faulty action appears to go unnoticed at the point where it occurs. CasePoint generated a next question – the film projector question – based on the prior, **Blurred image or text** choice and we can see from the transcript that the CSSR almost immediately asks the customer that next question. When the customer answers 'no' to the film projector query, this answer is promptly input by the CSSR, which generates another CasePoint question (see screen 5.4; again, this question is actually now the first on a list of questions): **Is the stock being used within the recommended specifications?**

The CSSR then asks this new question to the customer, who answers 'Far as I know.' Translated as a 'yes' response into CasePoint by the CSSR, this answer causes the system to select Case 374, **CQ Blurry – Escalate**, as the 'winning' case, as shown on screen 5.5 under the 'Cases' heading (the colour of the text on the CSSR's computer screen for that case title and action has changed from black to blue-green, and its point total has increased to 85, both of which signify its 'winning' status).

The faulty **Blurred image or text** action has thus led to what is likely a faulty decision: CasePoint has concluded that the customer's problem indicates software rather than hardware trouble, and that the call should therefore be escalated to a software analyst rather than dispatched to a service technician. Whether or not the CSSR understood that he had

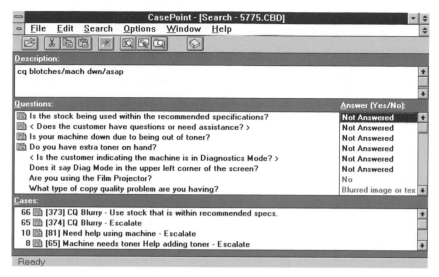

Screen 5.4

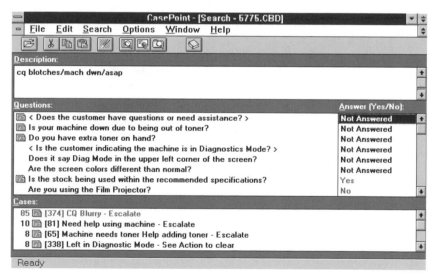

Screen 5.5

made an error earlier in the call is not known. What is clear from our data is that if and when such trouble – or another, related kind of trouble, where CasePoint's questions and actions are manifestly confusing or non-sensical – is recognised by a CSSR, the source for the trouble is difficult (if not impossible) to reconstruct because of the way the system is designed to operate and, more important, the constraints on CSSRs developing sufficient expertise to undertake such reconstructions.

There is another reason for why troubles with CasePoint use are difficult to repair or reconstruct: *interactional* constraints. CSSRs worry about whether customers would be comfortable spending the time and effort needed to start over (often the simplest step in terms of system manipulation, but the most awkward interactionally) or revisit earlier descriptions and accounts, or would be willing to wait while the CSSR tried to ascertain and correct the trouble on their own. CSSRs also worry about customers' perceptions of their competence, and what conclusion customers might draw from their actions. It is much easier, interactionally, for a CSSR who is experiencing any kind of trouble with CasePoint or with a customer to simply exit the expert system and tell the customer they will notify their technician.

Earlier, we alluded to the problem of interactional constraints and contingencies by noting that there were some difficult issues involved with initiating and, especially, sustaining the kind of diagnostic interrogation necessary for using CasePoint. We would now like to take up the problem directly, extending our analysis of expert system use *in situ*.

Obviously, CasePoint was designed for use during interaction on the phone with customers. Indeed, it relies on a problem description that has to be elicited from the customer in order to identify likely cases, and then lists questions that are to be asked to the customer. But our observations suggest that the logic underlying its design, which is exhibited in its assumptions about the role of CSSRs, treats that interaction as relatively unproblematic, as easily scripted and very straightforward. Little, if any, attention has been given to the local, collaborative nature of talk-in-interaction or its social accountability, and thus to the issues posed by the natural organisation of that activity for system design and use.

For example, consider the fact that customers most often begin their calls in the following manner:

[Call 7]

    CSSR: MMR ↑Customer Support, this is ↓Charley how
               can I help ya?
➡   CUST: yeah I wanted to place a service call?
    CSSR: ↑Sure::, what's the serial number.

[Call 8]

> CSSR: MMR Cust:omer Support this is Jimmy, how can
> I ↑he:lp you.
➡ CUST: I want to put in a service call?
> CSSR: Okay 'n the serial number please?

Traditionally at MMR, 'placing a service call' was tantamount to having a technician notified. As we have noted, only a few CSSRs possessed the knowledge or skills necessary to solve problems over the phone. Although this sort of opening turn is not an explicit, unabashed request for a service technician visit, the customer's expectation or need may be made explicit later in the call, as we saw in Call 6:

> CUST: He's supposed to come back out and he said it was
> <u>run</u>nable but it- now it's to the point it's- we
> can't even <u>run</u> it and >we've got these huge orders
➡ and we h- need somebody out here to fix it like
> A S A P.<

At the very least, an utterance like 'I want to put in a service call' can be heard as making a request (and exhibiting a need) for expert help, which then sets up an expectation that the help they receive will in fact be reasonably 'expert'. Verifying the customer's business name, address, phone number and the like can all be heard as leading to the delivery of that assistance, as can a straightforward query about the nature of the problem for which they are seeking help. But starting to then ask further questions about the problem, questions that are hearably diagnostic or 'analytic' in character, raises a new interactional issue for both parties. CSSRs face the problem of establishing how this different, more extended sort of questioning can be heard as relevant to the delivery of the expected expert assistance (for example, unlike service technicians, CSSRs are not 'machine experts' simply by definition). Concomitantly, if the interrogative activity is to be sustained, customers must somehow align as a recipient of that diagnostic work. Moreover, customers are sometimes unhappy or irritated about the fact that their machine is not working. Answering a series of questions takes time, and CSSRs are aware that customers may not see the payoff of that time investment (a problem that CSSRs recognise and talk about among themselves). In addition, questions that ask the customers to do something with the machine, or ask if they have done something, can be problematic in so far as they place, or seek to place, customers in a certain position with respect to *their* knowledge, expertise or actions and those of the CSSR.

If these various but related – and fundamentally interactional – issues are problematic for CSSRs and their interrogation of the customer, we would expect to see this revealed in their actions both when presented with CasePoint questions and in the design of their questioning turns; that is, in *how* they ask those questions. For instance, the simplest way to deal with such matters is to not ask any questions at all, not even opening up CasePoint, or as we mentioned just above, to open it but quickly exit if the customer displays any frustration, reluctance or obstinacy. CSSRs who lack expert knowledge of document machines do not have the resources to establish the legitimacy of their questions, to pursue a diagnosis when a customer appears reluctant to do so, or to counter a customer's resistance to their questioning. However, in most calls that we observed, CSSRs did open up CasePoint, and began to question the customer. Here, we found some revealing patterns when we examined turn and utterance design. The significance of these patterns is underscored by the fact that CasePoint's developers expected CSSRs to ask the questions to customers as they are worded on their computer screen (in keeping with their 'CSSR as information conduit' user model).

Consider in this regard Call 1. We focused earlier on the problem description entry, **cq lines across print**. We now take up the issue of what the CSSR does with the questions that are generated by CasePoint following that input of data. The CSSR's use of the **cq** abbreviation in Call 1 brings up the same, bracketed **What kind of copy quality problem are you having?** question and accompanying window, listing the available answers to this question, that we observed in Call 6. In this call, the CSSR selects **Other (marks, spots, lines, faded, etc.)** as the answer. That selection brings a new question (see screen 5.6): **How often does the Copy Quality defect occur?**

This question *is* one that the CSSR should ask the customer. Notice that he asks it almost exactly as it is worded, in CasePoint:

```
    CSSR:   Okay with this line
            (4.0)
➡           and how often does this uh::
            (0.4)
➡           (defect or)  [occur          ]
    CUST:               [>every copy<]
```

This is not unusual. CSSRs do indeed phrase some questions similar to or even exactly like CasePoint's phrasing. Notice, however, that this 'copy defect' question is a straightforward and unadorned request for information, and it does not indicate or even hint at something the customer may have failed to observe or do. This is *not* the case with the next two questions that CasePoint presents to the CSSR. When the customer answers 'every copy' to the CSSR's query, that answer (once selected in CasePoint) generates the following question: **Is the defect also on the originals?** (see screen 5.7)

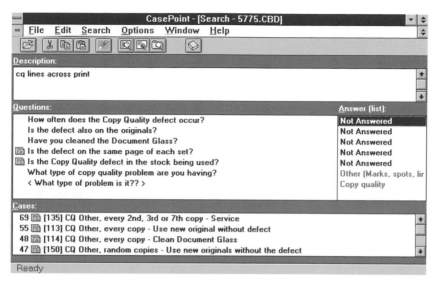

Screen 5.6

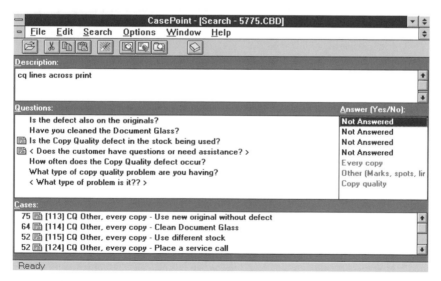

Screen 5.7

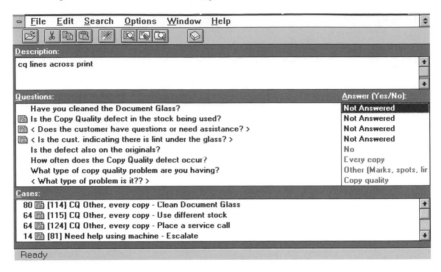

Screen 5.8

Observe how the CSSR asks this particular question:

CSSR: Every copy
CUST: Mmhuh
CSSR: Alright
     (1.3)
➡   good clean originals?
CUST: Yep

When the CSSR selects the **no** answer to this question (here, 'yes' from the customer means 'no' for CasePoint because of his rephrased question to achieve that affirmative response), CasePoint presents him with the next question to ask: **Have you cleaned the Document Glass?** (see screen 5.8).

Here is how the CSSR asks it:

CSSR: O:kay
     (4.0)
➡ CSSR: An' nothin' on the glass? You've checked that?
CUST: na⌈no no
CSSR: ⌊Okay

In both instances, then, the CSSR has significantly altered the phrasing and thus the interactional import of the CasePoint question. They have designed their question-utterances so that they project an affirmative response. This practice is directly responsive to the exigencies of interacting with MMR customers. In Call 1, the customer has already suggested a diagnosis ('somethin' scrapin' the paper') for the problem, and in this interactional context any hearably diagnostic questions from the CSSR run the risk of being interpreted as evidence that the customer's diagnosis has been ignored or rejected. A shared feature of these two particular questions compounds this eminently practical problem. Not to have noticed that an original has exactly the same defects as can be seen on a copy, or not to have cleaned the glass when the copies have marks on them, could be seen as a sign of ignorance, or at least ineptitude. Put plainly, CSSRs do not wish to appear to be suggesting a customer is dumb. Their rephrasing of these CasePoint questions shifts their import away from a possible insult, where they could be heard as implying that the customer is inept because the customer has not yet performed an action that any competent machine user would have performed, and toward a presumption that the customer has in fact performed those actions. As the CSSR who handled this call explained it to us:

> The reason I do that is because a lot of times the customer will react to what we say . . . It is almost like you're making them look stupid. Some customers will take offence to 'Have you flipped the paper or have you?' 'Is the defect on the original?' Then they'll pause, like, 'No, it's not on the original'. So I'll word it, 'Is it a good clean original?' because it's short and it's a little easier for the customer to swallow and they can just say 'Yes'.

This practice is quite common in our data. Additional instances can be found in the following call extracts.

[Call 9] 95.07.13 CSSC FM1

      CSSR: okay, the first question it's asking is
             have you cleared all the paper fro- from
             ( ) from areas one-A, B, and C.
➡   I'm assuming that you've done that,⌈correct?
      CUST: ⌊I've done
             that o:h about >three or four< ti::mes.

[Call 10] 95.07.13 CSSC JS12

➡   CSSR: a:n obviously you have cleaned the do:cument
             glass on that right?
      CUST: right
➡   CSSR: Yeah, I figured you did. I feel silly asking
             it but it never hurts . . .

In the first of these two examples, the CSSR asks the CasePoint question quite literally, and even makes reference to the fact that it is a question being produced by a help system of some type, but then adds 'I'm assuming that you've done that, correct?' thereby projecting an affirmative answer as the preferred one. In the second of these examples, observe that the CSSR actually formulates the concern underlying the 'projecting an affirmative response' practice, referring to how it makes him 'feel' to ask a question that implies the customer may not have done something a competent customer would 'obviously' have known to do. This comment provides an account for asking that question. Questions, then, are not just 'requests for information', which is how MMR's 'CSSR as information conduit' approach to expert system design treats them. Asking a question is an accountable social action, just like any other utterance in conversation, and CSSRs are well aware that customers can and do hold them accountable for their actions. This is one major reason why CSSRs sometimes make explicit, to the customer, that a question is being read or taken from a help system, as we saw in Call 9. This practice 'protects' the CSSR, since she cannot then be held personally accountable for the question she is asking, while also providing some legitimacy for her questioning.

We are not suggesting that the wording of these questions in CasePoint is at fault. Undoubtedly, questions about cleaning the document glass or scrutinising the quality of the originals have to be included in any help system for doing remote diagnosis on copiers. Service technicians occasionally encounter copy quality complaints where the cause is a dirty document glass or defective original, and usually check for these causes if the problem description warrants. And CSSRs will undoubtedly remain oriented to the particular, local contexts within which their questions must be asked, and to how MMR's customers will hear any particular interrogative action (these are surely provisos heeded by all conversational participants). Rather, in identifying communal practices for asking such questions, our intention is to provide further documentation for the pivotal significance of this orientation in the work of doing remote, telephone diagnosis, and most specially in the use of any help or expert system in this work.

We do want to suggest, however, that this practice of adapting CasePoint questions to the local context of the conversation can be more complicated when the CSSR knows little about document machines or CasePoint's workings. In these circumstances, when the CSSR alters a question's wording in an utterance to a customer, their orientation appears to be almost exclusively confined to protecting the service-oriented nature of the conversation. They have no way to express the rationale for the question or its wording because they often do not understand its foundation or purpose. Thus, when these CSSRs project the affirmative responses they inevitably receive, there is often a hearable sense that they are not seriously attempting to diagnose the problem and the customer's request for service does not really depend on the answer received. One gets the sense instead that these CSSRs are engaged in a kind of unspoken collaboration with the customer, are actively helping the customer to answer the questions in such a way as to make the whole process as quick and painless as possible. Although it is impossible for anyone to judge whether the customers' answers to these paraphrased questions are, in actuality, truthful or not, it is likely that there are instances where customers give the projected and thus preferred affirmative answer without actually knowing the true answer.

In any case, systems like CasePoint cannot assume that questions are asked literally, and that answers are straightforward. As our data demonstrate, the CSSR and the customer are engaged in a conversation where the appropriateness of a question or any other action is not purely dependent on the current state of a diagnostic reasoning process, but foremost on the local sequential context of the conversation. For the work of the CSSR is not simply to transmit the system's requests for information and to feed the information back, but instead to skilfully adapt the next CasePoint question (or any other action) to the immediate circumstances in the conversation. By treating the conversational interaction required for using the expert system as an activity that can be readily scripted, the 'CSSR as information conduit' approach fails to properly appreciate, in its design assumptions, basic features of that system's natural environment.

Additional evidence of the CSSR's adaptive work when dealing with CasePoint questions can be found in a variety of other practices. For example, CSSRs modify questions in other ways in response to immediate interactional contingencies. They also skip questions entirely – even when customers have answered prior questions – if a next question seems somehow nonsensical given what has been said so far, or may appear to be pushing interrogation a bit too far, or could have its answer somehow inferred, if searched for, in the customer's prior responses. Moreover, they answer questions in CasePoint before (or without ever) asking them of the customer.

Consider in this regard the following call.

[Call 11] 94.12.09 WC CD screen/call 3/rough
```
    CSSR:  °and° what's: the problem Brian?
    CUST:  uh >we're gettin' a< serial- (.) uh, a
           code coming up it's P O eight one seventy
           one?
           (8.0)
    CSSR:  'n you've cleared out eight (.) and: nine (.)
 ➡         [j a m ]s and s[tuff  ]like that.
 ➡  CUST:  [yeah ]        [yeah ]       Yeah, it's
           continuous
           (4.0)
```

➡   CSSR: uh::, Brian >the phone number I'm showing<
              is five three <u>five</u> (.) seven one one four.
              is that ri⌈ght? ⌉
      CUST: ⌊yup ⌋
      CSSR: oh↑kay, well that's about all we need:,
              we'll go ahead and put that <u>call</u> up

In this exchange, the CSSR modifies his question turn, more or less in mid-delivery, with that adjustment (and his subsequent actions in CasePoint) manifestly responsive to the customer's overlapping of that turn with 'yeah . . . yeah'. This adjustment involves use of the terminal phrase 'and stuff like that'. The CasePoint-based question being posed to the customer by the CSSR deals with jams in certain areas of the machine (a fault code has indicated a paper jam of some type), asking whether the customer has attempted to clear them. It reads in CasePoint, **Have you cleared the jams in areas 8 and 9?** At the time the CSSR begins the turn where he poses this question (''n you've cleared out…'), however, he has already answered it in CasePoint by selecting yes, and this answer has brought another, quite different question to the top of the list on his screen: **Have you powered the printer off and on in switches?** The CSSR's mouse pointer is moving back and forth over the text for this new, 'powered the printer off and on' question at the very moment he is delivering the 'areas 8 and 9' utterance to the customer. The CSSR may well have intended to ask the 'powered the printer off and on' question to the customer, possibly as a second part of a single turn that began with the 'areas 8 and 9' query. But regardless of whether the CSSR was intending to do this, his 'and stuff like that' is assembled on the spot, so to speak, and oriented to what the customer was doing at that very moment. That is to say, 'and stuff like that' is produced as soon as the customer begins to overlap the CSSR's turn-in-progress with an abrupt, somewhat dismissive answer – an answer the customer quickly repeats, and then repeats again, essentially indicating that there is really no point in asking him anything, that he has done everything he should or could do. The CSSR never asks the **Have you powered the printer off and on in switches?** question of the customer; instead, immediately after his 'and stuff like that' finish, he selects **yes** as the answer to that question, which leads to a 'winning case' determination by CasePoint and the notification of a service technician.

Consider also the CSSR's actions in Call 1:

      CUST: Na' it's it's I've seen it do this before an'
              it's it's somethin' scra:pin' in there I believe
      CSSR: Okay
      CUST: 'Cause its goin' to the f- full edge of the
              paper which (0.6) you know didn't copy it all
              the way to the edge=

CSSR: =Okay=
CUST: =so there's somethin'
      scrapin' as it goes through
CSSR: Do you need the log number
CUST: <u>Nope</u>

Recall that at the point where this particular series of turns begins, the CSSR has just asked the customer, 'An' nothin' on the glass? You've checked that?' The customer's 'Na' it's it's .. '. (the first line shown in this fragment) is his reply to that query. The CSSR then chooses **yes** in CasePoint as the answer (because the question on the screen is **Have you cleaned the Document Glass?**), and that selection generates, as the system continues its search for the best case, the next question: **Is the Copy Quality defect in the stock being used?** In this call, however, the CSSR does not ask that particular CasePoint question to the customer, or proffer any modified version of it. Rather, he answers that question on his own by quickly selecting **no** in CasePoint (this occurs just as he says, in response, 'okay'). This action is but one instance of the more general practice of answering CasePoint questions without first asking them (whatever the choice of wording) of the customer and, once again, can be attributed to the CSSR's orientation to the local interactional context. Here, notice that the customer has just restated ('it's it's somethin' scra:pin' in there I believe') a hypothesis for the problem he is experiencing that he first proposed ('looks like somethin' scrapin' the paper') several turns before, during his initial account of the problem. Moreover, that restatement is doing some distinct interactional work in the customer's turn. The customer is not only responding negatively to the document glass query from the CSSR, he is also casting doubt on the entire line of questioning to which he has been subjected. The restatement is being proposed as an alternative approach to diagnosing the problem, requiring a visit by a service technician (observe that the customer restates his hypothesis yet again – 'so there's somethin' scrapin' as it goes through' – just before the CSSR indicates by his 'Do you need the log number?' that such a visit has in fact been scheduled).

However, none of these interactional events is available to CasePoint; in fact, as we have emphasised, the expert system's access to any of the evidential or interpretive resources available to the CSSR through conversational interaction is gravely limited. As a consequence, the system's posing of the question, **Is the Copy Quality defect in the stock being used?** at that particular point in time takes into account only the data it has just received from the CSSR. That is, the only data that CasePoint can make use of is the CSSR's selection of **yes** as the answer to its prior question concerning the document glass. In contrast, and as we have emphasised, the CSSR must take the prior conversational actions of the customer into account in order to craft an accountably relevant and appropriate next action.

Taken together, then, the detailed series of observations we have presented on interrogating the customer suggests that an expert system strategy that fails to recognise the *active* participation of the user in the questioning of customers has fundamentally misconceived the ways in which those users actually participate in the diagnosis. In diverse but systematic ways, discrepancies may arise between the 'context' invoked by the system to diagnose a machine problem by generating questions and using answers to then eliminate or select cases, and the interactional context invoked by the CSSR in asking, not asking, or modifying those questions and entering those answers. If all CSSRs had expert knowledge of document machines, this discrepancy might be less worrisome with respect to achieving accurate diagnoses, since they could then draw on better knowledge in making such judgements than is now available to them. This raises the crucial question of how remote diagnosis is demonstrably more effective, and expert system use significantly improved, when CSSRs do have this expertise, when they are not 'blind'. We conclude this chapter with an examination of this issue, followed by some brief remarks on an alternative approach to expert system design for this type of work.

Expert systems versus systems for experts

As one example of how expert knowledge can dramatically improve problem diagnosis, consider a call where the CSSR does not use CasePoint or any help system whatsoever (although he has CCA available on his computer), and where any expertise is thus vested entirely with the CSSR. In this encounter, the caller, in response to a customary 'and the problem please?' query from the CSSR, responds, 'Uh, the copies are coming out faded.' This occasions the following exchange (we have normalised the transcript data here, with only minimal detail concerning prosody and timing):

[Call 12] 95.04.26 CSSC CL/Call #16
CSSR: Faded copy?
CUST: mhmh
CSSR: Okay by faded it's >part of the copy is
       missing?< or::?
CUST: no no⌈uh it-
CSSR: ⌊it's lighter than the rest of the copy
CUST: right

CSSR: I know how to fix it
CUST: You know how to fix it?
CSSR: yeah

Observe that the CSSR probes and clarifies the meaning of the customer's problem description. He does not let 'faded copy' stand alone as a statement of the problem, because he is aware that the term 'faded' may refer to several different kinds of real-world phenomena, with different causes and solutions. Consequently, his subsequent clarifying question includes one of those possible meanings, with an offer to the customer to provide an alternative should that possible definition be incorrect. Moreover, as soon as the customer indicates that this candidate definition for 'faded' is not appropriate, the CSSR offers an alternative, which the customer immediately accepts.

Having now achieved a reasonably clear, shared understanding of the problem, the CSSR makes his status as a 'machine expert' explicit: 'I know how to fix it'. This expression of confidence by the CSSR in his diagnostic abilities serves to establish the legitimacy and relevance of any 'fixing it' work to follow, which should contribute to the customer's willingness to answer any additional questions and, especially, to follow instructions. Effective remote diagnosis relies not only on machine knowledge but also on the interactional confidence and 'leverage' this knowledge affords; after all, diagnosing and fixing a problem over the telephone requires conversational as well as intellectual adeptness, and there is a close, interdependent relationship between the two.

This interdependence is clearly evident in the subsequent talk, which begins with the CSSR asking, 'When was the last time you had the dry ink cartridge checked or replaced?' 'Just recently', the customer answers. This response is followed by the CSSR's explanation of the cause of the problem:

CSSR: Okay and what we have here is like a small
       air bubble that's in the ((pause)) the ((pause)) dry
       ink line
CUST: ⌈okay
CSSR: ⌊(heading) towards the photo receptor belt

That account is followed by an extended and carefully parsed sequence of instructions on how to fix it. While he is giving these instructions, the CSSR is physically manipulating an imaginary machine in front of him, opening and closing the (imaginary) access panel.

CSSR: it:'s so simple here's what you need to do
CUST: okay
CSSR: the access panel ((pause)) where the dry ink cartridge is?

```
CUST:  uh huh
CSSR:  open it
       ((longer pause))
CUST:  you want me to through it right now?
CSSR:  yes
CUST: ⌈okay
CSSR: ⌊here's what you're gonna – open the access panel
CUST:  okay⌈just a minute
CSSR:       ⌊wait about five seconds and then close it
       after you've closed it you're gonna have a
       humming or vibrating noise coming from that
       side of the copier
CUST:  uh huh
CSSR:  wait for that noise to stop and then repeat this
       process two more times
CUST:  Just open it?
CSSR:  yes just open it
CUST:  and close it?
CSSR:  and then close it
```

When the customer then asks, 'I don't have to touch the dry ink cartridge or anything?' the CSSR answers 'no' and is able to explain why in some detail, as well as offer more information about what will be happening in the machine as the customer carries out the instructed actions. Much as he did just before, the CSSR moves his hands to simulate physical actions, in this case, within the machine itself – the turning of the auger, the ink being pushed from the cartridge toward the drum – in concert with his explanation.

```
CSSR:  . . . see 'cause every time you open that
CUST:  uh huh
CSSR:  that uh panel
CUST:  uh huh
CSSR:  you trigging you're triggering a sensor
       within the auger
CUST:  uh huh
CSSR:  which helps advance the dry ink from the
       dry ink cartridge over towards the drum
       so when you close it you're gonna hear a
       humming or vibrating noise
CUST:  haha
CSSR:  that is actually the auger turning within the
       dry ink tube itself
CUST:  okay
CSSR:  by pushing the dry ink out of the tube
       ((pause)) along the f- the dry ink line over
       towards the drum
```

Finally, the CSSR is able to produce a detailed explanation of why and how these particular actions will fix the problem, by drawing an analogy between these document machine actions and the workings of a machine with which the customer may be somewhat more familiar, an automobile (once again, he accompanies his explanation with hand gestures, this time simulating turning a key in the ignition).[7]

> CSSR: it's kind of like the same principle that
>   happens when you run out of gas you pour
>   gas into the, the- the gas tank
> CUST: uh huh
> CSSR: but there's nothing in the carburettor so by
>   sitting there and hitting the ignition hitting
>   the ignition hitting the ignition ((pause))
>   it's cranking over it's pulling it's sucking
>   everything out of the gas tank over towards
>   the carb.
> CUST: uh huh
> CSSR: same principle applies here

The CSSR then urges the customer to 'go ahead and try it now'. When the customer returns to the phone, after completing the instructed actions, she is asked to now make some copies. That takes the customer about a minute and a half, and when she comes back, she gleefully reports that the problem is fixed.

Still, it may be unrealistic to expect all CSSRs to develop the level of expertise displayed by the person in this call. And even with this level of expertise, CSSRs may encounter problems that cannot be diagnosed or solved without access to additional information or a help system of some kind (particularly with multipurpose digital machines or software troubles). This brings us to the problem of how to build a support system that works in conjunction with the CSSR's knowledge and practical reasoning, complementing the skills of a moderately expert user, and that can be easily integrated into the interactional environment of telephone diagnosis. Some indications of the effectiveness of this kind of system – a 'system for experts' that artfully couples machine and human capabilities by recognising the distinct contributions of the latter – can be found in calls where CSSRs use CasePoint to supplement their own expertise.

To illustrate, in one call from our data set that exhibits this practice, the caller describes the problem in this fashion: 'Well, I put a (pause) like a smaller piece of paper in the automatic feeder . . . and it's stuck and we can't find the paper anywhere'. Hearing this account, the CSSR – much like her colleague in the call we just finished examining – promptly announces, 'I can probably help you with this problem' and begins to impart the solution: 'Basically, what you need to do is push a manila folder through there.'

As was the case in the prior call, then, the CSSR's announcement evidences her expertise and legitimises the instructed actions (and the time and effort) that will now be required. Before the CSSR can proceed any further, however, the caller says that she wants another person at her site that is actually at the machine to take over the call. Consequently, the CSSR repeats, to this second customer, 'Pam', the instructions about pushing a manila folder into the feeder to dislodge the jammed piece of paper.

[Call 13]

> C S S R: Pam, uh, they said that you have a automatic
>   document feeder jam?
> C U S T: Umhm ⌈m
> C S S R: ⌊Umm, what uh, you could probably do is
>   uh ((pause)) hold on jest a second ((pause)) um you could
>   probably push a manila folder through there ((pause))
>   and, it would uh ((pause)) and it would uh shoot out the uh
>   paper that's jammed in there.

This CSSR knew the basic shape of the solution to this kind of paper jam without using CasePoint. She is married to a service technician, and (she told us) learned about the operation of MMR's machines and the solutions to common service problems from her husband. But this moderate level of expertise, while absolutely necessary for quickly recognising the problem and the form of the solution, is not sufficient for instructing the customer in detail, for dealing with all the difficulties that may arise in carrying out the required actions. Thus, to support her instruction-giving, the CSSR opens CasePoint soon after the second customer gets on the line. As she starts to work with that second customer, she quickly moves through CasePoint, answering (by selecting one of the choices presented on her screen) several of its questions – none of which she asks the customer – in order to force the system to select what she knows is the appropriate 'winning case'. This will then allow her to use a feature of CasePoint we have not yet described, a 'browse' utility that allows the CSSR to access a detailed explanation of certain terms and recommended actions.

It turns out that this detailed explanation – essentially, a set of instructions – proves quite useful as the customer begins to have difficulty performing the actions first proposed to her by the CSSR.

> C U S T: We:ll, lemme try it. Oooh! Just shove it in
>   there?
> C S S R: Um hmm.
>   ((sounds of folder being pushed into feeder))

```
═                    CasePoint - [Browse - To clear jam in the...]
□   File   Edit   Search   Options   Window   Help
    [🗁] [✂][📋][📋] [✖] [🔍][🔍][🔍]   [◇]
```

Title: To clear jam in the Document Feeder, do the following ...

Description:

HINT: If there is a lost original, manually push a piece of cardstock through the the Sing the ADF raised. Feed the short edge first. You will need to do this twice once on the fai far right.

For the 5018 and 5028:
1.] Remove all originals from the ADF.

2.] Raise the Single Sheet Feeder input door and remove originals (follow instructions or

3.] Close the input door.

4.] Open the document feeder and remove paper from the ADF and the document glass.

5.] Close the document feeder.

6.] Smooth and fan the originals, reorder them, reload them and try the copy operation a

To clear the jam in the automatic document feeder for the 5034:
1.] Raise the Single-Sheet Feeder Cover and remove any misfed paper.

```
Ready
```

Screen 5.9

CUST: How far?
      ((pause))
CSSR: Um, just far enough to get it where it's gonna
      pull out
      ((pause))
➡ CUST: Okay, I've pushed a manila folder all the way
      in and it's still- ((short pause)) jammed.
      ((sounds of folder being manipulated in feeder,
      followed by a pause, then by more sounds of the
      folder being manipulated))
CSSR: Did you raise the single sheet feed cover and
      re – ((machine sounds begin))
CUST: Umhm
CSSR: and look under there too?
CUST: Um hm ((short pause)) Sure did.

The CSSR is able to bring the browse utility's screen for the 'manila folder' ADF-jam solution (see Screen 5.9) up on her computer during the customer's turn that begins, 'Okay, I've pushed a manila folder all the way in . . .'

The CSSR is scrolling through those instructions at the point where she then asks, 'Did you open up the single sheet feed cover and look under there too?' Note that the instruction dealing with this particular action was listed first on her screen. When the customer replies that she did in fact perform this action ('Um hm . . . Sure did'), the CSSR then reads directly from her screen to instruct the customer in the precise manoeuvres required to dislodge the jammed paper (and note how she exhibits that she is *reading* by the manner in which she begins her turn):

> CSSR: It says if the- uh ((brief pause)) there's a lost
>   original mainly- manually push a card stock
>   through the single. sheet. feeder. With the
>   automatic document feeder raised, ((brief pause))
>   feed the short edge first, ((brief pause)) you
>   will need to do this twice ((brief pause)) once on the
>   far left and once on the <u>far</u> right.
>   ((sounds of folder being manipulated in the feeder))

After the customer carries out those instructions, she finally achieves success (and expresses enthusiastic appreciation of the CSSR's help):

> CUST: Well ((brief pause)) Now it's tellin' me to wait,
>   that my copier's warmin' up.
> CSSR: Yeah.
>   ((pause))
> CSSR: It should shoot it right on outta there.
>   ((pause))
> CUST: Oh! There it is. ((brief pause)) Alrighty then, you
>   found it!
> CSSR: Umm!
> CUST: and now I learned a new way to fix my copier!

It is the *combined* capacities of the CSSR and CasePoint's explanatory 'browse' feature that make this result possible. Although this example only points toward the possibilities for artfully integrating support tools like CasePoint into the work of telephone problem diagnosis, we have more than enough evidence of the troubles and dilemmas that result when there is no such integration, because of limitations in both the system and the knowledge of the CSSRs who have to use it. And one lesson thus stands out quite clearly: the role of the knowledgeable human is essential.[8]

An alternative approach

'Ethnomethodologists interested in technology and design', Button and Dourish (1996: 21) remark, 'have thus so far, and after much effort, managed to make the first step from the study of the use of technology to the critique of technology'. To this point in the chapter, our analysis has proceeded along these same lines: developing an ethnomethodologically informed critique of expert system technology in a particular work setting.[9] We would like to conclude, however, by shifting from critique to design – a next step that, as Button and Dourish (1996: 21) rightly observe, 'will be more problematic' and, in ethnomethodological analyses, has rarely been taken.

Our step in this regard will necessarily be small, as space limitations preclude any detailed exposition of a comprehensive design strategy, let alone actual design specifications. In addition, our design concerns will be unlike those usually found in ethnographic studies (whether informed by ethnomethodology or not) of workplace technology. As we stated at the very start, we are concerned less with technology design, with the technical features of the expert system alone, than with problems in the design and deployment of socio-technical systems. Plainly, this requires a radically different approach to 'the design problem'. Developing tools and technology systems to support or enhance work performance, or to enable people to work together more effectively, is not sufficient. We need to devote equal attention to questions of how people learn to use that technology to do their work, and how they learn about and strive to master their work projects and tasks more generally. This is not simply a 'training' problem. It is rather a problem in understanding the foundations of work practice, including the epistemological history behind that practice.

Accordingly, we shall outline an approach to the work of CSSRs that integrates a learning strategy with a technology strategy. Our goal is to enable CSSRs to develop sufficient expertise about document machines while also providing them with help systems that assist and enhance their diagnostic, problem solving abilities when working with customers on the phone.

It is important to note that this is not merely an exercise in design theory. We recommended most elements of this approach to MMR in presentations to CSSRs and their managers that followed our fieldwork, and some of these recommendations have since been implemented. Moreover, CSSRs and managers who were dissatisfied with certain aspects of the company's technology strategy, and with whom we had worked during our research, have since developed and tried to implement other elements.

In our discussions with MMR, we summarised our analysis in the following manner. First, we stated that our observations of CasePoint use plainly indicated that expert systems do not and cannot make experts (or employees who can function like an expert) out of novices. That is to say, without some knowledge of document machine operation and problems, effective diagnosis is quite difficult, no matter how well designed the expert system. Related to this, we pointed out that CSSRs who lacked such knowledge appeared to have difficulty establishing themselves as a trusted, reasonably expert problem solver in the eyes of the customer, and did not exhibit much confidence in their diagnostic efforts during their interactions on the telephone. Because effective diagnosis over the phone is so deeply embedded in the dynamics of conversational interaction, lack of confidence and inability to establish expert status seriously under-mined CasePoint's effectiveness.

Second, we emphasised that we had collected a great deal of evidence – including data like Call 12 and Call 13 above – that CSSRs could and did acquire knowledge of document machine operation, common problems, 'easy fixes' and the like. This knowledge was demonstrably important in the success of most if not all of the 'telephone solves' in our data. Moreover, our analysis suggested that knowledgeable CSSRs were more confident diagnosticians and more easily gained the trust of customers, who were then more likely to answer the CSSR's questions and engage in problem-solving work.

In line with these findings, we recommended that CSSRs needed to learn about document machines. This learning, we argued, should centre on those operating principles and problem areas that would prove most useful for and amenable to telephone diagnosis, rather than on every aspect of machine operation, and on solutions that were relatively easy to explain and implement over the phone. In response to these recommenda-tions, some MMR senior managers (those outside the call centre organisa-tion) and the members of the CasePoint development team argued that the kind of expertise demonstrated by the CSSR in Call 12 above (the 'faded copies' call) was exceptional. Consequently, they believed few CSSRs were capable of acquiring this level of expertise. Thus, rather than demonstrating that CSSRs were capable of far more than had been previ-ously imagined in the company's planning, these managers and develop-ers took examples like Call 12 to indicate the opposite.

They also argued that the cost of training all CSSRs in document machine operation was greater than the cost of deploying an expert system like CasePoint, and that this was especially true when you consid-ered the level of turnover in the CSSR workforce (close to 25 per cent annually). Of course, this last argument was based on the assumption that CasePoint would prove to be more effective, in terms of the 'solve' rate, than was currently the case. From this view, our data documenting prob-lems in its use were the result of the deployment being at an early stage and the expert system's relative immaturity. As time went on, and system development believed, the results would significantly improve.

Our answer to these objections was based in part on the results of data the development team had themselves collected. After the team viewed some of our early recordings, they were disappointed with the infrequent use of the CasePoint system revealed by these data, and decided that the key problem was that CSSRs were not properly motivated to use the system. They attributed this to the inadequacies of the call centre's incentive structure, in which CSSRs were evaluated primarily on the number of calls they took, not on whether they had attempted to solve the customer's problem. The development team then created a month-long incentive campaign in which CSSRs would get a financial reward for each 'solve' (whether they used CasePoint or had access only to CCA).

At the end of this campaign, the top performing employee – not surprisingly – was the same CSSR who achieved the successful solve in Call 12 above, an eight-year MMR veteran with some college experience. But the second highest performing CSSR had been employed at the centre for only four months, had only a high-school diploma, and prior to coming to work for MMR had no previous experience with document machines. In addition, she had access only to CCA (at that time, many CSSRs did not yet have PCs, which were required to run the CasePoint software, and used so-called 'dumb terminals' and the CCA help screens). Thus, her performance could not be attributed to CasePoint's workings or her effective use of that expert system.

The developers had not thought to inquire into the actual reasons for this woman's high level of performance, however. When we decided to investigate, we discovered that she was indeed fairly knowledgeable about document machines and some of their typical problems. Most important, though, was the fact that she had first learned about machines from the CSSR who handled Call 12. As it turned out, she sat opposite him during her first two months on the job, and overheard him talking customer after customer through a diagnosis and solution to their problem. She was intrigued, and asked him to help her learn how to do that. He began to teach her about the machines. During their breaks, they would walk over to the different MMR copiers in the building, and he would explain how they worked and what problems the customers experienced most frequently. Moreover, she also noticed that the few other CSSRs who were skilled at telephone solves had collected, completely on their own, various types of information about machine operation and problems – company manuals, product specification documents and the like – and so she started to build her own collection of these materials. She used these documents to learn more about MMR machines, and as an aid during problem diagnosis.

For us, this story not only confirmed how important machine knowledge was to diagnosing and resolving problems over the phone, but also proved that new employees could acquire the knowledge efficiently by learning from their peers. Further, it was clear that CSSRs were motivated and capable of assembling different kinds of support tools and materials for this diagnostic work, and that they had a much broader notion of useful job-aids for that work than was imagined by MMR's technology strategy, which relied exclusively on CasePoint. Accordingly, we recommended that the foundation for the 'document machine learning strategy' for MMR's customer support centres should be built on these indigenous sharing and collaborative-learning practices. This approach would be less costly and more effective than one based solely on classroom training, which required taking people off the floor for extended periods of time and, when no other teaching methods were employed, unnaturally divorced learning from the actual work practice and work environment.

Peer-to-peer teaching or coaching was only one way that CSSRs developed expertise in document machine operation, however. As we pointed out earlier in this chapter, knowledgeable CSSRs often learned about copiers and service problems by talking to technicians who, before the introduction of automated notification, had to phone the customer support centres to report on the outcome of service calls and receive information about pending calls. We therefore recommended that this indigenous, highly effective practice, which ended when these kinds of routine phone conversations between CSSRs and technicians were no longer possible, should be partially restored by having a few technicians placed in each of the customer support centres on a rotating basis (to minimise long-term impact on field operations). These technicians would work side-by-side with CSSRs and – as before – would play an informal teaching role (they could also help identify the problems that were most easily fixed over the phone, which would provide a focus for both the learning strategy and the design of any help system).

With respect to the design of CasePoint itself or any other help system, we argued that such systems needed to be much more transparent to the user. As our data demonstrated, the CasePoint system can be incomprehensible because the CSSRs often do not know where it is going, where their actions are leading it, and because the system rather than the CSSR essentially 'decides' where it is going to go. We proposed that they either revise the system or develop a new one that users could navigate with greater ease and know where an answer will take them – and why. Making the same point that other ethnographic, 'user-centred design' researchers have frequently made, we argued that users needed to be closely involved in this design process (not just consulted occasionally on usability questions), and that the system should be evaluated on a regular basis under natural, everyday conditions. By following this approach, whenever MMR designed or adopted new technology, the work of the people for whom the technology was being created could be understood *before* decisions about the particulars of the design were made. In this case, the managers and designers had unfortunately started from an unrealistic vision about how the system would be used and an inadequate understanding of the nature of the everyday work of CSSRs.

Related to this, we proposed that another lesson for MMR was that special care should be taken with expert system technology. Expert systems are typically developed with the idea that the system will make inferences based on input the user provides. The potential problem with this approach is that these inferences are necessarily based on the designers' model of the problem domain. Our research showed that in the actual practice of doing the work the users of expert systems often find the designers' logic or model wanting in the particular situation in which the system is used. Whenever this occurs, serious usability problems arise. The only remedy is a reasonably expert user and a flexible system, one that can be easily adapted to the varied situations of actual, practical use. This called for additional changes in the design of MMR's system.

The response to these recommendations was mixed. The commitment by senior management in the major customer service organisations to CasePoint was unshakeable, and they did not want to invest in any modifications in the design or deployment of the system. They were also sceptical about the costs and effectiveness of our proposed learning strategy for CSSRs. The MMR staff responsible for developing and maintaining the CasePoint system were equally committed to the 'blind leading the blind' strategy, and wanted to see how far they could go in relying exclusively on (expert system) machine expertise – as an alternative to CSSR knowledge – with respect to problem diagnosis and solution. To be fair, their approach had proved itself reasonably effective for sorting out hardware from software problems. This had resulted in significant cost savings for the corporation.

In contrast, several of the call-centre managers and their front-line managers were convinced that the kind of learning strategy we proposed was essential if their employees were to ever reach the solve rate they believed possible. Although there was little or no official support for it, one centre manager set up a small 'lab' where CSSRs could learn about copiers. This manager, together with a second centre manager, also encouraged CSSRs to use their own knowledge about copier problems and solutions, rather than just the CasePoint system, to diagnose and solve problems when on the phone with customers. In addition, all of the MMR call centres designed and implemented a peer-to-peer coaching model like the one we proposed as the basis for their CSSR training, and included some training in document machine operation in their planning.

The most interesting development to date, however, is a learning programme called 'Approach', which was initiated and is being led by one of the CSSRs. 'Approach' combines hands-on training in machine operation and problem diagnosis with on-the-phone coaching in how to better approach and interact with customers in determining what was wrong with their machine and taking actions to try to fix the problem. The programme is built in part on the same observation we had made in our discussions with MMR: knowledgeable CSSRs are more confident diagnosticians and thus able to gain a customer's trust, and that customers are then more likely to answer questions and do problem-solving work with the CSSR. It also takes seriously the idea that the work of a CSSR involves certain conversational-interactional skills and, more specifically, that the work involved with using CasePoint is fundamentally embedded in the local and collaborative organisation of talk-in-interaction. In taking this line, 'Approach' breaks sharply from the view of the CSSR as simply an information conduit between the customer and CasePoint, and thus from the model of the user that decisively informed MMR's expert system design strategy. Performance results with 'Approach' have been encouraging, with CSSRs who have gone through the training showing significant increases in solve rates.

Finally, at the time of this writing, several call-centre managers and their staffs have expressed interest in developing new, 'community knowledge sharing' methods and systems for supporting the work of CSSRs, whether they are doing remote call assistance or any other problem-solving task. This type of socio-technical system, organised around a database created and maintained by the work community itself, could function alongside of or even on top of CasePoint's database. While there are significant organisational obstacles to overcome (as evidenced by the cost concerns and strategic objectives of other managers we noted above), we are very much encouraged by this interest. A knowledge sharing system developed along that line – one that could also include diagnostic software to support reasoning through problems in certain situations – would be very close to a true 'system for experts'.

Acknowledgements

We would like to express our deep gratitude to 'MMR Corporation' – especially the employees of their customer service and support centres – for the opportunity to conduct this research and complete access to

MMR's activities and records. Our thanks to Jon Hindmarsh, Paul Luff, Christian Heath, Kathryn Henderson and especially Marilyn Whalen for many helpful comments and suggestions.

NOTES

1 The debate about the possibility of 'intelligent machines' has been plagued by a misunderstanding over what persons could mean when they say that a machine is or can be 'intelligent'. A computer may be able to more or less *simulate* human action, but this is not to say that can be endowed with human capacities (like 'intelligence'), only that it can be equipped with programming rules to generate such simulacrums (see e.g. Button and Sharrock, 1995: 118–19). Of course, many artificial practitioners make a point of distinguishing between 'computer intelligence' and 'human intellect', and define the former as requiring simply the mathematical description of human thought and action (see e.g. Wagman, 1998). From this view, the discipline of artificial intelligence is seen as directed towards the continuous augmentation of this distinct, computer-fixed type.

2 There is a striking lack of studies of expert systems in practice. Most AI systems reported in the literature operate on experimental problems or in specially designed environments; they are evaluated not on the basis of their support of ordinary users' work and decision-making, but on the basis of their performance on a test-set, commonly a well-chosen group of cases. For example, a medical diagnostic program named *Internist* was tested based on data from case records (Miller *et al.*, 1984). But these records were 'cleaned up', such that the same terms were used for every case. Also, to test the system, all cases with diagnoses that were not available to the *Internist* program were deleted. 'The diagnostic program cannot conclude a diagnosis that is missing from the knowledge base', Miller *et al.* (1984: 201) argued; 'such a case would not be a fair test for the system.' The evaluation was based on a comparison of the expert system's performance on the cases with the performance of clinicians on the same cases. Note that, although this may be an interesting exercise for the clinicians, this is hardly representative of doing a diagnosis *in situ*. Although we recognise that this type of testing is a necessary step in the development of such systems, it cannot anticipate the problems that may arise when the system is actually used by people in their daily work.

3 Our research on expert system design and use was conducted as one, rather small part of a business re-engineering project by MMR. MMR was attempting to reorganise all of its various teleservice operations by integrating previously separate functions (selling supplies, resolving invoice or product delivery problems, and processing calls for service on MMR equipment). We were full members of the MMR re-engineering project team, working under a contract at that time with the Institute for Research on Learning (IRL) with two colleagues, Marilyn Whalen and Kathryn Henderson. Our group used our research capabilities to address a wide range of problems related to the integration effort, such as work organisation, technology design and deployment, physical set-up design, learning strategy and work support documentation.

Most of our research on MMR's expert system took place in the early stages of the project, several months before the experimentation with integrating different jobs or functions began.

4   In the more typical expert system architecture, rules and frames are used to model the application domain. The problem with this approach is that making such a model is a time-consuming task, and arguably unnecessary: one can perform diagnosis on a copier quite well without an extensive model of how the copier actually functions. Case-Based Reasoning systems therefore start from a different premise, namely that humans commonly solve problems by comparing the current problem with problems they have encountered before. The remedy associated with the retrieved case may then well provide a solution in the current situation as well. The reasoning in case-based systems lies in the process of finding the right case, not in reasoning about the problem domain. Of course, as one can imagine, the reasoning to retrieve the right case can be quite involved, and based on representations of the domain. In those architectures the differences between the two techniques diminish, and they are sometimes referred to as hybrid architectures. Besides these differences in architecture, however, both knowledge-based systems and case-based systems are designed to perform some specialised task that was previously done by a human expert.

5   In some instances no definite cause will be identified. But this is no different from the experience of service technicians in the field, who do not use an expert system but rather rely on their wits, along with proven and documented 'repair analysis protocols', to try to diagnose and fix reported machine problems. In many situations, service technicians work with 'possible causes' that then have only possible solutions. In addition, the reported problem may be difficult or impossible to characterise as a definite machine fault, with the technician concluding that the real issue is the customer's relationship with (and understanding of) their machine (see Orr, 1996).

6   Questions that are bracketed (< >), like the last one displayed on the list in screen 5.3, **<What type of problem is it?>**, are 'internal' questions, meant to be answered by the CSSR based on information obtained from the customer through prior queries or heard in prior accounts, rather than asked directly of the customer.

7   Being able to exhibit expertise provides the CSSR with an interactional advantage in difficult situations. For example, knowledge of machine operation can give a CSSR the confidence to gently counter a customer's resistance or reluctance to performing actions with the machine that could fix a problem.

8   It is worth noting that over the course of some twenty months at MMR, we never witnessed a 'solve' where the solution had been achieved by the use of CasePoint; that is to say, in every 'solve' where CasePoint was employed, human expertise was still the most important factor.

9   Lest we be misread as claiming to critique expert system technology in general, we want emphasise once again that CasePoint represents only one approach to AI and expert system design, Case-Based Reasoning. Moreover, the application of that approach at MMR is but one among a range of possibilities.

6   The critical role of workplace studies in CSCW

Kjeld Schmidt

While there is no question that workplace studies play a prominent role in Computer Supported Cooperative Work, the exact nature of this role has been a subject of much reflection and debate over the years. So far, the deliberation has been inconclusive, and, moreover, in the last few years a certain sense of disillusionment and even scepticism has arisen concerning the ways in which and the extent to which such studies in fact contribute to CSCW systems design.

Plowman *et al.* (1995), for example, have raised the question 'what are workplace studies for?' To investigate this issue they undertook a survey of a large part of the workplace studies published in the area of CSCW – altogether seventy-five papers – and found what they called a 'paucity of papers detailing specific design guidelines' (Plowman *et al.*, 1995: 313). While they hesitated to conclude that 'workplace studies do not produce specific design guidelines', they did feel confident that the observed paucity 'can be attributed to the lack of reported research which has developed to the stage of a system prototype' (Plowman *et al.*, 1995: 313). Discussing these observations, Plowman *et al.* (1995: 321) surmised that the reason for the apparent failure to bridge the gap is 'a big discrepancy between accounts of sociality generated by field studies and the way information can be of practical use to system developers'.

While agreeing with the characterisation of the state of affairs advanced by Plowman *et al.* (1995), Anderson (1997) has challenged their tentative explanation, arguing that the issue of how ethnographic findings are formatted is a distraction; ethnography can be highly formal when *that* is appropriate for the research programme at hand. Instead, Anderson argued that the problem has deeper roots. Observing that not all kinds of qualitative studies of social life in the 'real world' are ethnographies and that the idea of ethnography 'as a method for the specification of end-user requirements for systems' is 'predicated in a misunderstanding of ethnography's role in social science', he stated flatly that 'designers do not need ethnography to do what they wish to do' (Anderson, 1994: 153):

designers way well work closely with users, engage in fieldwork among the end-user organizations for whom they are designing; and focus on the intersection of the technological, the organizational, and the social dimensions of the working environments within which their designed systems will find a place, all without ever engaging in the kind of analytic ethnography ... found in the social sciences. In fact, doing ethnography may prove a barrier to achieving the goals that designers want to set themselves. (Anderson, 1994: 155, emphasis deleted)

While Anderson's observations that not all kinds of qualitative studies of social life in the real world are ethnographies and that ethnography cannot serve as a requirements analysis methodology are topical and appropriate, he did not get to what I consider the root of much of the confusion, namely the mix-up of two distinct questions: first, the role of workplace studies of particular settings with a view to the design of specific CSCW systems for the same or similar settings, that is, the role of workplace studies as a requirements analysis method; and second, the role of workplace studies of particular settings as contributions to the development of the conceptual foundation for CSCW and, thereby, to the development of CSCW technologies. While workplace studies in both roles might be said to contribute to 'systems design', albeit in very different senses and through quite different mechanisms, the latter role is critical whereas the former is highly problematical.

First, let me address the role of workplace studies in the development of the conceptual and technological foundation of CSCW.

Cooperative work is a tricky phenomenon. We are all engaged in cooperative activities of various sorts in our everyday lives and routinely observe others working together around us. We are all experts from our everyday experience. And yet this quotidian insight can be utterly misleading when applied to the design of systems to support cooperative work.

As participants of a cooperative effort we routinely take its orderly accomplishment for granted. We have to do that, in order to get the job done. In depending on the activities of others, we are 'not interested' in the enormous contingencies and infinitely faceted practices of colleagues, unless these may impact on our own work (cf.Schutz, [1932] 1967, [1943] 1964, [1953] 1962). An actor will thus routinely expect not to be exposed to the myriad detailed activities by means of which his or her colleagues deal with the contingencies they are facing in their effort to ensure that their individual contributions are seamlessly articulated with the other contributions. Conversely, an actor will routinely avoid to publicise those contingent practices which colleagues do not 'need to know', not only in order to appear competent in the eyes of colleagues and managers, but also and more importantly in order to not to add to the complexity of the work of his or her colleagues. The individual activities of cooperating actors are *made to appear as if* they are seamlessly integrated and meshed. Disclosing only those aspects of the work required to articulate the distributed and yet interdependent activities which are relevant to the concerns of colleagues – that is, knowing what to make publicly visible and what *not* to make publicly visible in a given situation – is a crucial aspect of competent conduct in any cooperative work setting. Just like illusionists and acrobats strive to make their acts appear as if performed effortlessly, cooperating actors strive to 'dampen the noise' from the contingencies of their own work and from the concomitant efforts of articulating their own activities with the other contributions to the joint endeavour by skilfully modulating which aspects of their work are made visible, and how, and which aspects are performed such that they are inconspicuous to colleagues.

The notion of orderliness which cooperating actors take for granted and have to take for granted and which they, in turn, convey to colleagues through the way they make publicly relevant aspects of their own local affairs publicly accessible and visible, is not an illusion or some kind of 'false consciousness'. The mutual projection of order is rarely deceptive to competent members. It reflects the fact that myriads of cooperative activities usually are accomplished, integrated, meshed, articulated successfully, day in and day out, and it reflects this fact perfectly adequately by 'escamotating' the detailed practices by means of which this orderliness is achieved.[1] It is rather a necessary simplification, indispensable for us to be able to cope with the routine complexities of our daily work.

The problem arises when the categories in which these notions are generalised as common-sense constructs (e.g. 'task', 'goal', 'shared', 'context', 'role', 'procedure', 'team', and 'organisation') are used uncritically beyond the realm of everyday work. It may for example make a lot of sense to refer to a 'shared goal' in a particular setting, for instance if one actor has asked the other participants in a meeting, 'Do we all agree this is what we want to do?', and they have nodded their consent. While the category of a 'shared goal' can be seen to escamotate the ways in which the members arrange the multiple, partially dissonant, motives and interests into a workable compromise and handle the unavoidable indications of continual discord and diverging interpretations of the compromise, competent members of the particular setting know the extent to which and the sense in which the 'goal' is 'shared'. But if a joint effort – for other purposes, for example for the purpose of sociological theory or for the design of organisational information systems – is conceived of as constituted by a 'shared goal', the notion of a 'shared goal' becomes utterly misleading. For a brilliant example, cf. Sabbagh:

Each person working on Worldwide Plaza had a different goal: for a bricklayer, during 1987, to see the gleaming, soft-beige-and-rose expanse of crisply laid brick reach up to six hundred feet; for a steel fabricator in Houston, to see nineteen thousand tons of steel erected into a soaring framework of complex ellipses and sturdy rectangles; and for the developers, to see an investment that would transform the West Side of New York, and bring profits for decades to come. Linked to any major construction project are men and women with every type of personality, intellect, and qualification. Scientists and engineers, welders and electricians, artists and writers, salesmen and real-estate brokers, accountants and bankers, canteen managers and dynamite experts, seismologists and calligraphers – all feeling entitled to think of a building as 'their' building in the same way as the architect or the principal developer. This possessiveness can be a driving force behind each craftsman and his task. It can lead to the excitement of competition, as the mason, the waterproofer, and the window installer will the steel erector to complete *his* stage in the building to make *their* work possible. (Sabbagh, 1989: 1–3, original italics).

Thus, in his studies of the engineering design process as it unfolds within design projects, Louis Bucciarelli found that

different participants in the design process have different perceptions of the design, the intended artifact, in process . . . The task of design is then as much a matter of getting different people to share a common perspective, to agree on the most significant issues, and to shape consensus on what must be done next, as it is a matter of concept formation, evaluation of alternatives, costing and sizing – all the things we teach. (Bucciarelli, 1984: 187)

That is, the 'shared goal' is not there in advance; it is constructed by the members in the course of the project, and it is in the process of agreeing to a 'shared goal' that the designers arrive at an agreed-to design. When the designers have a 'shared goal', they have – for all practical purposes – finished the design task. In fact, they may not even agree on anything but the design when they finish; agreeing on a 'shared goal' may require additional effort and participants may simply decide, tacitly, that it is not worthwhile: 'Design decision in this instance is best seen as an overlay of interests rather than their synthesis within some flat, cognitive domain' (Bucciarelli, 1988).

Similarly, the notion of 'shared knowledge', which spontaneously crops up in CSCW contexts, ignores the work required to make knowledge 'shared': determining the adequate level of abstraction for a given purpose, eliminating aspects of less relevance to the intended audience and formatting according to the expected use situation, providing indexation and so on (cf. Bowker and Star, 1991). Even such ubiquitous and seemingly innocuous categories as 'task' and 'collaboration' are problematic, in that they introduce a conceptual separation of 'individual' and 'collective' which, at closer inspection, turns out to be misleading since 'seemingly individual and specialised work tasks are produced with respect to the actions of colleagues' (Heath and Luff, 1996a: 97).

In order to develop computer-based technologies which can enhance the ability of actors to accomplish their cooperative endeavours we cannot take the orderliness of cooperative work for granted. On the contrary, we need to go beyond the common-sense notions of everyday working life. We need to understand *how* orderliness is accomplished in cooperative endeavours; we need to uncover the practices through which the myriad distributed and yet interdependent activities are meshed, aligned, integrated, because it is the very practices through which such orderliness is accomplished that must be supported. The primary role of workplace studies in CSCW is thus to dismantle the common-sense conceptions of cooperative work, take them apart, unpack and disclose the hidden practices of articulation work, and thus give us access – analytically and conceptually – to the intricate ways and means of the production of social order in cooperative activities. This role is critical in the sense that it is crucial, but it is also critical in the Marxian sense of uncovering the social practices through which categories that are otherwise taken for granted are produced as necessary 'thought forms' and thereby determining the boundaries of the validity of these categories.[2]

Indeed, those workplace studies that have had the strongest influence on CSCW research have been studies which did not aim at arriving at specific design recommendations for specific systems but instead tried to uncover, in minute detail, the ways in which social order is produced in cooperative work settings, whatever the design implications of the findings might be.

In this respect the studies of office work conducted by Suchman and Wynn in the early 1980s are exemplary. They undertook to demonstrate empirically that the conceptions of 'office work' then prevailing among managerial ideologists, designers of 'office automation' systems, office equipment vendors, etc. were misleading. In particular, they subjected the common-sense presuppositions about the status of office procedures *vis-à-vis* the actual course of action to a critical analysis and demonstrated that office procedures do not determine action causally; they could thereby show that the design visions of the office automation movement were misguided (Suchman, 1982, 1983; Suchman and Wynn, 1984; Wynn, 1979). In doing so, they were highly influential in shaping the agenda of the research programme which a few years later became CSCW.

Since then, workplace studies have had and continue to have a profound impact on the development of CSCW technologies. Not in the form of a direct relationship of 'requirements specification' with respect to the design of specific systems, but by contributing to the conceptual foundation of CSCW. Most significantly, a series of studies such as the Lancaster study of air traffic control (e.g. Harper and Hughes, 1993; Harper *et al.*, 1989, 1991; Hughes *et al.*, 1988) and the study of the London Underground control room (Heath and Luff, 1992a, 1996a) have made the CSCW community understand the delicate interplay of individual and cooperative activities and appreciate the crucial role of 'awareness' in ensuring that individual activities are seamlessly integrated. This has incited and inspired computer scientists to explore ways in which the production of awareness in cooperative ensembles can be supported in CSCW systems through 'shared object servers' (e.g. Rodden and Blair, 1991; Rodden *et al.*, 1992; Trevor *et al.*, 1995), awareness models (e.g. Benford and Greenhalgh, 1997; Rodden, 1996; Sandor *et al.*, 1997; Simone and Bandini, 1997) and so forth. Other areas of CSCW research can tell similar stories of how workplace studies have informed the development of CSCW technologies. For instance, ethnographic and other in-depth workplace studies have played a crucial role in the development of the concept of 'computational coordination mechanisms' and of the corresponding software environment (Schmidt and Simone, 1996; Simone and Schmidt, 1998; Simone *et al.*, 1995).

That is, the observed 'paucity of papers detailing specific design guidelines' (Plowman *et al.*, 1995: 313) does not reflect on the *relevance* to CSCW of ethnographic or other in-depth workplace studies informed by sociological programmes such as ethnomethodology or symbolic interactionism. Nor does it, in fact, reflect on the actual impact of workplace studies on the development of CSCW technologies.[3] That is, 'designers' of novel CSCW technologies – as opposed to application of existing technologies to the requirements of specific settings – indeed do need ethnography and other sociologically informed kinds of workplace studies 'to do what they wish to do'.

Instead, I shall suggest that the paucity of specific design guidelines reflects first, on the state of CSCW technology, and second, on a lack of appreciation of how radical the CSCW programme really is.

Conducting a requirements analysis presumes a mature and reasonably understood technology. The analyst investigates a particular work setting or a set of settings in a particular work domain in order to determine if a given family of technologies might be usefully deployed, to determine which aspects of the work activities in the domain would benefit most from computerisation, and to sketch a design. Without knowing the general characteristics of the potential technologies, the analyst would be faced with an infinite space of possibilities and would in fact, in order to give specific guidelines or recommendations, be expected to develop the new technologies more or less from scratch.

In terms of technology, CSCW has a long way to go. Discussing the state of CSCW technologies in any kind of detail is, of course, completely beyond the scope of a brief set of comments on the role of workplace studies. Allow me to mention one point, however, just to illustrate the situation: as pointed out by foundational CSCW workplace studies such as the ATC study and the London Underground study, cooperative and individual activities are inextricably interwoven in daily work practice, and a CSCW system should thus support a fluent and seamless meshing of individual work and cooperative work. However, current operating systems are basically designed to support work conceived of as individual work. They do not provide facilities for supporting the articulation of cooperative activities with respect to the shared data structures and functionalities as represented by applications. Thus, although CSCW facilities supporting mutual awareness and adaptation (monitoring the activities of colleagues, making one's work appropriately visible to colleagues, directing attention to anomalies and so on) are orthogonal to applications such as word processors, spreadsheets, and drawing tools, CSCW designers attempting to build shared work spaces are forced to incorporate such facilities in the domain-specific data structures and functionalities, that is, in applications. As a result, users are suddenly faced with 'individual' as well as 'cooperative' word processors, spreadsheets, drawing tools and so on, and an impedance is consequently created between individual and cooperative activities. CSCW facilities providing 'shared work spaces' should not be conceived of as applications or be implemented as part and parcel of applications but as extended operating system functions that can be accessed from and combined with, in principle, any application. Otherwise the delicate and dynamic relationship between cooperative and individual work breaks down. (For an attempt to outline the implications of workplace studies for the architecture of a CSCW software environment, see Schmidt and Rodden, 1996.)

In the absence of appropriate computing environments – and I have indicated only one example of many equally fatal deficiencies – it is no wonder if workplace studies do not result in *specific* design recommendations or CSCW prototypes for specific settings. We are still in the murky prehistory of CSCW, and there is a long way to travel until environments that support articulation work fairly adequately become available. Until then, there will remain a big discrepancy between accounts of sociality generated by field studies and the way information can be of immediately practical use to system developers.

However, while CSCW technology is still far from mature, important practical steps in the development of CSCW technologies are of course being taken in the form of experimental systems, sometimes developed as attempts to explore possibilities of supporting certain modes of interaction (Fitzpatrick *et al.*, 1996; Fuchs *et al.*, 1995; Ishii, 1990; Ishii *et al.*, 1992; Roseman and Greenberg, 1996), sometimes to explore the feasibility and limitations of certain existing technologies for CSCW purposes (for example media spaces, workflow technology, hypermedia and so on) in particular work settings (Grønbæk and Mogensen, 1997; Shepherd *et al.*, 1990) or more generally (e.g. Heath and Luff, 1992b; Heath *et al.*, 1995), and sometimes even to solve very practical problems in particular work settings (e.g. Pougès *et al.*, 1994). In any case, these experimental systems inevitably support only certain modes of interaction and thus provide quite limited support for articulation work. These unavoidable limitations notwithstanding, the experiments provide indispensable insights, not only in the advantages and problems with applying those technologies for CSCW purposes, but also often – when the experience is carefully documented – in the (perhaps unforeseen) problems that can arise when such technologies are introduced in the social organisation of work.

In the development of experimental CSCW systems, designers often – as pointed out by Anderson (1997) – work closely with users and engage in fieldwork in the settings for which they are designing; they may even invite sociologists and psychologists to assist in investigating the setting and evaluating the system and its impact. In these cases, however, the objectives of the experiment are clearly defined and the technological options identified and bounded in advance.

Thus, while requirements analysis – in line with other ways of developing requirements such as user participation in design – plays an important role in the development of experimental CSCW systems that investigate the applicability of specific technologies for specific aspects of articulation work, the impact of this kind of requirements engineering is limited by the fundamental inadequacies of existing software environments for CSCW purposes.

Ironically, however, when the new technology eventually matures and the adequate software environments become available, to a large extent due to the long-term impact of sociologically inspired workplace studies, it may very well turn out that this technology does not leave much room for requirements analysis as a distinct kind of activity which requires specialised qualifications. In the 1980s much attention was paid to developing a methodology for requirements analysis of 'office work'. Most of that effort was made redundant with the development of modern graphical user interfaces and inexpensive 'shrink-wrapped' software. As a result, contemporary users do not need to hire experts to conduct a requirements analysis and devise a requirements specification to configure, for instance, a Macintosh.

In fact, a radical conception of CSCW and CSCW systems argues that a CSCW system should provide an environment that supports users in designing and manipulating the coordination mechanisms that are appropriate for the particular setting (Ellis *et al.*, 1995; Kaplan *et al.*, 1992; Malone *et al.*, 1992; Schmidt, 1991; Schmidt and Simone, 1996). In a similar vein, Bentley and Dourish (1995: 134) have suggested that a CSCW system should be seen 'as one whose behaviour can be adapted through high-level customisation to meet the needs of its users'. From this perspective, they argue, in-depth requirements analyses will no longer be necessary in order to design effective systems to support cooperative work.

That is, if the radical programme in CSCW proves realistic, and I for one am convinced it will, the conventional notion of the product life cycle as constituted by distinct stages defined by the involvement of different professionals – 'requirements analysis', 'design', 'use', 'evaluation', 'maintenance' and 'redesign' – will not be adequate for the design of CSCW systems.

In sum, then, the role of workplace studies in CSCW is crucial and critical: to dismantle prevalent common-sense notions of cooperative work by uncovering how orderly cooperative work is routinely and inconspicuously accomplished. On the other hand, there does not seem to be much room for workplace studies – such as ethnographies – in the design of specific CSCW systems, in part because the technology is not mature yet and requirements analysis therefore as yet is a problematic undertaking, and in part because CSCW represents a radical technology in which requirements analysis may eventually turn out to be gratuitous anyway.

NOTES

1 'Escamotating' is derived from the French *escamoter*, to remove something diligently and surreptitiously, normally used to denote the skilled practices of illusionists and conjurors.
2 Cf. the subtitle of Marx's *Capital: Critique of Political Economy*.
3 Notice that the trails of this impact – the histories of how workplace studies inform the development of CSCW technologies – are not always readily visible in papers reporting on findings from workplace studies. The transfer of findings and insights typically happens in the course of discussions within cross-disciplinary research teams and is often documented only in design-oriented papers.

7 From individual action to collective activity and back: developmental work research as an interventionist methodology

Yrjö Engeström

> Having emerged as an individual exception from the rule in the labour of one or several men, the new form is then taken over by others, becoming in time a new universal norm. If the new norm did not originally appear in this exact manner, it would never become a really universal form, but would exist merely in fantasy, in wishful thinking.
>
> (Ilyenkov, 1982: 83–4)

Introduction

Since the 1980s, ethnographic and cognitive studies of work have taken important steps forward. Powerful micro-level methodologies and theories, such as ethnomethodology, conversation analysis and distributed cognition, have been developed. However, a nagging question sometimes arises (e.g. Hughes *et al.*, 1993; Rogers, 1997): what difference do these studies make in practice? In this vein, Grudin and Grinter (1995) write about 'the ethnographers' deep professional bias against intervention'.

> Although ethnographers know that introducing technology disrupts work, they are not trained to invent organizations, to assess the costs of change, or to determine the likelihood of successful adoption. And even change that some would regard as positive might be questioned by ethnographers. (Grudin and Grinter, 1995: 56–7)

After examining the problem in some detail, Rogers (1997) draws the following conclusion:

> Rather than always take a backseat role, researchers need to become more proactive in their involvement with the people and objects of their study. This means engaging more in an ongoing dialogue with the various groups of people working or designing together (i.e., the users, the managers, and the designers). Researchers should stop shying away from being involved. On the contrary, they should be seeking ways of taking a more active role in the design and implementation process, even becoming 'change agents' (cf. Blomberg *et al.*, 1993) where appropriate. In doing so, ideas can be fed back, discussed, and negotiated as part of the ongoing practice of research. (Rogers, 1997: 69)

Rogers emphasises that such ongoing dialogue is informal and opportunistic, moving 'with the ebb and flow of the tide of obstacles, problems and developments' (Rogers, 1997: 72). Rogers emphasises refraining from taking sides. The researcher is depicted as a mediator and facilitator. Rogers noticed that 'there was even a joke at the end of this process that the company could usefully employ me as a secretary to type up the lists [of problems experienced by the workers]' (Rogers, 1997: 71).

The basic stance described by Rogers is of course not new. It is common to many variations of action research, including the Scandinavian version called 'democratic dialogue' (Toulmin and Gustavsen, 1996). From my perspective, informal and opportunistic dialogue is an unsatisfactory alternative to the delivery of packaged prescriptions by designers and consultants. Remaining a mediator or secretary with only improvised substantive input is too modest an alternative to decontextualised principles and technical guidelines.

The dichotomy of obtrusive prescription from above versus minimal informal facilitation is actually quite prevalent in the available micro-level approaches. Ethnographic studies have traditionally been preoccupied with observing and understanding stable orders, routines and repeatable procedures. The issue of change has been relatively alien to them. In this regard, they seem to be inherently handicapped in dealing with the turbulent worlds of work and technology.

In this chapter, I argue for a radical reconceptualisation of the possible role of workplace research in facilitating practical change. Ambitious interventions require an ambitious theory. At the core of any intervention is the question of development. Developmental theorising has been largely avoided by ethnographers, possibly fearing deterministic and evolutionist implications. In the face of the pervasive and often dramatic changes going on in workplaces, such avoidance amounts to hiding one's head in the sand.

I shall present activity theory and developmental work research as an alternative approach to the dilemma of research versus intervention. I briefly discuss two central ideas of this approach. The first one is understanding change as grounded in disturbances experienced in daily work actions and in corresponding concrete innovations. The second one is seeing change as driven by expansive reconceptualisation of the object and motive of the collective activity. The crucial issue elaborated in this chapter is movement between these two levels as a key to the methodology of developmental work research. I concretise this idea with an example taken from an ongoing intervention project in the children's hospital of Helsinki. Finally, I summarise the implications of my argument for our understanding of development and developmental methodology.

Starting with actions: grounding change in disturbances

The lesson from various intervention studies in hospital settings is that change and development imported from the outside and implemented from above do not work. For instance in the case of 'Parkside' Hospital (Hanlon *et al.*, 1985), the attempts to get employees involved in efforts to change their work boiled down to discussions of isolated random problems and ideas with no apparent connection to an overall vision or direction. In a more recent intervention in the Karolinska Hospital (Kaplinsky, 1995), even such attempts were missing – the consultants seem to have believed that their rational approach and glossy materials would be sufficient to convince the staff.

In activity theory, developmental transformations are seen as attempts to reorganise, or re-mediate, the local activity system in order to resolve its pressing inner contradictions. The emergence, aggravation and resolution of contradictions may be regarded as a developmental cycle in the life of the activity system (Engeström, 1987).

As an example of contradictions of work in the medical field, let us consider the following extension to Leont'ev's account of a village physician.

The doctor who buys a practice in some little provincial place may be very seriously trying to reduce his fellow citizens' suffering from illness, and may see his calling in just that. He must, however, want the number of the sick to increase, because his life and practical opportunity to follow his calling depend on that. (Leont'ev, 1981: 255)

Every day the doctor faces the primary contradiction of patients as people to heal versus patients as sources of income. But he has to live with the contradiction and mostly is able to suppress it out of his conscious awareness. The tension grows as his patients begin to change. A new district hospital is built in the nearby city, and the patients are starting to ask for modern lab tests, X-rays and other wonders of medical technology as they visit the doctor. Of course the village doctor does not have such tools. This leads to a secondary contradiction between the new kind of object – demanding patients asking for technological medicine – and old tools based on the handicraft mode of doctoring. As this contradiction is aggravated and spreads across the nation, it leads to a crisis and eventual reorganisation of medical practice in primary care (for an examination of this development in Finnish health care, see Engeström, 1993; for consequences in medical cognition, see Engeström, 1995).

If actors are able to identify and analyse contradictions of their activity system, they may focus their energy on to the crucial task of resolving those contradictions by means of reorganising and expanding the activity, instead of being victimised by changes that roll over them as if forces of a natural catastrophe.

Contradictions do not manifest themselves directly. They manifest themselves through disturbances, ruptures and small innovations in practitioners' everyday work actions. The task is first, to make these disturbances visible to the practitioners, and second, to engage practitioners in analyses in which these seemingly random incidents are connected with and interpreted in the light of contradictions in the activity system that time and again give rise to such disturbances and innovations.

Making disturbances visible requires a lot of groundwork from the researcher – namely powerful field data that lead to an 'ethnography of trouble'. In the intervention studies conducted at the Center for Activity Theory and Developmental Work Research,[1] we typically videotape numerous problematic work situations and associated on-site interviews where practitioners and their clients reflect upon events as they unfold or immediately thereafter. In medical settings, we use doctor–patient and nurse–patient consultations and other interactions, as well situations of coordination and collaboration between different staff members and their artefacts. These are displayed, viewed and discussed with groups of practitioners and clients, including those who appear on the tape. In other words, we erect a collective mirror in front of the practitioners. These encounters evoke personal involvement and tense debates on dilemmatic situations seen in the data.

Connecting disturbances with contradictions requires another kind of groundwork, namely digging deep into the history of the activity system under scrutiny. Historical documents and accounts, including interviews with long-time practitioners and clients, are collected in order to identify past cycles of development and transformation in the activity system (Engeström, 1987). Historical data from the different phases are analysed and modelled using as template the model of activity system depicted in figure 7.1.

Figure 7.1 calls attention to both the personal perspective of the subject – any given subject involved in the collaborative activity may be selected – and its relationship to the systems perspective that views the activity from the outside. An individual artefact-mediated action may be depicted as the uppermost sub-triangle in figure 7.1. Such individual actions are embedded in collective activity systems. This collective aspect is represented by the bottom part of the diagram, consisting of the community, its division of labour, and its rules. In the model, systemic contradictions are depicted as tensions within and between the nodes of the activity system aggravated by the asynchronous development of the different elements. For example, the emergence of new kinds of symptoms, illnesses and

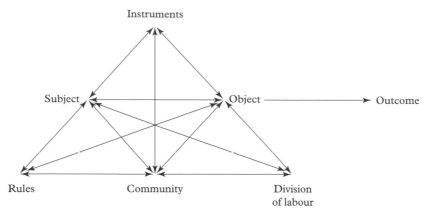

Figure 7.1 The mediational structure of an activity system (taken from Engeström, 1987:78)

patients often leads to an aggravated contradiction between this new object and the old instruments (including conceptual tools, such as diagnostic categories). This is not only because of a general resistance to change; more importantly, the existing instruments are invested and identified with a certain motive for and perspective on the work, and their vigorous persistence is fuelled by other, interconnected activity systems which produce and update them for the practitioners (see e.g. Berkenkotter and Ravotas, 1997).

The tentative identification of past and current contradictions enables the practitioners to distance themselves from the disturbances viewed on the video and to a recognise recurring patterns and types of trouble as manifestations of systemic contradictions rather than personal failures. This, in turn, leads to elucidation and enriched conceptualisation of the contradictions.

This dual move from experiential encounter with troublesome actions to conceptual modelling of the activity system and its contradictions is schematically depicted in figure 7.2. In the figure, the notion of contradictions in the activity system is represented by means of two-headed lightning-shaped arrows.

Modelling the activity: building object and motive in the zone of proximal development

Common to most intervention accounts is an unshaken trust in the idea of explicit goals as the guiding perspective of change, in other words, a

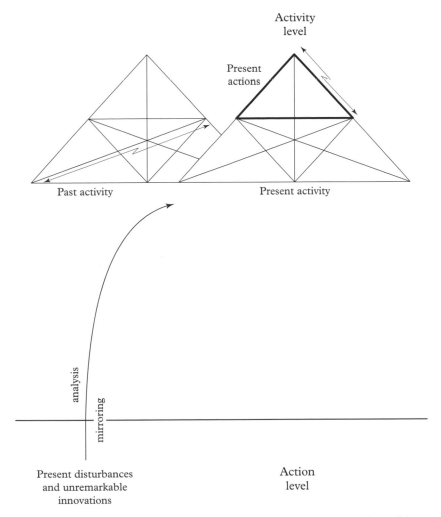

Figure 7.2 From troublesome actions to contradictions in the activity
system

goal-rational view of change. Suchman's (1987) study of plans and situated actions and Weick's (1995) work on organisational sense-making
make convincing cases for assigning a much more limited role to conscious goals and plans. Instead of determining and directing actions in
the strict sense, explicit goals and plans typically function as resources
in accounting for actions after their accomplishment. Individuals do
set goals and try to pursue them, but goal-directed actions always have

unintended consequences. Above all, goals are pitifully insufficient as motivators of major change in people's routines of thought and action. To be reachable, goals must be specific and relatively short-term.

In activity theory (Leont'ev, 1978), the distinction between individual goal-directed action and collective object-oriented activity is of central importance. A collective activity is driven by a deeply communal motive. The motive is formed when a collective need meets an object that has the potential to fulfil the need. The motive is thus embedded in the object of the activity. The object, in turn, is to be understood as a project under construction, moving from potential 'raw material' to a meaningful shape and to a result or an outcome. In this sense, the object determines the horizon of possible goals and actions. But it is truly a horizon: as soon as an intermediate goal is reached, the object escapes and must be reconstructed by means of new intermediate goals and actions.

It is important to realise that one and the same goal-directed action may accomplish various different activities and transfer from one activity to another. On the other hand, the object and motive of a collective activity may typically be sought after by means of multiple alternative goals and actions.

The object of hospital work is the patients, with their health problems or illness. To maintain that the patients are the object and motive for hospital work is not an idealist statement advocating selfless devotion to a higher calling among employees. What more than anything arouses involvement, effort, emotion, excitement and frustration among frontline hospital staff is encounters with real, live patients, no matter how cynical or instrumentally oriented the individual employee may be.

This is not to say that the very object of hospital work would be harmonious in itself. To the contrary, I find it fruitful to think of the object of any activity as internally contradictory. In capitalism, the pervasive primary contradiction is that of commoditisation: between the use value and the exchange value of objects. In medicine, this takes the form of patient as person to be helped and healed versus patient as source of revenue and profit (or on the flip side, as opportunity to profit by cutting costs).

Paradoxical expectations about physician behavior are also built into those cost-containment programs that reward physicians for saving money in the care of their patients . . . Creating economic incentives that encourage providers to perform fewer services or to discharge patients from the hospital more quickly makes sense only if providers can be trusted not to be excessively influenced. (Gray, 1991: 324)

How can the energy stemming from the tension-laden object be translated into change efforts? The key is the realisation that the objects – the patients with their problems – are constantly changing, and this historical

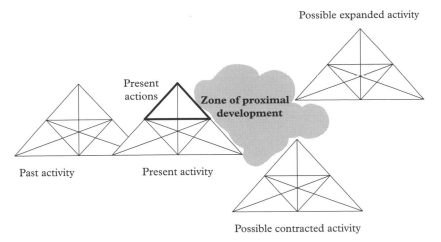

Figure 7.3 The zone of proximal development

evolution of the patient is partly constructed by the hospital itself. Any transformation of the hospital is also a transformation of the patient. The motive for change efforts arises from analysing the contradictions and possibilities in the object and from projecting a new historical form of the object as an expansive solution to the present tensions. Such projection means sketching a zone of proximal development for the collective activity of hospital work.

The notion of zone is crucially different from the notion of goal. While a goal is a fixed end-point or end-state, a zone is the distance or the area between the individually experienced present and collectively generated foreseeable future (Engeström, 1987). If such a zone is not worked out, specific goals are built on sand, or pinned on to thin air. You get the 'failures to endogenise' change processes, vividly described in the two hospital studies mentioned above.

The zone of proximal development may be depicted as a grey area between actions embedded in the current activity with its historical roots and contradictions, the foreseeable activity in which the contradictions are expansively resolved, and the foreseeable activity in which the contradictions have led to contraction and destruction of opportunities (figure 7.3).

Modelling the possible expanded activity requires yet another kind of groundwork from the researcher. Alternative models of the future must be brought to the table, to be debated, analysed and compared. These alternative visions are available among competitors, managers, and design experts. Instead of regular benchmarking which typically aims at identifying strengths and weaknesses in advanced practices without questioning the criteria of success, modelling of the zone of proximal development looks for radical change in the very object and criteria of the activity. Such expansive change has to resolve the historically accumulated contradictions presently plaguing the activity.

Back to actions

The zone of proximal development can be crossed only by means of new kinds of concrete actions. This calls for a move back from activity to actions, a move of design and implementation.

Interventions of the kind depicted in figure 7.3 are based neither on prescriptions from above nor on random complaints and ideas from below. They are based on an introduction, collaborative application and production of new tools – literally on re-mediation or re-instrumentation, originally envisioned by Vygotsky (1978). Previous Vygotskian theorising and research has, however, mainly focused on a single individual or a dyad of two subjects using a single, well-defined mediating tool or artefact. Language as mediator has required a more complex approach – but studies of semiotic mediation have commonly excluded material instruments and tools. In interventionist studies of expansive learning, the mediational set-up is complex and multilayered both semiotically and instrumentally, yet the crucial events are temporally and spatially constrained so as to allow the collection of comprehensive high-fidelity data by means of videotaping. Analysis of such data forces the researcher to adopt a new view of mediation: instead of single instruments, one has to analyse a whole interconnected instrumentality.

The concept of instrumentality implies that the instruments form a system that includes not only multiple cognitive artefacts and semiotic means used for analysis and design, but also straightforward primary tools used in the daily practice and made visible for examination, reshaping and experimentation. In such a dense mediational setting, a set of interconnected new socio-cognitive processes is called for – literally, a new mentality is to be generated. The very complexity of the set-up means that the instrumentality is constantly evolving; old tools are modified, new tools are created and tested in action.

This type of design requires a bold experimental attitude rather than the attitude of a casual observer and facilitator. Bringing about and traversing collective zones of proximal development is experimentation with activity systems. When practitioners face a mirror depicting their own actions and disturbances, they often experience them as personal failures

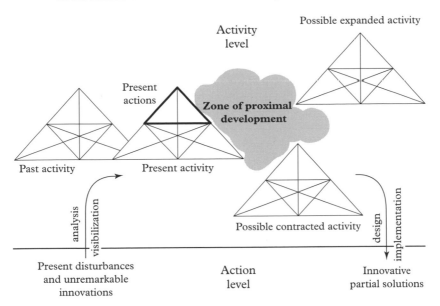

Figure 7.4 The movement from actions to activity and back in developmental work research

or even crises. Powerful and unpredictable cognitive, emotional and social dissonances are triggered.

The developmental interventionist needs to record, analyse and support these processes. The researcher needs to record and analyse also his or her own actions and interactions. Interventions themselves must become an object of rigorous study: the mirror is used both ways (figure 7.4).

Putting theory into practice: remodelling children's medical care in Helsinki

The Helsinki University Central Hospital (HUCH) Hospital for Children and Adolescents (hereafter called simply the children's hospital) is struggling with the need to cut the disproportionally high costs of care typical to Helsinki. The current phase of their change efforts is focused on coordination and collaboration between the children's hospital outpatient clinic, the hospital wards, the other hospitals of the area and, most importantly, the primary health care centres of the cities in the area. This phase has been facilitated by my research group, using a method called Boundary Crossing Laboratory. Approximately sixty invited representatives of physicians, nurses, other staff and management from the various institutions responsible for children's health care in the Helsinki area met around a round table in ten three-hour sessions, the last one of which was held in mid-February 1998. The participants viewed and discussed a series of videotaped patient cases which in various ways demonstrated troubles caused by lack of coordination and communication between the different care providers in the area. The troubles took the form of excessive numbers of visits, unclear loci of responsibility and failure to inform other involved care providers (including the patient's family) of the practitioners' diagnoses, actions and plans.

The historical background behind these troubles was dug up and discussed. In the 1970s, the Finnish primary health care services were reorganised so that each municipality was required to create a health centre which offers comprehensive primary care services to the population free of charge or for a small fixed fee. During the 1980s, the health centres were plagued by classic symptoms of mass production and bureaucracy: minimal continuity of care, faceless service, long lines and waiting times, and low satisfaction among both staff and patients. Reforms were carried out, based on the principles of 'personal physician', 'population responsibility' and teamwork. These reforms have effectively increased the continuity of care, replacing the isolated visit with the long-term care relationship as the object of the practitioners' work activity. The notion of care relationship has gradually become the key conceptual tool for planning and recording work in health centres.

A parallel development has taken place in hospitals. Hospitals grew bigger and more complicated in the decades following the Second World War. Fragmentation by specialities led to complaints and was seen to be partially responsible for the rapidly rising costs of hospital care. In the late 1980s, hospitals began to design and implement critical paths or pathways for designated diseases or diagnostic groups.

These paths are a crucial part of a team's (physician, nurses, and support professionals) efforts to manage and/or coordinate the patient's care. A critical path should be developed based upon diagnoses with similar patient care needs. The critical path should then be organized to help the health care team know what intervention on any given day of a patient's hospitalization is most likely to produce the best outcomes for a given patient population. (McDonald, 1994: 141)

With these reforms spreading and taking root, should not the problems with coordination and collaboration be under control? Evidence presented and discussed in Boundary Crossing Laboratory sessions led to the conclusion that this is not the case. Care relationships and critical paths were solutions created in response to particular historical sets of contradictions. These contradictions are rapidly being superseded by a new, more encompassing configuration of contradictions.

Care relationships and critical paths respond to contradictions internal to the respective institutions. Care relationships are seen as a way to conceptualise, document and plan long-term interactions with a patient inside primary health care. Their virtue is that the patient can be seen as having multiple interacting problems and diagnoses that evolve over time; their limitation is that responsibility for the patient is practically suspended when the patient enters a hospital. Correspondingly, critical paths are constructed to give a normative sequence of procedures for dealing with a given disease or diagnosis. They do not help in dealing with patients with unclear and multiple diagnoses, and they tend to impose their disease-centred world-view even on primary care practitioners. Fundamentally, both care relationships and critical paths are linear and temporal constructions of the object. They have great difficulties in representing and guiding horizontal and socio-spatial relations and interactions between care providers located in different institutions, including the patient and his/her family as the most important actors in care.

The need for such horizontal and socio-spatial coordination across institutional boundaries was powerfully spelled out in an article entitled 'A Health Lesson I Never Wanted' by Eric Caines, a former high-ranking official involved in the market-oriented reform of the British National Health Service (NHS). He encountered the contradictions when his own father-in-law became terminally ill.

What was absolutely clear to us . . . was that each episode of illness had been treated separately on the basis of what appeared to be the distinctive characteristics at the time . . . The glaringly obvious problem was that nobody was in overall charge of the case. My father-in-law was, in effect, treated as a number of patients, each presenting different problems and requiring different treatments. The basic failure was one of ownership – or, more precisely, lack of it. The delivery of health-care is still organised to suit the requirements of professionals in their specialisms, not focused on patient needs. Whenever my father-in-law was transferred from ward to ward within the same hospital, or between different hospitals or units in different Trusts, everything started again from scratch. No records appeared to travel with him on his various peregrinations around the NHS – on some occasions, no one even seemed to know under whose care he had previously been. (Caines, 1997: 24)

The experiences that Caines had with the care of his elderly father-in-law are common among child patients who suffer from multiple parallel medical problems or whose diagnosis is unclear. Asthmatic and allergic children with repeated respiratory problems are the clearest case in point. Such a child may have a dozen hospital visits, including some stays of a few days in a ward, and even more numerous visits to primary care health centre in one year. Some of these visits are serious emergencies, some of them are milder but urgent infections, some are for tests, control and follow-ups.

One of the cases we presented in the Boundary Crossing Laboratory was Simon, age 3. In 1997, he had three visits to the district hospital of his municipality, eleven visits to the HUCH ear clinic, fourteen visits to his personal physician at the local health centre, and one visit to the out-patient clinic of the HUCH children's hospital. Another case we presented, Andrew, age 4, had in 1997 four visits to the HUCH hospital for skin and allergic diseases, nine visits to his local district hospital, and fourteen visits to his primary care health centre.

The newly emerging constellation of contradictions is schematically depicted in figure 7.5. A contradiction emerges between an increasingly salient aspect of the object – namely patients moving between primary care and hospital care – and the rule of cost-efficiency. This contradiction is about to reach a crisis. In Finland, the costs of health care, including hospital care, are basically covered by the municipal health centres who are supposed to monitor the referrals to hospital care. In Helsinki, these costs are clearly above national averages, largely due to the excessive use and high cost of services provided by the Central University Hospital (HUCH), of which the children's hospital is a part. Thus, there is an aggravated tension between the primary care health centre and the university hospital. Health centres in the Helsinki area are blaming the university hospital for high costs, while the university hospital criticises health centres for excessive referrals and for not being able to take care of patients who do not necessarily need hospital care.

Finally, a contradiction emerges between the new object (patients moving between primary care and hospital care) and the recently established instruments, namely care relationships in primary care and critical paths in hospital work. Being linear-temporal and mainly focused on care inside the institution, these tools are inadequate for dealing with patients who have multiple simultaneous problems and parallel contacts to different institutions of care.

The participants of the Boundary Crossing Laboratory constructed an expansive solution to this set of contradictions. The solution distinguishes between two layers of responsibility: each practitioner's traditional responsibility for his or her patient's specific care, and the shared responsibility for the formation, coordination and monitoring of the patient's overall network and trajectory of care. This expansion of responsibility forced both the practitioners and the researchers to realise that not only does expansive learning concern the temporal and socio-spatial dimensions of work, but also a third, ethical dimension of the object of work is always involved.

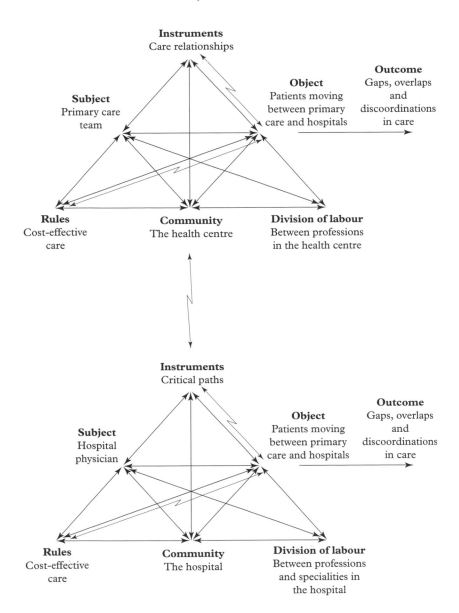

Figure 7.5 Contradictions in children's health care in the Helsinki area

To ensure that the expansion is achieved, four new tools were created. First, the patient's personal physician or a general practitioner in the local health centre is designated as the coordinator in charge of the patient's network and trajectory of care across institutional boundaries. Second, whenever a child becomes a patient of the children's hospital for more than a single visit, the hospital physician and nurse in charge of the child draft a care agreement which includes a plan for the patient's care and the division of labour between the different care providers contributing to the care of the child. The draft agreement is given to the child's family and sent to the child's personal health centre physician (and when appropriate, to the physicians in charge of the child in other hospitals) for their scrutiny. Third, if one or more of the parties find it necessary, they will have a care negotiation (by email, by telephone or face to face) to formulate a mutually acceptable care agreement. Fourth, care feedback, in the form of a copy of the patient's medical record, is automatically and without delay given or sent to the other parties of the care agreement after the patient's unplanned visit or changes in diagnoses or care plans.

This solution aims at resolving the contradictions depicted in figure 7.5 by creating a new instrumentality. This instrumentality, when shared by practitioners across institutional boundaries, is supposed to expand the object of their work by opening up the dimension of horizontal, sociospatial interactions in the patient's evolving network of care, making the parties conceptually aware of and practically responsible for the coordination of multiple parallel medical needs and services in many patients' lives. This does not replace but complements and extends the linear and temporal dimension of care. The solution also aims at relieving the pressure coming from the rule of cost-efficiency and the tension between the children's hospital and health centres by eliminating uncoordinated excessive visits and tests and by getting the health centre general practitioners involved in making joint care decisions that are acceptable to all parties.

Conclusion: so what is development?

On the view advocated in this chapter, development is local qualitative reorganisation, or re-mediation, of activity systems, attempting to resolve their historically evolving inner contradictions. Development goes on in the systems we study; they have their own developmental dynamics. Decontextualised prescriptions typically lead to solutions alien to the local system's developmental dynamics and are thus rejected or unpredictably altered in practice.

This would seem to support the minimalist approach suggested by Rogers (1997). However, there is nothing untouchable or sacred about the local developmental dynamics. To the contrary, outside influences from neighbouring activity systems constantly enter into the local systems and trigger novel developmental processes. It is this very triggering that is tremendously interesting for researchers curious about developmental potentials. Why do some developmental processes lead to dramatic expansions while others stagnate and die away? Why is the yield of some small interventions tremendous, while many large-scale interventions lead to miserable results?

Cultural-historical activity theory suggests that the answer is closer than we often realise: dig where you stand. In other words, 'to understand how a practice may enable or disable, how it may figure in development, we must know its social history' (Modell, 1996: 488).

While history helps us uncover the contradictions and potentials of an activity system, it does not directly tell us how those contradictions are to be resolved.

'Development' is a directional notion, an idea concerned not with contingent behavior alone (however processually conceived) but with origins and destinations, with transformations assessed in view of 'potential' and thus teleological . . . Change does not merely accrete. (Modell, 1996: 492)

In the approach advocated here, the direction of development – 'which way is up' – is an issue of local negotiation and struggle. Research aims at developmental re-mediation of work activities. In other words, research makes visible and pushes forward the contradictions of the activity under scrutiny, challenging the actors to appropriate and use new conceptual tools to analyse and redesign their own practice. The normative or teleological determination of the desirable direction is viewed as a mundane performance, accomplished by people on a daily basis. Thus, it is not something that researchers should fear and shy away from. Instead, the mundane accomplishment of directionality can be made explicit. This means that the different voices involved in the determination of direction (including the voices of the researchers) are identified, and clashes between them are regarded as an opportunity to get toward a clearer view of the contradictions. Such an approach does not eliminate the power relations and constraints at play, but it helps demystify them and potentially to rearrange them by capitalising on grey areas of uncertainty.

These grey areas of uncertainty or 'under-determination' may be opened up if we reconceptualise our very notion of development. Drawing on Peter Høeg's (1994) important novel *Borderliners*, I have suggested some points of departure for such a reconceptualisation (Engeström, 1996). Instead of just benign achievement of mastery, development should be also viewed as partially destructive rejection of the old.

Disturbances and ruptures involving negation, rejection and destruction are often the first decisive indications of significant developmental processes.

Furthermore, instead of just vertical movement toward higher levels of performance or mastery in some domain, development should be also viewed as horizontal movement across borders. In other words, developmental transformations involve shifts between and new combinations of contexts. The transformation of an activity system is never an isolated process; it also means redefinition of its boundaries and thus renegotiation of its external relationships. Galison (1997) has powerfully argued for physical and conceptual 'trading zones' as sites of development and innovation. The Boundary Crossing Laboratory briefly described in this chapter may be regarded as a deliberate attempt at organising such a trading zone to foster and facilitate expansive learning. I suggest that in order to be developmentally effective, such a zone needs to include a cyclic movement from actions to activity and back.

This view implies that ethnography is not in itself a sufficient or privileged method. Yet ethnography is definitely needed. More specifically, we need a new kind of developmental ethnography in studies of work, technology and organisations. While promising, attempts at bringing together ethnography and developmental psychology (Jessor *et al.*, 1996) are still largely limited to the level of individuals and to the notion of development as acquisition of cultural context which is assumed to be stable. It is an appropriate task for developmental studies of work and organisations to go beyond that, answering affirmatively to Modell's (1996) question: 'Can context really be at risk?' Such a developmental ethnography of collective activity systems is particularly attuned to recording and analysing troubles and disturbances, as well as innovative deviations from the normal scripted course of work actions.

NOTES

1 The research team, representing the Center for Activity Theory and Developmental Work Research of the University of Helsinki, consists of Yrjö Engeström (principal investigator), Ritva Engeström and Tarja Vähäaho. When I use the pronoun 'we', I refer to the research team.

Part 2

The interface between research and design

8   Analysing work practice and the potential role of new technology at the International Monetary Fund: some remarks on the role of ethnomethodology

Richard H. R. Harper

Introduction

The International Monetary Fund's main building is situated a short distance from the White House in Washington, D.C. From the outside the building is nondescript, and indicates nothing of the institution's importance in world affairs nor about the activities that are undertaken within. From the inside, however, the building offers a much more spectacular and informative view. The building has an enormous atrium ensuring that nearly all of its offices have a window. Most, of course, face outward, towards the World Bank across the way on 19th Street, for example; but the remainder face in and the occupants can gaze across the atrium at their colleagues on the other side of the building. For those who do not have an office – an ethnographer for example – the landings by the lifts offer vantage points on to the atrium. Here the ethnographer can view the institution's staff in action: as they sit around conference tables in meetings, move from one office to the next, or crouch over their workstations keying in data. Indeed, during my own ethnographic vagabondage in Washington, these landings provided me with havens in which I could wait in between interviews or could jot down notes from a meeting I had just finished. Sometimes I would simply rest here and dreamily watch the theatre of bureaucratic life before me.

In this chapter I want to explain what some of the activities I observed involved. I want, if you like, to give those activities the meaning that they so obviously lacked from the windows on to the atrium. Such a goal is of course the fundamental task of ethnography. It is also the concern which is claimed to make ethnography so useful in generating resources for the design of computer systems. That description of meaning is the main goal of ethnography does not mean, however, that providing such descriptions is easy to do. Unfortunately, and as many ethnographers have explained long before the designing sciences took an interest in them, achieving the

169

right description – whatever that might mean – is part of the conundrum that lies at the heart of all ethnography.

Part of what might be defined as the right description is determined by the concerns an ethnographer brings to bear. Here there starts to be a distinction between what one might call the traditional concerns of ethnographers within sociology and anthropology and those which motivate ethnographers who are wishing to generate materials for design issues. It is this last category into which I fit myself. Within this category an ethnographer does not simply report on whatever organisational actors do, but instead searches for those properties of their activities salient to design issues.

This much is obvious. But it is altogether much less obvious how one determines those salient properties. It is my concern in this chapter to demonstrate that one can determine some of these properties by taking lessons from the more orthodox perspectives of ethnography (i.e. those already current in anthropology and sociology) and partly through concerns driven by technological possibility.

More specifically, I would like to argue that the sociological research programme known as ethnomethodological studies of work is powerfully suggestive of how there are basic elements to the social organisation of work.[1] I would like to argue that these elements are likely to be relevant to any examination of work, design oriented included. A concern with these can enable the ethnographer to begin the task of characterising the work in question. Second, I want to argue that a concern with a particular type of technology will also direct an ethnographer's inquiries in design-related directions. This follows on from the preliminary stage when the ethnographer needs to sketch out the basic elements of work. More particularly, I want to suggest that a concern with networked technologies enables an ethnographer to draw attention to what can and cannot be shared over a network, or if you like, it draws attention to the social organisation of information sharing. Knowledge of this can be particularly helpful in informing the design of collaborative technologies.

I illustrate this argument by reporting some of my research into the work of economists at the International Monetary Fund (or 'the Fund' for short). More specifically, I want to report on some of the activities of a subset of these economists, namely, area department desk officers. Without saying anything about what their work involves for the moment, my concern will be to distinguish between what one might call the arcane expertise of the individuals in question – an expertise in such things as analysis of the aggregated money flows in economies – and the mundane, practical, organisational context in which that expertise shows itself.

I shall explain that an ethnomethodological approach helped me map out issues to do with the variegated character of the information these individuals use in their work, as well as the practical time limits restricting the analytical work they can undertake with that information. I then report on my investigations of the implications of providing networked access to the information that desk officers collect. I shall show that such inquiries led me to equally basic facts about their work, such as how their expertise is deployed, for example, within a particular division of labour wherein some staff are responsible for certain views and recommendations. Furthermore, these recommendations are made within certain cycles of work. Outside of these cycles the work does not lead to such recommendations and indeed has a quite distinct character.

To explicate my arguments I organise the chapter in the following way. Having briefly outlined what the Fund does and why, I then describe desk officers' work at a kind of abstracted level. By this I simply mean the kind of level that desk officers themselves typically offer as a first cut at describing what they do. These descriptions most often turn around the nature of economic reason, and as a consequence assume some kind of expertise in economics. Without wanting to pretend any such competence, I shall attempt to explain what I understood as the kinds of 'economic reason' desk officers employ by reference to one of the tools of their trade, specifically, a flow of funds analysis. Such analyses are intended to enable economists to recognise the basic models that underscore how a national economy might be conceived of by policy administrators.

I then show that if ethnographers look beneath this abstract level, they will find that such tools are used in a setting where other more fundamental tasks have to be undertaken. These tasks involve, for example, gathering and sifting all the information that is delivered to desk officers. This information arrives in a variety of forms: in paper mail, in email, in journal articles, in government publications and in spreadsheets from colleagues. Managing all these materials results in desk officers engaging in a kind of bricolage. It is only once this bricolage has been done that desk officers can turn to a flow of funds analysis. Or, to put this another way, it is this bricolage that provides the resources for doing so.

I will also draw attention to how this bricolage is undertaken within practical time constraints. Desk officers cannot spend all their time dealing with the information that comes their way. Nor, even if they did, would it be certain that they would finish their bricolage. For this work is never quite done; it is always being added to, worked on a little more.

Having done this, I go on to show how a concern with what technology might support provides another angle on important properties of organisational action. These properties, too, are mundane in just the same way that the ethnomethodologists mean them, but are more likely to be uncovered when technological innovation is considered. I illustrate my arguments by reporting my inquiries into what might be the benefits that would accrue to desk officers (and indeed the Fund at large) if a computer network was introduced that allows access to the information that desk officers gather and analyse. I shall suggest that the ethnomethodological approach helped me to understand that this information is often partial and incomplete. This has obvious implications for the application of network technology. But I argue that by inquiring into and further clarifying these implications, I was led to understand that another factor supersedes the importance of this. In particular, I learnt that although this is mainly the case in desk officer work for large periods of the year, in contrast, when desk officers participate in what is called the mission cycle, they reorient their work to ensure that their data collection and analysis work get completed. There is then a contrast between patterns of work (and associated information gathering and production tasks) within different points of the working calendar. This in turn has another implication. For if one focuses on the mission component of this calendar, one will discover that there is another set of basic or elemental parameters as regards what is treated as the information that is shared and distributed and what is treated as private and unshareable. These too are matters that are of consequence when considering the potential of new technology.

I shall argue that these various mundane properties need to be understood as an *amalgam* if one wants to properly characterise the work of desk officers. This amalgam can provide the basis upon which to investigate the design and potential role of any new technologies, and not just the networked information applications I discuss. Needless to say, there will be many other properties that one would need to map out if one wanted to do a thorough job. Furthermore, I would not want to claim that one would only be able to uncover them in the manner I describe. I am sure that, for example, many ethnomethodologists with no interest in design type issues would uncover similar materials. My concern, however, is to report on a way of proceeding – a practical approach to the problem of determining the matters of relevance in design informed ethnography.

The International Monetary Fund

One can think of the Fund as a financial 'club' whose members consist of most of the countries of the world. Member countries contribute to a pool of resources which can then be used to provide short duration, multi-currency loans should a member find itself facing balance of payments problems, and be willing to undertake corrective policies. It has some 3,000 staff, of which 900 are professional economists. These economists analyse economic policies and developments – especially in the macroeconomic arena. They have particular interest in the circumstances surrounding the emergence of financial imbalances (including those that lead to a balance of payments crisis), the policies to overcome such imbalances, and the corrective policy criteria for making loans. This involves going on 'missions' to the country in question. The resulting assessments and criteria for lending to member countries are contained in documents called 'staff reports' (and associated documents) which are used by the organisation's Executive Board for its decision-making.

The Fund is divided into departments and bureaux. There are 'area departments' which are responsible for particular member countries divided up into contiguous geographic blocks (Western Hemisphere, Middle Eastern and so on); 'functional departments' which either support and review area work (such as the Policy Development and Review Department); or other service or information departments. The area departments (of most concern here) are divided into front offices (consisting of the senior staff, the director, the senior advisers and chiefs) and divisions, each with responsibility for certain countries. The divisions are populated by desk officers and chiefs. Desk officers are economists who develop and maintain expertise on any particular country. A chief will manage several countries and desk officers, and hence will be responsible for the information that the Fund has about any particular set of member countries. The chiefs and their desk officers are the main mechanism of information gathering and production at the Fund. There are approximately 180 desks at the Fund, one more or less for each and every member country. Some desks are populated by several economists while others are staffed only on a part-time basis. The result is that there are about 200 economists who have the official title of Fund desk officer.

Basic aspects of the fieldwork

The fieldwork centred around the life-cycle of a mission, from the first draft of what is called the 'briefing paper' (the team's terms-of-reference) prepared before a mission commences, through the mission process itself, to the post-mission review and preparation of the staff report, and then that report's translation, printing and circulation processes. This was accomplished by:

1 Following a hypothetical staff report around the organisation and interviewing parties that would be involved in its life-cycle. Interviews were conducted with desk officers and chiefs who author staff reports,

with administrative and research assistant staff who help in the composition of staff reports, with participants in the review process, including junior economists, and with front office chiefs and senior managers (including the deputy managing director). Staff involved in the post-authoring and review stages were also interviewed, including the clerical staff who issue and release staff reports once they have been 'cleared', with those who copy and print staff reports, with translators, and finally with archivists. In all, 138 personnel (including ninety economists) were interviewed.

2 Observing a Fund 'mission' and its allied document production practices. This involved observing meetings between the mission team before the mission commenced, between the member authorities and the team during the mission, and observed post-mission meetings. All related documentation was examined.

3 Subsequent to the fieldwork, a set of descriptions was generated and circulated around the Fund. Written comments were gathered and discussed with a number of key 'informants', ranging from senior staff, through to junior economists.

The work of desk officers

I want to start my discussions with the kinds of materials that I was first confronted with during my research, namely the kind of descriptions that desk officers typically offered as an introduction to their work. I do not mean that they always offered the same or identical accounts, only that in general terms these descriptions had a similar flavour. A quote from one of the ninety economists I interviewed will indicate what I mean. Having asked him to describe his job, he replied:

I see my responsibilities as being as informed as possible about the current developments and I think most importantly, to have a basically coherent, albeit explicit analytic framework of understanding. Without it there are a million and one different traps, but I think when you have it, you know, having put together the pieces of the puzzle and having taken on the dynamics of the economy, you know what it is important and what is not.

In my early interviews I was also told that such an understanding is crucial in enabling desk officers to comprehend the authorities of the member country in question. It was explained to me on several occasions that it is no good building up a conception of how an economy operates if that conception – that analytic framework – does not allow for effective exchange and mutual understanding between desk officers and member authorities. This is not to say that there is only one analytic framework that needs to be shared by one and all, only that the conceptions must be sufficiently similar to allow sensible discussion, critique and exchange. As another desk officer put it:

Here is an important point, it reveals the way which policy-makers think about the economy because that's the data set they work with themselves, and I have found – I think equally throughout Europe – is that you have to understand the model that the policy-makers have in their own head. Otherwise you have, no em, the model [you have] is wrong . . . or it's a different model. You have to be able to argue with them about the economy in terms of their model.

I asked him to explain what these models looked like or involved, but we soon traversed matters of economic reason beyond my understanding. In a subsequent interview with another desk officer, I explained my predicament and was offered some advice:

Look, read . . . [referring to the author of a training manual], take the flow of funds bit, that will give you some idea of what desk officers mean when they talk about [frameworks and] models.

I duly followed his advice. Reading this manual did not by any means give me all the things I wanted, but it certainly did help me begin to develop what Geertz (1983) calls a sensibility for the kinds of things that the first desk officer I quoted had in mind. The manual explained, and this is to paraphrase, that a flow of funds analysis enables desk officers to understand (at least in broad terms) which part of an economy generates resources and which consumes them. This, apparently, is fundamental to macroeconomic analysis and to understanding the financial imbalances that may lead a member country to seek Fund resources. The manual went on to say that to understand how it does this, one needs to know some basic facts.

First, the Fund collates economic data (disregarding what those data might be or where they come from for the moment) into four broad categories: data about the government or non-financial public sector, data about the non-financial private sector, data relating to the financial sector, and lastly, data about the external sector. The flow of funds analysis is an integration of these, showing to the desk officer the flows of revenue and expenditure between sectors. So, for example, it can show that investment in the non-financial private sector is financed by savings in the external sector. Thereby, it can highlight which sectors are running a deficit and which a surplus.

It is these relationships, I learnt, that are important elements in what the desk officer quoted called an 'analytic framework of understanding'. There are, needless to say, other elements in this framework. My point, however, is not to explicate those elements; it is rather to draw attention to how it is that when one starts to talk to desk officers, one is presented with remarks about analytic frameworks or models. If one burrows away a little more with the desk officers, they will start to talk about the kinds of tools they might use to build up these models. What one learns thereby (about the desk officers) is still superficial, and I would imagine that the reader is only a little less flummoxed by such things as a flow of funds analysis as I was when first presented with one two or three days after I started my fieldwork. But such things are the stuff that is talked about when one first meets desk officers.

Having gone through this stage, desk officers will then typically start talking about the details of what they do, or as one of them put it, 'what I actually do'. I did not take this to refer to some platonic essence in their work so much as a reference to the mundane, everyday practical realities of their work, all too often dismissed as the things that actually get done rather than what ought to be done. Such a contrast can of course be misleading, and many ethnographers, especially within the so-called constructivist camp, have turned this distinction into an excuse to ironicise the work they describe (for a discussion of this see Woolgar, 1993). Certainly I do not want to do so myself, being more concerned to take these partly self-mocking observations as pointing towards what for me (if not for them) are the interesting aspects of the work.

In any case, what this real work consists of, I learnt, had to do with such things as where the numbers used in such things as a flow of funds analysis came from. I had presumed from the first that they did not come from thin air, and, from more or less the first interview, I had gathered that desk officers did not find them placed on their desk first thing Monday morning (delivered from the hands of say, a research assistant). What I began to learn is that desk officers have to dig out those numbers from a variety of sources. They have to sift through various materials to get the raw stuff for their analytical work.

One desk officer explained this by starting with a complaint:

What do I actually do? I am a traffic cop. I get so much information here that I seem to spend all of my time sorting it out and sending it on elsewhere.

What he was alluding to was the myriad sources and modalities of information that came his way. These materials consist of such things as newspaper editorials and articles in *The Economist*. There are also the documented analyses of other somewhat similar organisations to the Fund, such as the Organisation for Economic Co-operation and Development (OECD) and the World Bank. Occasionally, scholarly work in economics journals is also collected. But there are also such terse texts as government bills for financial or economic legislation, ministry of finance budgetary statements, and financial statements from commercial banks. Most desk officers also get such things as quarterly statements of foreign currency holdings from central banks; a somewhat smaller group get estimates of government fiscal revenues faxed them.

The desk officers have to juxtapose these bits and pieces, these newspaper reports and monetary tables, these faxed notes from central banks, and editorials from the *Financial Times*, into a position where numbers can be found that constitute the stuff used in such things as a flow of funds analysis. It is in this respect I would suggest that desk officers engage in bricolage.

Desk officers are not unique in undertaking bricolage, of course, since numerous commentators on bureaucratic life have drawn attention to the bricoleurs that one finds within most bureaucratic institutions. But there is something unique about the Fund's desk officers. In this setting, this bricolage does not result in nice tidy, sorted, systematic filling systems. For irrespective of why it is that, say, French government bureaucrats can create orderly systems of materials, the Fund's desk officers find it much more difficult to do so.[2]

To explain: some desk officers keep notes or compilations of important economic information in what are often called 'black books'. Others keep AREMOS time series and Lotus spreadsheets. But during my discussion of what the 'real work' consisted of, I was told that desk officers do not keep these artefacts continually up-to-date.

I try and update some of my time series when I can but to be honest I don't do that very consistently. It depends how much time you have. You know there are so many other things you have to do. In any case I don't give it much priority.

Additionally, desk officers do not aggregate their numbers into some kind of whole. They may keep a variety of spreadsheets, notebooks and data, some of which will be more up-to-date than other parts, but one will not find an integrated representation of any country, even an out-of-date version.

What databases? There is no database! This is something that people have to understand about operational countries. Even for Article IV countries. Sometimes there may be some general time series but I have not seen any operational country with a database in the sense of a large composite file that has all the series for the country you may need. The thing simply does not exist.

What I began to learn, then, was that limits of time, practical constraints if you will, are enormously consequential in terms of the up-to-dateness and completeness of the numbers and more generally the data that desk officers keep. They do engage in bricolage, but it is a job that would appear to be rarely finished. By and large, desk officers undertake their data gathering in a somewhat *ad hoc* and piecemeal way and as a result, such things as flow of funds analyses are the kinds of undertakings that desk officers would like to undertake, but for practical reasons they rarely have all the information they might ideally require to do so. Instead, they have rough and ready resources, partial, incomplete, the kinds of materials that are likely to be revised and completed if another day was given to them. In other words, desk officers were telling me that they have to make do.

Now, what I am trying to do here is not say that desk officers have excessive workloads or have poor resources; my concern thus far has been to report the kinds of descriptions of their work that desk officers themselves provided at the outset of my fieldwork. I have remarked earlier that one should recognise that these descriptions are first cuts, offered as a guide to the ethnographer; in this sense they are instructions for how to see. I want to say in a moment that on the basis of these instructions I was able to go further and understand their work in more detail in subsequent interviews, later on in my fieldwork. As it happens, the characterisation of desk officers' work I have just begun to sketch on the basis of these instructions turned out to be, in important respects, flawed. But what I have been wanting to convey in these remarks is how even at this first cut, what I began to see, albeit in a flawed and shadowy way, where what the ethnomethodologists would call primordial features of work. Such features are to do with such things as the relationship between the time people have and the work they do and, related to that, the quality of the materials they have in hand; and finally, the kinds of practical goals that motivate work. It is my view that these primordial properties should always be the first concern of an ethnographer concerned with design issues. But it is also my view that on this basis they can then develop and refine their analysis by moving on to refer to technological possibilities in their fieldwork activities. It is to report on how I did so in my own fieldwork that I now turn.

New technologies and desk officers

So, having begun to appreciate some of the elemental features of desk officers' work, I then directed my inquiries to focus on what would be the implications of introducing a network at the Fund. In simple terms, such a network would allow ease of access to the information that desk officers store. Of course, there are many other tools that could be introduced and indeed I discussed many of these during my interviews.[3] But the outcome of my inquiries into a network is sufficiently interesting to serve my needs here, as I shall show. More specifically, I used an interest in how a network might affect the relationships between desk officers and the rest of the organisation to deepen my understanding of desk officers' work. If, at first, I simply asked the desk officers to give me an overview, a first cut as I have described it, after the first few dozen interviews I began to focus on the issue of technological possibility.

Before I can discuss this, the reader needs to be aware of two assumptions I made. First, I disregarded all issues to do with how the desk officers' collections of 'raw materials' (the stuff in the black books, in the Lotus spreadsheets and so on) might be stored, located and accessed over a network. During my interviews with desk officers, I simply assumed that it could be.[4] A second assumption was that there were no technological barriers in the way of ensuring that with a network, whoever wanted and needed information from desk officers could get access immediately.

Assuming this, the network I had in mind would provide an information system where any and all individuals could access information as and when needed. Thus I would suggest to desk officers that with such a network, one could imagine the senior staff of the Fund browsing through the files the desk officers kept. Thereby senior management could find out what was known about some member country, to keep themselves up-to-date. Not only senior management could do this, of course, but also so could others who, for one reason or another, have some concern with the country in question. In this sense, I suggested that the use of the network would help make the Fund an 'informated organisation', a phrase originally coined by Zuboff (1988).

On the basis of my preliminary understandings of desk officers' work, it seemed that such a network – irrespective of whether it was technically feasible – would not be particularly beneficial since the kinds of material that desk officers gathered and stored were too 'rough'. In other words, I expected my reference to the informated organisation to become a rather crude stalking horse. Desk officers would laugh and say 'if only!' But in fact the responses I had to my questioning took a different tack and this in turn resulted in my deepening and making more subtle my understanding of desk officers' activity.

More specifically, my discussions with desk officers made it clear that to use a network to informate the organisation was inappropriate for current work practices not because of the compromised nature of the information on the system (for example, because the information was often incomplete, a collage of materials, or bits and pieces). Rather, it had to do with what was wanted for sharing and what was not. As one desk officer put it:

You could make sure that all the data we keep on the workstations was up to date and properly annotated. Doing that could be made a management priority and data management could be something that we get measured on. I don't think that would ever happen but in any case, even if we were required to do that no one would use it, no one would use [it]. The only person who wants to use the information is the desk officer himself.

This struck me as peculiarly interesting for at least two reasons. First, information is one of those categories of material that is often spoken about as if any number of persons might become users of it. This is especially the case when information becomes digitised, for this creates a

new universe, a parallel universe created and sustained by the world's computers and communications lines . . . the realm of pure information. (Benedikt, quoted in Nunberg, 1996: 117)

In being 'pure', anyone can have access to this information. According to this vision, digital technology allows information to become free of the physical fetters that bind it to its original creator. So, in this case, the kinds of diverse materials used in the desk officers' bricolage, the newspapers, faxes, the electronic spreadsheets and of course the infrastructure that supported this – the filing cabinets, paper-based mailing systems and so on – might be thought of as constituting the fetters that tie information about member countries to particular desk officers. It is these fetters that also ensure that the analyses that desk officers generate have that incompleteness, that make-do quality that I have already mentioned. Yet what I was told when I brought up the technological possibility of an informated organisation is that the information is indeed tethered to desk officers, not because of its physical medium, but for other reasons.

Before saying anything about that what those reasons might be, let me remark on the second reason why I found this interesting. In my second week of interviews, one of the more senior members of the Fund said to me:

'Look, have you ever seen a staff report?' I explained that I hadn't. He went on: 'It's not the staff report that is so important, it's this bit.'

at which time he pointed out that on the first page of the text there was a footnote stating that the figures in the report were based on discussion with the authorities and staff estimates. He wagged his finger at the word 'estimates'.

This is crucial, Richard. This makes the materials we use quite different, quite special. You have to understand this to understand the Fund.

I say this was interesting to me because it is almost commonplace to say that one of the outputs of bureaucratic life is a collection of anonymous documents; that a crucial achievement within bureaucratic organisations is to transform the materials gathered by unique individuals in unique

circumstances into the objective, voiceless documents of modern bureaucratic enterprise. These are the salient claims of authors as distinct as
Weber, Foucault, Giddens and Smith.[5] Yet here was I confronted with a
document that specifically identified the authors and which linked the
materials used in that document to those authors. This was the point that
the senior official was wanting to make. Fund documents are, in important respects, *authored*.

This, however, was still far from sufficient to explain why information
on desk officers' workstations would not be used by anyone but the desk
officer. So I asked the same senior member of staff if he was suggesting
that there were issues of ownership as regards data on desk officers' workstations.

No. The data is shared but only in certain circumstances and in any case is never
shared widely. What you have got to understand is how desk officers have responsibility for delivering the right information. They do so as part of the mission
process, as part of the team that does that. You have to realise that is their job and
not anyone else's.

He then explained that I needed to learn more about the mission process
and the patterns of information production and sharing that were constit-
utive of it.

I did so primarily by direct observation of a Fund mission (cf. Harper
1998: chapter 8). I learnt that during the mission process (or rather, 'the
cycle' as it is more often called by the desk officers themselves), the desk
officers will 'work up' their individual data sets. That is, they will endeavour to complete their bricolage activities to produce the raw materials
they need for such things as flow of funds analyses. But they do not do so
alone. They collaborate with other mission team members (there are normally four economists working on each mission). More specifically –
although this is merely to sketch the activities in question – they corrobo-
rate their own data against the data 'worked up' by their colleagues.
Gradually, a commonly specified set of interpretations is agreed upon by
the group. This is used to compile such things as the staff report, the final
product of the mission process. One important feature of this process is
that data stored on any individual workstation reflect that stage in the
social process of agreement and iteration undertaken by the mission
team. Hence at some point in the mission cycle, the data are rough and
incomplete; the social process of figuring out the data being only begun.
At another, later stage, the data are more complete, more effectively
understood and developed, the social process of which it is part being
nearer completion.

One can put this another way. When a team starts work on a mission, when data have just begun to be gathered and the first meetings between the economists have occurred, data are too rough to be shared among the team, although each member will have some understanding of other team members' data. Towards the end of the mission cycle, data can be more readily shared, since by that time data will have been more thoroughly worked up, assessed and cross-validated. Therefore, at any specific moment in time, the adequacy of data is only visible to participants in a mission team, since it is only they who are aware of what stage of completion the data have reached. All others outside the mission team and outside the mission cycle, will find those data opaque and unsuited for use.

Revisiting the characterisation of work

As I understood this, I began to worry that what I had originally understood as the work of desk officers, that is to say, what I understood as its unfinished nature, the endless work of bricolage and so on, had been incorrect. To clarify things, I went back to some of the desk officers I had first interviewed.

They explained to me that to understand their work does not just mean recognising the variegated character of the materials they subject to bricolage, nor the time limits they have in this work, the stuff I had been learning about once I had got through such things as talk about flow of funds tables. They explained to me that it also means understanding the significance of the distinction between what they do in Washington and what they do on mission. For, in a somewhat oversimplified sense, the process of gathering and analysing data in Washington is perceived as producing only partial, or more accurately, 'provisional' information. It is only when missions are undertaken that these desk officers will endeavour to get the data required into what one might call a complete condition.

You can spend a great deal of time keeping all this stuff [information] but in between missions, it kind of, look, you have got to realise that it's only during a mission that you really get to grips with this data.

And another:

You have got to distinguish between what they do during the mission process and what they do at other times.

From this view, I had been correct in understanding what desk officers do, but these doings related only to those periods outside of the mission process. My original questions had been treated as being directed to that concern. Thus, I was correct to understand that outside of the mission process, when economists are working on their own, the data they store will be very difficult for anyone to use but themselves, and even then they are often too rough and ready for desk officers to make use of. They are better thought of as a kind of residue of their work, the detritus from tasks that are all too often incomplete. This may be contrasted with their work during the mission cycle, where they orient towards working up their information into shareable stuff. But the sharing in question is strictly limited to their fellow mission members.

In understanding this, I also began to appreciate why it was that desk officers could not see what a networked information-sharing system would be used for. From their perspective, the only people with an interest in accessing information are those they work with on a mission. Making information available to anyone within the Fund is unnecessary. Thus it made perfect sense for one of them to ask:

What would senior staff do with the information I have?

He asked such a question since he knew that outside the mission process, the information he kept was too rough and ready for anyone but himself to use; and though in contrast, during the mission cycle his information would be more thoroughly marked up and completed, it would still not be useful to those outside the mission team.

Finally, it was this that made me understand the import of the senior member of the Fund wagging his finger at the footnote in a staff report. For the Fund consists of a division of labour wherein the production of information is certain persons' demonstrable responsibility. His concern was not to distinguish the Fund from any other bureaucratically organised institution, so much as to underline the basic fact that the Fund operates around a division of labour.

Conclusion

That an institution is so organised is hardly news, of course. The value of my analysis – if it has any – is in how I highlight the *social organisation* of this division of labour. This organisation has implications for how information is gathered, used and shared, and for the value placed on that information at different points in the working year.

As I have already remarked, this is just a sketch of the issues, and only points towards many things that would need to be understood to thoroughly appreciate the work of desk officers and the institution they are part of. But my concern has not been to provide a comprehensive description of their work so much as to report on the approach I used to unpack it. In this sense, the import of this chapter has been both empirical and methodological. As part of those concerns, I have wanted to underscore how ethnography with design as a motivating force takes on a different hue from ethnography concerned strictly with sociological and anthropological concerns.

In particular, I have wanted to argue that though one type of 'orthodox' ethnography – namely ethnomethodological – might start with a similar concern with the basic facts of work practice, an interest with particular sorts of technology will focus design oriented ethnography in a different direction. This results in a supplementary set of social organisational features being uncovered.

To demonstrate how the social organisation of work may be uncovered I have reported the actual process of one element of my research at the Fund. I have wanted to be frank, and have made it clear how this research process consisted of a journey during which I gradually unravelled and developed my understanding of the work in question. This may have given the chapter a semi-biographical air. This must not be taken as indicating that the procedure I deployed was personal, idiosyncratic or serendipitous; I organised my fieldwork this way.

I now want to conclude my discussions by briefly remarking on how findings from the research programme I deployed were used by the Fund itself to assess some of its own design activities. For, during the latter part of my ethnographic vagabondage in Washington, the Fund's bureau of computer services started to implement a pilot version of a system that would allow the deputy managing director and other senior staff to have direct access to area department desk officers' workstations. The system was known as System X. System X had been developed for two reasons, first, as an investigation into the rather complex technological requirements to ensure ease of navigation around an organisation-wide network, and second, to draw attention to the fact that new systems like it could have considerable impact in collaborative activities, though the bureau of computer services did not know what that impact might be.

As part of my original agreement with the Fund, I presented some of my key findings, and argued that System X might be resisted by desk officers not because they felt it was intrusive or forced them to radically alter their working practices, but because they would not see what benefits it would bring about. In particular, they would not see why senior members of the Fund would want to access information stored on the desk officers' own workstations. I explicated this by reference to the social organisation of the Fund's division of labour, as sketched out above. As a result of this analysis and other factors, the pilot System X was withdrawn from use, and further plans for its development halted.

System X aside, my presentation was sufficiently well received for the

Fund to recognise that new procedures and techniques would need to be deployed to fully understand the collaborative aspects of work affected by new technologies, particularly networked ones. Furthermore, the Fund recognised that ethnographic techniques may be particularly useful for this. As a result, the Fund funded a further stage of research during which the use ethnographic techniques for future design work at the Fund was investigated in collaboration with my then research institution, Rank Xerox Research Centre in Cambridge, England. Of concern were not only information sharing technologies like System X but also other networked technologies, including work flow and multimedia conferencing systems.[6]

The Fund's use of ethnographic research techniques is, of course, worthy of a chapter in its own right. My concern in this chapter has been to report on how the approach I used in my ethnographic research took its cue from the ethnomethodological studies of work programmes and how this was then developed by reference to a particular set of networked applications. Doubtless, reference to a different set of applications would have led my research in other directions. Be that as it may, in this short chapter I hope to have justified the claim that the procedure I followed enabled me to understand at least some elements of the work of desk officers, and thus has provided me with the wherewithal to give some meaning to those activities one can observe from the landings on to the Fund's atrium.

NOTES

1 When this programme was first developed, the materials outlining it consisted of a mix of unpublished manuscripts and only a handful of published articles and books (one early text was Garfinkel, 1986). Those on the inside of the ethnomethodological community were able to share copies of the relevant manuscripts; those on the outside of the ethnomethodological community – postgraduate students for example wanting to learn more – found it difficult to get access to such documents. However, some recent texts have begun to remedy this unhappy situation. See, for example, the methodological appendix in Lynch and Bogen (1996).

2 My allusion to French bureaucrats derives from the work of Bruno Latour (1990) who argues that the centralisation of power in Paris over the past two or three centuries has occurred because officials within the various ministries of the French government have been able to sort out the vast seas of information they have. More particularly, instead of being buried under this information they have been able to organise it so that they can use it for their own ends. My point is that in contrast, desk officers do seem to get buried under the information they gather, at least at certain points of the year.

3 For discussion of shared information repositories (e.g. Lotus Notes) see Harper (1995). For the potential of workflow technologies see Sellen and Harper (1996). For discussion of video technology see Harper (1997).

4 There are clearly many questions to do with how this may be achieved, especially given the various media currently used by desk officers As it happens, many of my discussions with desk officers focused on this topic.
5 For a discussion of Weber, Foucault and Giddens on this issue, see Dandeker (1990). For Smith, see D. E. Smith (1993). For further discussion of this issue in relation to the Fund, see Harper (1998).
6 This project also involved M. Eldridge, W. Newman and A. Sellen of RXRC and C. Dub of the IMF (see Harper, 1996; Harper and Newman, 1996).

9 Ethnography, communication and support for design

John Hughes, Jon O'Brien, Tom Rodden and Mark Rouncefield

> Design is a distributed social process, and, as such, communication plays a vital role.   (Erickson, 1996: 32)

Ethnography, workplace studies and design: the problem of communication

Since the late 1980s, and much to the surprise of many of its practitioners, ethnography has risen to a position of some prominence within CSCW research (Bentley *et al.*, 1992; Hughes *et al.*, 1994). This rise has not, of course, gone unchallenged; even from relatively sympathetic critics serious questions have been raised, and quite rightly, about the value of the approach in actually informing system design (see e.g. Plowman *et al.*, 1995). Although this criticism is well taken, it does point to a problem recognised from the outset, namely, how are the results of ethnographic field studies to be conveyed to designers? In fact, there are a host of problems involving, for example, the scope of the design, the size of the design team, the stage of the design and more (see Hughes *et al.*, 1994). Such communication problems have been at the heart of system design for some years even before ethnography and workplace studies came on the scene, and in this connection the 'story' related by Cooper *et al.* (1995) – though pertaining to designers and users – can be adapted to portray something of the state of affairs between fieldworkers and designers:

Systems design used to be done by a bunch of techies, deep deep deep within some head office building somewhere. Here they would build their system. Test it, test it, test it, until they were sure it would work, and then they would throw it over this great high brick wall, and hope that the user would catch it, on the other side.

As fieldworkers we would continue the 'story' something along the following lines:

Meanwhile in another part of the organisation the ethnographers were conducting their observational studies of work, layering on the detail until they were reasonably satisfied that they had adequately described the sociality of work. The study would be so heavy that they would have no need of a brick but, having given the designers ample warning to stand clear, would simply lob it over the great high brick wall with a message attached, 'read this and then build something'.

In other words, to call the problem one of 'communication' between fieldworkers and designers glosses a whole host of practices, procedures and tools which need to be developed if field studies are to become a valuable part of the design process. This emphasis on communication and design also highlights a number of other issues concerned with how communication can best be facilitated among a likely changing design team with varying communication needs and throughout the life-cycle of a design.[1]

In this chapter we want to present an outline of the approach that we have been developing as a means of bringing ethnographic field studies more systematically into the design process.[2] We do so through a consideration of the emerging use of a particular prototype tool for the organisation and presentation of ethnographic material. In doing this we wish to stress that this work is part of a *research* endeavour exploring just the question of the ways in which field studies can be brought to bear upon the design process. We do not, of course, suppose that it can be the only approach.

Some background considerations

From the beginning of our interdisciplinary collaboration we accepted that, in practical terms, there would be differences in outlook, experience, training and approaches between the ethnographers and the computer scientists involved, while not trying to over-dramatise these differences into a 'gulf' or a 'chasm' which could be bridged only by the most arcane species of psychobabble.[3] These differences, though real enough, we treated as essentially *practical* issues, ones which quickly settled into the routines of a working division of labour within which the assignment of tasks was fundamentally governed by the nature of the problems faced and the known competencies and skills of each side in the design process.[4]

We also accepted that the design process itself conformed to no simple model and that, as a result, the role and point of ethnography could vary (Hughes *et al.*, 1994). Further, if ethnography was to move from the small-scale team which, through debriefing, could quickly imbibe, guide and direct the fieldwork as an integral part of the design process, it would have to develop a means of presenting fieldwork materials and analyses to latecomers to the team, a means of reviewing fieldwork materials time and again as the design develops, a means of focusing the fieldwork on to design problems, and so on.

This last point about focus turned out to be important not least because one of the major issues in requirements elicitation is identifying the various members of an organisation who have an interest in the formulation of the requirements, including users, designers, organisational power brokers, customers, organisational heads, trade unions and more, and all of which are groups which could be 'unpacked' even further. But even a relatively simple conception of an organisation will quickly bring out the different viewpoints on what the organisation is and what it does. Different viewpoints are not necessarily antithetical, though they may be, but draw attention to, bring out, features of organisational life which are more relevant, more salient, for the work of the particular group which holds to a distinctive viewpoint.

However, it was not so much this feature of organisational life that we wanted to capture with the notion of viewpoints, since it was felt that fieldwork is precisely the method through which these can be captured and identified. Instead, we aimed to use the notion of viewpoints as a means of representing generic features of workplaces and through which the fieldwork materials could be organised in ways useful to design.

Accordingly, the approach to bringing ethnography to bear more systematically on design which evolved had the following ingredients. First, the development and utilisation of a framework for the analysis and presentation of the social organisation of work settings – a framework which would encourage a sensitivity to the domain of application. Second, tool support to allow the structured ethnographic record to be used for the development of requirements, prototype designs, design variants and so on. Third, to enable the process to be presented to a variety of interested parties. Fourth, to facilitate the complementarity of fieldwork, organisational research and system design. Integral to all of these was the exploitation of 'viewpoints' as a means of structuring the ethnographic material and, through this, enable the construction of abstract models of work and/or process, but models grounded in ethnographic findings. In short, the facilitation of what Anderson (1994) calls 'the play of possibilities for design'.

In the remainder of the chapter we describe the facilities offered by the Designers' NotePad, the system which eventually emerged as the tool to realise, in part at least, the aims just set out. Its use will then be illustrated on some fieldwork materials gathered from a study of lending control in a major high street bank. The relationship between 'viewpoints' and the 'framework for the analysis of work' is explored and illustrated. Throughout the emphasis is on how these representations might improve communication between the different members of the design team.

A brief outline of the Designers' NotePad

The Designers' NotePad (DNP) is a prototype flexible information management and browsing system providing a range of facilities for representing, changing, rearranging and referencing information (Sommerville *et al.*, 1993b). Originally, the DNP was conceived as a support tool for designers engaged in the software engineering process. The DNP is essentially a flexible hypertext system that supports the rapid construction of the directed graphs widely used in structured methods. The focus of the DNP is on the rapid construction of networks to support the generation and structuring of ideas in a manner similar to Cognoter (Stefik *et al.*, 1987). The flexibility of the DNP has led to its use in a variety of contexts.[5] Initiated in late 1992 the usage of the DNP has undergone significant change. Its use as a presentation device and means of communicating the results of ethnographic studies has enabled a more systematic approach to informing system design. This restricted account of its facilities and use concentrates on its employment in the organisation of data produced during an ethnographic study of work processes. The intention here is further limited to an examination of a small number of the facilities of the DNP – sub-designs, text notes and cross-references. It is certainly not intended to produce a definitive list of features, although this account does cover those features currently most utilised.

Representing designs in the DNP

The DNP is designed to allow information stored in it to be reorganised flexibly and easily. Designs are seen by the user as a window on which entities – shapes chosen from a menu and which can be used in a variety of ways, for example, to represent people, processes, information stores and so on – can be placed and moved around. The cross-references, text notes and sub-designs are structured annotations to entities or links.[6] The DNP supports hierarchical decomposition by allowing an entity to represent a sub-design. This sub-design behaves in the same way as its parent design so that entities, links and sub-designs can be created in it. As a simple example, in the case of ethnographic fieldwork notes, the worksite can be represented as a simple plan which utilises entities (to represent desks, workers, filing cabinets and so on), links (where, for example, the same worker may appear in another design), text notes (such as accounts of work activity) and sub-designs (for example of the outline of the day's tasks, or the organisation of a desk or filing cabinet) to valuable effect (figure 9.1). Various colours and symbols can be used to signify the social actors, their positions and spatial relationships. A sub-design can be used

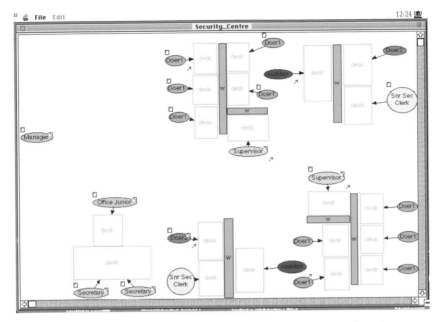

Figure 9.1 Using a design in the DNP to represent a work setting

on an individual worker in order to display information concerning their workflow, the organisation of work and so on.

Text notes

The manipulation of text notes in the DNP is a key feature for ethnographers in the representation, management and organisation of their fieldnotes, since the text notes will conventionally contain the bulk of the ethnographic observations. Text notes are annotations, similar to sticky Post-it™ notes, that can be attached to any type of entity or link. So, for example, they might be attached to a particular worker giving an account of this person's observed activities at any particular time; they might be attached to a desk, giving a list of files, folders and forms contained in the drawers; or they might be attached to a computer listing the software packages available on that particular machine. They can take a variety of forms, be it simple unformatted text areas or complex, lengthy user-defined terms. Text is usually typed into the DNP and then attached to the entity or link – it can also be pasted in from any word processing application. Any number of text notes can be attached to an entity and they can be browsed, edited, searched (for example, for particular key terms or activities) and printed.[7]

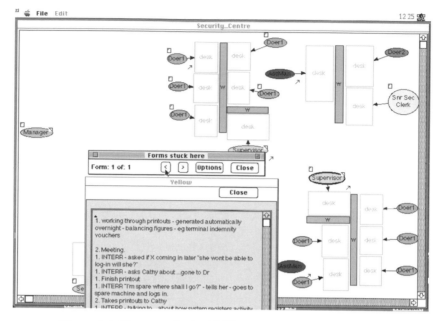

Figure 9.2 Text notes in the DNP

However, this very simple and straightforward account of the use of the text note facility effectively disguises or ignores the gradual evolution of the use of the DNP in the face of a number of (largely mistaken) criticisms of its representation of ethnographic text. (See e.g. Bowers and Pycock (1994) for an account of the early use of the DNP and Calvey *et al.* (1997) for a response to the criticisms and a description of its evolving use.) What gradually emerged through continuing use of the DNP was a principle for structuring and presenting the ethnographic field-notes. As shown in figure 9.2, the details of the observations of particular workers are attached to their representation but within, or alongside, a contextualising ecological 'schematic' derived from sketches of the work-site. This use of the DNP has close parallels with the practice of ethnographic fieldwork in several ways.

First, although there is no particular methodological justification for this, a common technique by which ethnographers familiarise themselves with the research site is by collecting, even as first impressions, details of what is in view, we have termed its 'ecology'. This will include the layout of desks, filing cabinets and typewriters where people are routinely located; and what the site looks like as a daily working environment.[8]

Second, one of the main rationales of ethnography is to obtain an effective understanding of the actual work done and this, inescapably, will involve close observation of particular individuals; individuals not simply in the sense of isolates but importantly as members of a division of labour, of a team, whose work has to be coordinated with that of others.

It was this combination of a graphical way of representing the ecology of the work (never envisaged in the original conception of the tool) with the facility of attaching descriptions of the person, the work and their interrelationships which proved a fruitful means of structuring fieldnote materials. In other words, this simple device showed considerable promise in thinking about one of the problems of relating the textual representations of fieldnotes and the more graphically based modes of representation used in system design. In this case the text note transcriptions of the fieldworker's own notes are attached to the relevant 'entities' in the ecological overview and, accordingly, available to other members of the design team. What the DNP offers therefore is a new, readily accessible and, above all, legible means of organising and presenting the ethnographer's fieldnotes, a considerable achievement in itself given our constant (though happily unrealised) practical fear of 'what happens if the ethnographer dies?' The DNP thereby makes the detailed ethnographic accounts of the application domain continuously available for inspection and reinspection, analysis and reanalysis, by other members of the design team.

Cross-references

The DNP allows the construction of a hypertext network of links between different entities and designs in the system. The value of this cross-referencing facility clearly emerges in establishing links between different types of designs.[9] So, for example, a workflow design showing the temporal and sequential organisation of work within an office or organisation might be cross-referenced to an ecological design showing the geographical position of particular workers within the organisation, the importance of any particular workflow process in an individual's daily routine and fieldwork observations of how any particular task in that workflow is routinely and practically accomplished. Cross-referencing thereby facilitates the presentation (and comparison) of different views of the application domain (figure 9.3). In terms of improving communication and in the context of our particular research project this cross-referencing facility proved especially useful in facilitating the exchange of ideas and information between very different approaches (thematic workchains, management cybernetics and ethnography) to understanding work.

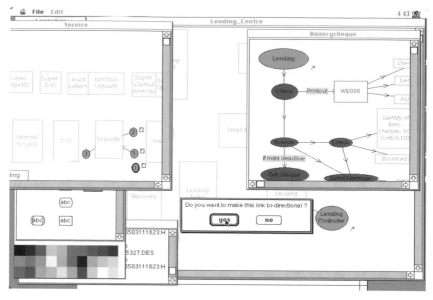

Figure 9.3 Developing links using cross-referencing

Viewpoints as a means of presenting ethnographic material

The DNP was originally envisaged as a flexible support tool which meant that it does not itself provide a structured way of organising or analysing the materials but, rather, provides the means for the fieldworkers to develop their own organisational approach. This feature of the original tool was retained and re-emphasised as the ethnographers slowly got to grips with the DNP and evolved practical methods of working use. Unlike many other tools for handling qualitative data such as NUDIST (Richards and Richards, 1991a, 1991b) and Ethnograph (Seidel and Clark, 1984; Seidel *et al.*, 1988; Tallerico, 1991), DNP was not intended to displace the judgement and the analysis work of fieldworkers but to support the work of representing and recording these analyses for a multi-disciplinary design team.[10]

In placing material within the DNP a structure eventually emerged for the presentation of information. Users placed information from field-work material within a number of distinct contexts, each of which emphasised particular perspectives on the fieldwork material. This parti-tioning of material led to the emergence of 'viewpoints' within the tool and the adopting of particular practices to support viewpoints. As we have noted elsewhere (Hughes *et al.*, 1995) the adoption of a technique based on viewpoints allows us to present information in a form that makes explicit the different but complementary interests involved in the design and implementation process and thereby provides the starting point for developing fruitful communication between designers, users and researchers, since the presentation of these different viewpoints allows alternative views and perspectives to be set beside each other as a resource. The reasons motivating the choice of viewpoints as a means of involving ethnography in the process of design include: the need to highlight the multiple orientations people may have to a supporting system; to provide a means of setting the multiplicity of user needs alongside each other; to facilitate and support multidisciplinary communication and working.

The idea behind viewpoint-based approaches is that different users of a system will hold different views of its operation, allied to the suggestion that these views must be identified in order that inconsistencies and conflicts between them can be avoided. Such an approach clearly lends itself to the design process: viewpoint analysis of an application domain or workplace can identify actors' relationships to the work process and to each other within the setting, and thus offers an account of the potential requirements of a system under development and in use.[11]

We use the notion of viewpoints as a sensitising and structuring device on a corpus of common ethnographic information that may be used in a variety of ways to inform the design team, users and facilitators of the system and other researchers. In this section we are concerned with extending and replicating ideas offered elsewhere (Finkelstein *et al.*, 1992; Kotonya and Sommerville, 1992) by examining the applicability of the viewpoint approach as a means of presenting ethnographic information, through the use of the DNP, in a form which can be used by system designers, users and others, and while it is a form that is primarily graphical rather than the dense text commonly associated with ethnographic accounts, this is because, at the same time, it also seeks to preserve the richness of the fieldwork materials.

Our earlier studies (Hughes *et al.*, 1995) specified a small set of viewpoints – the setting of the work, the social context of the work and workflow – each presenting a particular focus on the social organisation of work activities and chosen in order to highlight relevant aspects of the sociality of work.[12] Here we illustrate them by means of their application to an ethnographic study of part of the lending process of a major high street bank, specifically the process of 'bouncing' – returning unpaid – cheques.

The setting of work/ecology of work viewpoint

The setting of work viewpoint focuses on the development of a representation of the workplace seeking to represent the spatial distribution of the workplace in terms of its participants, the work they do as part of an organised division of labour and the local resources that they use. The purpose of this is to provide a sense of 'where the work takes place', it is a view upon the workaday character of the world within its setting, and the socially constructed affordances that this offers as an arena for the various kinds of interactions that take place.

Figure 9.4 gives an ecology of work viewpoint for the Lending Centre which performs the lending control functions for the branches in the region. Branch Lending Control is divided into a number of teams that service particular branches, generally consisting of a lending controller and two lending assistants. Overseeing these lending teams is an assistant manager and a manager. This division of labour is also a division of responsibility instantiated in the lending limits attached to each position and accessing the text notes and cross-references attached to the different members of the Lending Team presents a range of fieldwork observations of the daily accomplishment of the work of lending control, much of which centres on the perusal and 'actioning' of a variety of computer printouts.[13]

Without making grandiose claims, the point of providing this easy access to the ethnographic fieldnotes, as we have suggested earlier, is to facilitate their reading and analysis as part of systems design, and in a form that is, perhaps, a more accessible and digestible form of communication than that provided by the standard fieldwork report, debriefing or presentation. This extract from the fieldnotes, for example, available via the text notes in the DNP, illustrates the use of printouts in the team-working of the controller and the assistants; the relationship between printouts and computer use; the extent of checking and the deployment of local and tacit knowledge, all of which may prove fruitful for systems design.

3 Looking at printout WXYZ – accounts going out of order. Printouts produced centrally – written on by Controller for actioning by Assistants. Done 1st thing every morning – because of time scale for bouncing cheques. (In particular if the morning of the 4th day have to tell unpaids by 10:30 otherwise have to go and hunt out the cheques themselves; if past 12:00 – Bank liable.)

   . . .

   machines going down

   . . .

15 Logging in for details of Acc – using Acc No from printout.

16 Uses yesterday's printout – compares with today's. Supposed to write something next to every line – Red = action; Black = personal note – has to write on printout to show it has been dealt with.

17 'I know I spoke to him the other day and I want him to send me an income breakdown . . . I know he's got a cheque guarantee card – he's cashing them in a local newsagent.'

18 Continues working down list.

19 Decision-making – looking at screen – when payments come in; extent of OD [overdraft] in the past – 'because we haven't written to them since last February . . . I could bounce his cheque.

. . .

22 'Writes balance on piece of paper.' One of the first things I look at is the balance & I write it down – if Assistant is going to have to write a letter anyway . . . If I'm going to decide to bounce – I have to look if we've bounced before – otherwise I have to refer it to the Assistant Manager . . .'

. . .

30 Gives printout to Assistant for actioning.

The Service Centre (also illustrated in figure 9.4) deals with the wide range of back-office activities formerly associated with branch banking. The rationale for this concentration in specialised, centralised processing units is the expected efficiencies, improvements in processing and reduction in costs associated with centralisation. The Unpaids desk is where the necessary but complicated administrative processes for the return of cheques are carried out. The tasks include dealing with their own customers whose accounts are 'out of order' and require the return of cheques drawn on that account, dealing with cheques paid into their customers' accounts 'bounced' by other banks, and so on. Again through using the text note facility on the DNP, which gives access to the fieldnotes, the design team is able to see that these tasks involve various interactions between computer and paper, often under serious time pressures.[14]

In figure 9.4 the physical layout of the Lending Centre, where the initial decision to 'bounce' the cheques is made, is formally depicted. It shows a series of Lending Teams, each serving particular branches and consisting of a lending controller and two assistants. Figure 9.4 also shows the Service Centre and in particular the Unpaids desk and the individual workers who have the responsibility for the routine process of returning cheques unpaid. The cross-reference arrows in the illustrations, positioned next to the individuals, are designed to show their interconnectedness; other cross-references could also be used, for example, to the storeroom (or bookroom) where cheques are stored and from where they have to be retrieved before being returned.

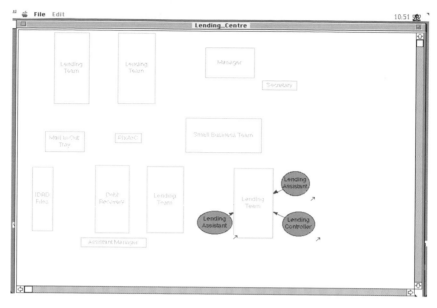

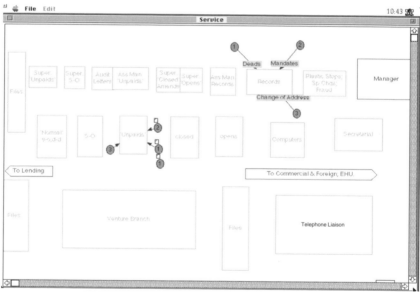

Figure 9.4 The setting of work/ecology of work viewpoint of the
Lending Centre and Service Centre

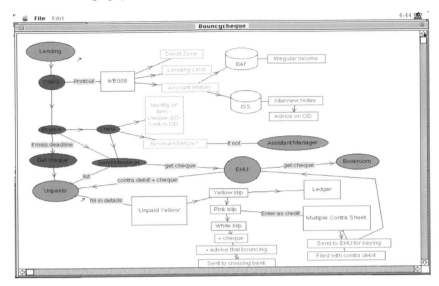

Figure 9.5 The workflow viewpoint for 'bouncing' cheques

The workflow viewpoint

The workflow viewpoint focuses on sequences of work activities and information flows, thereby attempting a representation of the division of labour within the work, together with its various interdependencies. Figure 9.5 gives a very simplified, abstract and idealised workflow view of the process of bouncing cheques, highlighting the various stages and individuals involved in decision-making. In the ethnographic fieldnotes this will often consist of reports of activities, the relationships among parties to the work, how the interdependencies are achieved as real-world, real-time phenomena, the various contingencies that arise and so on. Workflow is represented in the DNP through simple diagramming techniques, and cross-references to other designs and their associated text notes make the ethnographic material available to the reader. So, for example, following cross-references in the DNP workflow design for the process of bouncing cheques will take the reader through to the Lending Centre and accounts of bouncing decisions; or through to the Unpaids desk in the Service Centre and accounts of the administrative processes involved in returning cheques unpaid.

Social and organisational viewpoints on work

The final viewpoint – of social and organisational perspectives on work or views of work – is really a collection of potential viewpoints from which the ethnographic materials may be examined, depending upon the particular interests of the designers. As such it is a far less obvious viewpoint than either the work setting/ecology or the workflow viewpoint and is consequently far more dependent on both skilful ethnographic work and interpretation and on communication between researchers, designers and users. Included within this viewpoint might be, for example, the point of view of a particular actor within the work setting, an account of formal or informal teamworking and so on.

This viewpoint both highlights and draws upon the strengths of ethnographic studies, their emphasis on providing materials on the real-world, real-time, nature of work, of providing depictions of just how work is practically and routinely accomplished. Of particular importance is the notion of egological organisation, of representing via this viewpoint how individual workers necessarily have an informal, incomplete and often inconsistent model of the work taking place – a depiction of which, given our emphasis on the importance of communication issues in the design process, may well provide significant in the development of abstract models in systems design and redesign. The term 'egological' refers to the manner in which the individual actor fits into a complex division of labour and comprises the practical details of what the individual needs to accomplish and needs to know, to be able to answer in a practical fashion the worker's abiding concern and question, 'What do I do next?' (Anderson *et al.*, 1989).[15] This will typically include some understanding of processes and procedures, of the location of resources and so on. The depictions of 'how the work gets done' that arise from this viewpoint may prove valuable since the actual accomplishment of work may bear little relationship to the idealised models of the work process that occur, for example, in organisational process charts. Egological organisation can be represented on the DNP by a combination of sub-designs and text notes giving graphical representations of typical workflows; the organisation of desk space and access to relevant files; and accounts of how the work is practically accomplished, including the myriad of interruptions and disruptions that punctuate the working day. Figure 9.6, for example, presents an account of the everyday work of one of the workers on the Unpaids desk as she progresses through the routine administrative procedures involved in returning cheques unpaid.

Reconciliation of viewpoints: moving from ethnography to design

The final phase of the traditional engineering oriented viewpoints process characterised by Kotonya and Sommerville (1992) focuses on the reconciliation of information across viewpoints. Rather than seek a directed

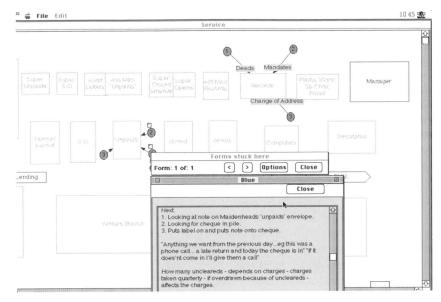

Figure 9.6 Organisational viewpoints: ecological organisation

transformation and reconciliation of viewpoints we seek to allow the different perspectives to be drawn upon and related to an emerging design. The last viewpoint to emerge in these systems is more closely connected with the abstract representation of work and the system structure developed by the designer and recorded along with the other viewpoints. (For a more detailed examination see Hughes *et al.*, 1995). The cross-referencing facilities encourage linkage between different viewpoints in order to permit validation and assessment.[16]

'Viewpoints' and the 'framework for the analysis of work'

This section attempts to integrate the viewpoints approach adopted in the presentation of the DNP with the perspectives that comprise an evolving 'framework for the analysis of work' that has been used for structuring fieldwork studies across a series of projects (see Comic Deliverables 2.3 and 2.4, 1995; Hughes *et al.*, 1997). In structuring the fieldwork materials we identified a number of ways of viewing the social organisation of work activities, designed to bring out key aspects of the sociality of work. The principal perspectives that have emerged so far, without suggesting that these are in any way exhaustive or comprehensive, are the interrelated notions of

- distributed coordination
- plans and procedures
- awareness of work.

These perspectives, we suggest, not only bring out important features of the social organisation of work but also highlight central concerns to CSCW design. (For more on the framework see Blythin *et al.*, 1997; Hughes *et al.*, 1997.) The value of reconciling, of integrating, viewpoints with the perspectives indicated in the framework, resides in the belief that viewpoint based approaches are focused on a recording of the detailed relationships between the computer system and users rather than a more general examination of the nature of systems within a context of work; and that such a general examination is, or can be, produced by the perspectives identified in the framework. We would, however, wish to re-emphasise that we see the viewpoint identification process as one that emerges from the ethnographic data, rather than from the simplistic application of an a priori set of analytic categories. Furthermore, the processes of communication between designers, users and researchers that the DNP is intended to encourage are integral to the identification of viewpoints in the fieldwork data and an assessment of the relevance and appropriateness of those viewpoints to instantiation in the system design.

Each of the identified perspectives motivates particular presentation viewpoints.

- A *setting of work* or *ecology of work* viewpoint is clearly linked with the *awareness of work* perspective. This perspective highlights the important role that the ecological setting of work, its physical layout and relationships, has to play in facilitating or hindering awareness.
- A *workflow* viewpoint reflects some of the central concerns expressed in both the *distributed coordination* and the related perspective of *plans and procedures.*
- A *views of work* viewpoint, perhaps not surprisingly given its collective nature, may be represented within any of the identified perspectives. So, for example, *egological organisation,* with its emphasis on the individual worker's perspective on the work process, is obviously linked to *awareness of work;* it may also, however, need to be related to both *plans and procedures* and *distributed coordination,* especially in respect of any revelations of the extent to which organisational plans and procedures are not routinely completed but are subjected to local logics and local knowledge.

This interrelationship between the viewpoints identified for use with the DNP and the perspectives outlined as part of a framework for the analysis of work might be simply illustrated, for instance, by reference to, and DNP diagrams of, the workings of the Lending Centre outlined earlier.

To take a single example, the perspective of 'plans and procedures' might be illustrated by reference to a *workflow* diagram of loan sanctioning, showing the various procedures involved in this process. A cross-reference might then be made to an *ecology of work* viewpoint which would display the physical arrangement of the lending manager's and lending manager's assistant's desks in the Lending Centre, their record files, access to computer support and so on, along with text notes detailing the various interactions involved in sanctioning a loan. Similarly an *ecological* viewpoint for either the lending manager or the assistant could then be provided showing how the process of sanctioning a loan is accommodated within their working division of labour and the various resources – records, action sheets, forms, computer packages and other workers – on which they draw.

Applying the 'framework' and 'viewpoints': using the DNP to communicate research on lending

This section is concerned with illustrating and applying both the viewpoints and the framework via the use of the DNP to communicate, to users, designers and other researchers, the results of long-term research into the lending process of a major high street bank, and the various prototypes designed to improve aspects of this process. The purpose of this particular piece of research (the 'SYCOMT' Project part of the DTI/EPSRC CSCW Initiative) was to provide a framework for recommending CSCW-related improvements to the design and organisation of work in financial services and communicating these ideas to an audience of bank management, system users, designers and researchers. This section considers how the DNP might usefully be employed in this communication process.

As part of the research, a series of descriptive models of the lending process were developed to gain an understanding of how the different parts of the bank worked together to carry out lending. These models illuminate areas where the 'theory in use' differs from the organisation's espoused theory (as articulated by working manuals and procedural guidelines). They also show how both in theory and practice the various parts of the bank – particularly the Lending Centre and branches – are closely interlinked by the flow of these work processes and the ways in which teamwork – a phenomenon that the bank wishes to encourage and improve – is either facilitated or hindered by organisational and system design. Teamwork can be rendered in a number of different ways using the DNP. Figure 9.7, for example, presents an *ecology of work* viewpoint of the non-personal lending team in the Lending Centre.

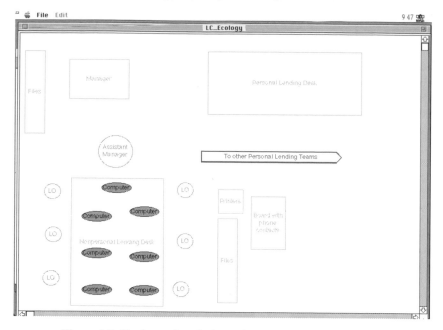

Figure 9.7 Ecology of work viewpoint: Lending Centre

Attached to each worker a sub-design can outline the egological organisation of their work and text notes, pasted in from the fieldnotes, can provide accounts of how their work is practically achieved as part of a lending team. These text notes, for example, suggest that the lending team appears to operate flexibly, sharing the workload out among themselves in an equitable way, with a good deal of mutual support, camaraderie and regard for quality of service. The layout of the teams, with their desks grouped together, facilitates the rapid exchange of information about particular cases or correct procedure. Among the usual office banter, advice and training on plans and procedures and developing the awareness of work are also dispensed in an informal fashion. In this example from the text notes the assistant manager has been overviewing a printout documenting the actions of the team; as he comes across specific accounts he talks across the table to the lending officer involved:

ASSISTANT MANAGER (AM):   I think you may have been a bit harsh on FF,
                          XX, check out the Business Account
LENDING OFFICER (XX):   me being harsh, I can't imagine that ... I don't
                          think there's much on the Business Account ...
                          there's £700 over on the ...

AM:	is he ... he's only gone £50 over on the other that's all. it's a little bit (harsh) ... I don't know whether you've written to him ... before
XX:	I think we've returned before
AM:	... oh we will have returned before ... whether at the £50 level ...
	(XX goes to chat)
XX:	... I was generous
AM:	... it's 3 months since we've written to him ... do an LC letter (letter of concern) *... LCH1 will do in this case ...*

The point we are, rather laboriously, trying to re-emphasise here is that the utilisation of the various viewpoints, the sub-designs, the cross-references and the text notes plays a significant part in communicating the results of the research to designers, management, users and other researchers in ways that may be more easily digested than the traditional research report. Furthermore it may be the case that just such a presentation of the research brings to the fore a number of design issues that might profitably be considered by these interested parties, for example, as in the case above, that there is some benefit in carefully considering relatively mundane issues, such as seating arrangements, in systems design; that sitting people next to each other or around desks may produce returns in the form of increased awareness of work and training, and that when such an option is not chosen in systems design it should be because of the consideration of some other tangible benefit that any alternative arrangement might have. Other issues that may be relevant for systems design concern the importance of informal monitoring and checking procedures – approaches that may well not be easily replicated or replaced by an automated system.

The more formal processes of loan sanctioning are outlined in a series of workflow diagrams in the (rarely consulted) Bank's Lending Manual, and can be illustrated via the *workflow* viewpoint using the DNP. Figure 9.8 presents a simplified representation of the formal, the idealised, process of sanctioning a loan and cross-references provide linkages to other designs and viewpoints of, for example, workplace ecology or egological organisation at the various organisational units.

In contrast to this idealised model the DNP can also be employed to outline models of the lending process 'in operation' that emerged from the research, deploying features of the framework such as the *plans and procedures* perspective and, when linked to particular organisational units and organisational actors, the perspective of *distributed coordination*. To illustrate, we outline and discuss DNP designs for one lending process, that of evaluating a loan application and initiating or rejecting the facility.

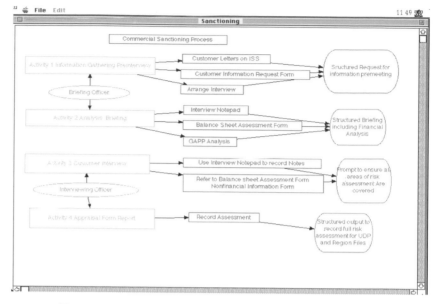

Figure 9.8 Workflow viewpoint: sanctioning a loan

Figure 9.9 presents a very rough overview (in the form of a modified *ecology of work* viewpoint) of the principal teams and the various linkages and relationships as well as the extent of computer support involved in the process. The various sub-designs and text notes attached to the design are used to give an indication, through furnishing examples from the fieldwork, of exactly how the process of lending is practically accomplished; the 'egological' organisation of the various individuals involved in the decision-making and administrative process, as well as accounts of lending interviews and decision-making.

Figure 9.10 shows two sub-designs and various text notes attached to the Customer Service Branch (CSB). One sub-design briefly outlines the various individuals that might be involved, and the other details the various stages of the lending process where the CSB is required to perform some role. The text notes attached to these entities contain descriptions, pasted in from the fieldnotes, of the accomplishment of the different stages. Similarly, figure 9.11 shows an ecological viewpoint created in a sub-design, together with the various text notes, again taken from the fieldnotes, associated with the Lending Centre.

Emphasising, yet again, the *communicative* role of the DNP, examination of the material presented in these viewpoints could provide evidence to users, designers and management, of the rather different approaches to

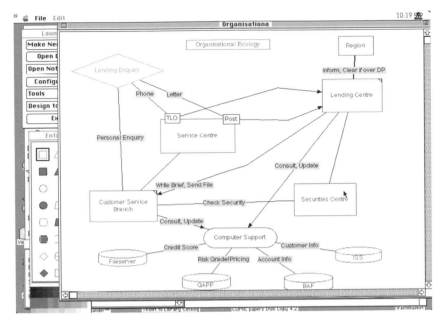

Figure 9.9 The lending process: organisational ecology

lending found in the CSB and the Lending Centre, suggested perhaps in one CSB lending officer's rather rueful comment, 'You have to have a letter from the Pope to get any unsecured borrowing round here.' Perusal of the text notes would also illustrate the ways in which, despite the various manuals and action sheets and computer software support, 'procedure' was routinely reinterpreted in the light of 'gut feeling' or, as one lending officer put it, 'in the end do you trust him to pay the money back?' Such perusal might, conceivably, have design implications in the sense that it might be valuable to know the circumstances in which routine is strictly followed and when and how it is subject to modification or rejection. It is also likely to reveal some of the observed differences between the different units in their approach to lending decisions with, for example in this instance, the Lending Centre appearing to be more rule or procedurally bound, and lending officers in the Lending Centre being much less free and much less likely to take an idiosyncratic view of lending proposals. Again this is likely to have some consequence for system design (or redesign) in a highly distributed organisation. Finally, since our interest is in communicating research results to a varied audience, there is an important methodological point to be made here which is that reading the fieldworkers' notes in the various text notes attached to the different designs will

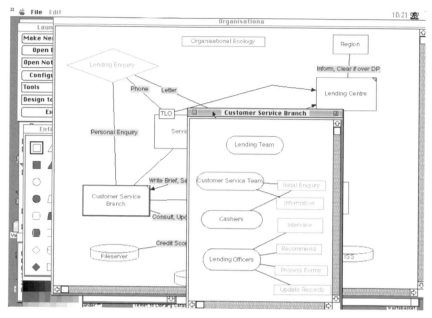

Figure 9.10 The lending process: CSB

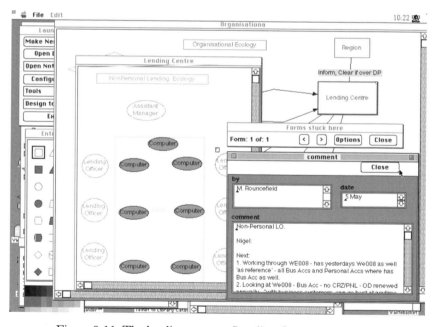

Figure 9.11 The lending process: Lending Centre

quickly bring home to the reader the sheer (and necessary) tedium of much routine work in a way that the 'illustrative vignettes' or 'storytelling' do not. What the DNP attempts to do is provide the detailed context within which such stories or vignettes occur and might be assessed. There is a danger that the vignettes, commonly found in research reports, and a feature of many ethnographic reports or debriefings, come to represent 'the data' and, of course, they do not. As we have already suggested such vignettes may exaggerate the unexpected, the unusual and the bizarre and the implications for systems design are not necessarily obvious in that since design is a 'satisficing' activity both designers and users of systems may prefer to live with and accommodate the exceptions that constitute the illustrative vignettes rather than opting for the uncertainties of system redesign.

One outcome of the research on the lending process was the identification of a number of 'problems' arising from the existing organisational arrangements, problems which were intended to be addressed by the different prototyping options. The suggested problem areas were those of 'geographical and organisational dispersal', the 'sales incentive scheme', 'functional baronies' and 'communication issues'. These can all be represented in a DNP design where again the cross-referencing and text notes facility enable the audience to read and evaluate the various accounts of the 'problems' and assess their importance in effecting the overall lending process.[17]

Finally, a number of options for the redesign of the lending process were suggested by the research, each of which could be presented in the form of DNP designs with their accompanying sub-designs, text notes and cross-references. The modified option that eventually was preferred for the redesign of 'non-personal' lending is depicted in figure 9.12

While this represents something of a novel departure for the DNP, in representing 'how things might be' rather than 'how things are', the suggestion is that the presentation of the prototype in this format, along with the accompanying cross-references to other designs and text notes that do display 'how things are' and which are part of the justification for the prototyping option, may encourage the kinds of debates and discussions that might usefully impact on systems design.

Conclusion

I have a repertoire of stories that I've built up over my years of design practice. I collect them . . . I use these stories to generate discussion, to inform, to persuade . . . Stories are very powerful tools (Erickson, 1996: 31)

In this final section the emphasis has been on the practical value of the DNP in communicating research to various interested parties in a way

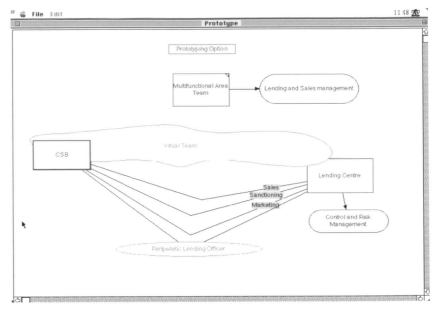

Figure 9.12 Prototyping option

that goes beyond either the standard debriefing or presentation with the inevitable glossing that involves or the ethnographic research report and the problems of understanding that (perhaps equally inevitably) ensue. As ethnographers involved in multidisciplinary CSCW research projects over a number of years we are well aware of the suggestive power of Erickson's (1996) stories or illustrative vignettes in conveying a rich picture of the application domain. We are also aware of how seductive and potentially misleading such stories can be for the practice of design. At the same time we are equally aware that the lengthy ethnographic fieldwork report, with its endless detail and frequently turgid prose, is less than ideal as a communicative device. The developing use of the DNP, accidental and serendipitous as it has been, is presented here as a working contribution rather than a solution to this particular problem of communication and design, being suggestive of the (admittedly problematic) practices of participative design. The interested parties in this communication process comprise designers, management, users and other researchers; the latter because it is not untypical in large organisations to find almost identical research projects unknowingly commissioned by different parts of the organisation on the same phenomena. This approach also involves a complex view of the design process; in this case not being confined to the initial requirements capture phase but taking place over time and in response to a changing array of organisational priorities and user demands. As Henderson and Kyng (1991) suggest:

As designers of technology we are usually confronted with the task of designing systems that will be used for long periods of time. And no matter how well they may have fitted the situation initially, circumstances of use change: the needs change, the uses change, the users change, the organization changes. Therefore the computer systems may well have to change to match the changed circumstances.

The complexity of the world makes it difficult to anticipate all the issues that will eventually be of importance in the final situation. (Henderson and Kyng, 1991: 221)

While ethnographic studies continue to remain influential as a means of understanding the everyday aspects of work settings, the presentation of these findings remains problematic and information from an ethnographic study relatively difficult to access. We have sought to resolve this by developing more structured techniques for presenting ethnographic information, specifically by the use of viewpoints and their incorporation into the framework for the analysis of work, thereby facilitating communication between ethnographic researchers and other interested parties to design. However, we continue to perceive the DNP as complementary both to the ethnographic exercise and the diagrammatic representations underpinning accepted design methods.[18]

We feel that the use of the DNP, or its like, to organise and present data from ethnographic research, as well as its possible use to present users' views of the application domain, facilitates the discussion across a broad development team of the representational viewpoints emerging from such data. The complex sociality of the work setting – which the system under development must support – as represented in the ethnographic record and delineated in users' experiences, is made available for information, assessment and interpretation by users of the DNP. We therefore continue to argue that the use of the DNP can provide a systematic means of viewpoint identification and representation and thereby represents an emerging development of a bridge between the complexities of an ethnographic account and users' experience and knowledge and the requirements of a system designer.

NOTES

1 Clearly the topic of 'communication' in the context of the relationship between ethnography and design merits further consideration. For us, the problem was primarily a *practical* one of presenting and getting our work understood within a multidisciplinary research team.

2 The research for this was funded from a variety of sources including the DTI/EPSRC CSCW Initiative and Esprit BRA 6225.

3 Ethnographers typically work with text – making notes, writing reports, transcribing tape recordings, interviewing and so on – while system designers prefer the formality of graphical notations. Clearly, this preference is more than just a preference but indicates differences in the ways in which problems are set up, characterised, displayed and resolved. Nevertheless, the difference was something that had to be faced.

4 Some computer scientists could have been quite adept at fieldwork but a more effective use of their time and skills was to concentrate on system design. The symmetry of the argument was not quite preserved with respect to fieldworkers and computer science, though it made practical sense for them to use their training in what they did best. However, through teamwork a greater familiarity of each other's approach and method of working was achieved.

5 The DNP has been used in a variety of contexts; as a basis for computer-supported learning, the development of safety cases for software systems; as a generic software design tool; and, in this instance, in the organisation of data produced during an ethnographic study of work processes.
http://www.comp.lancs.ac.uk/computing/users/mbt/dnp/dnp.html

6 An extensive symbol library is available so that users can define the graphical representation of the types required in their method. The ability to manage multiple families of types means that the DNP can support a comprehensive yet simple system of information hiding. The ability to create entities and links quickly and to rearrange them spatially has facilitated the use of the DNP as an outliner/ideas organiser. The free-format is very fruitful as ideas are put down as entities and then rearranged, grouped and deleted as they become more coherent.

7 A large number of different types of documents are created during a study. These can be transcriptions of conversations, interviews, statistics and observations etc. This information is often held in files created across a wide variety of applications. The information in text-notes need not be necessarily held within the DNP. A text note may be linked to a file so that its contents are derived from that file. This facility allows material generated in existing tools to be directly linked to material within the DNP.

8 We have tentatively explored the possibility of using digitised photographs of work settings instead of line drawings. However, on the whole these convey less information while providing a more realistic 'feel' for what the setting actually looks like. There is, of course, no reason why both types of representations could not be accommodated allowing users themselves to make the choice as to which they find the most useful for various purposes.

9 Such cross-references, which are designated by a small arrow next to that entity, can be bidirectional. If more than one cross-reference exists, for example where a worker is involved in a number of different teams or workflow operations, when asked to search these, the DNP lists them in an options menu.

10 URL for NUDIST is http://qsr.latrobe.edu.au/

11 Our emphasis here in using the notion of 'viewpoint' is on the practical requirements of system engineers as they set about the software development process. This approach represents a practical engagement with the problem of

relating the contribution of ethnography to the design process. As we have indicated elsewhere it is obvious that the notion of viewpoint, in a variety of forms, has its sociological supporters and precursors and appears, implicitly or explicitly, in a number of sociological accounts of the research process. Our adoption of what might be termed a 'weak viewpoints' approach reflects a concern that viewpoint identification is fundamentally an empirical exercise without necessarily carrying any ontological presuppositions. As we have pointed out previously, our objective is to make use of the idea to effect a practical bridge between ethnography and system design.

12 While not entirely arbitrary there is clearly a great deal of flexibility in the choice of viewpoints; the flexibility is a bonus as far as we are concerned. However, as a matter of record, these viewpoints were chosen because they represented our interests but, as important, they enabled us to explore the idea of viewpoints to see how it might work.

13 The routine work of the Lending Teams is essentially that first thing each day the controller deals with the daily computer printout – the WXYZ – that details the accounts that are 'going out of order'. This entails examining each account; calling it up on the AP (accounting package) (to see how the account has been and is being run) and the RD (relational database) to peruse the customer's notes (to see the history of the customer relationship, what action, if any, has been taken in the past, whether 'concern' letters have been sent, whether cheques have been bounced and so on); and finally making a decision on what course of action to take and indicating this in note form on the printout for actioning by the assistant. The two assistants, besides actioning the controller's decisions, also work from the printouts, looking at accounts showing limits marked expired, open loans, make more minor lending decisions and perform a range of other clerical tasks, get files, check the diary and, most important, field all the phone calls coming into the team. By making sure that the controller sees all the relevant post and letters, the team ensures that work on the printout – the WXYZ – takes place with, as far as possible, full knowledge of the circumstances of each account.

14 When cheques are returned unpaid from other banks the customer has to be informed either by standard letter or by phone, and the requisite paperwork completed and assembled for the debiting of the customer's account. Similar procedures take place with the return unpaid of their own customers' cheques and here the time considerations are most obvious in the case of 'late returns', that is, when the decision not to pay has occurred in the last half day of clearing. In these circumstances the Lending Manager must inform the 'Unpaids' desk by 10.30 a.m. in order for them to get the cheque from the bookroom. If the cheque is over £500 they have to phone the 'crossing bank' – the bank where the cheque was presented – by 12 p.m. The 'routine' work associated with these tasks consists of completing the forms – 'unpaid yellows' – for their records and to be sent for keying to the EHU (Entries Handling Unit) and other banks, sending out a range of standard letters or phoning customers and updating the records.

15 A not too misleading gloss for the term 'egological' could be 'how the work looks to the person performing it'. It acknowledges the fact that in most if not all work processes no one has detailed knowledge of the total.

16 What is perhaps interesting in our particular study was that just such an abstract representation had clearly already been undertaken by the bank and in the weeks following the fieldwork the process of lending control was radically redesigned with a new computer printout – the WRST – automatically making decisions on 'out of order accounts' and thereby significantly altering (effectively making redundant) much of the work of the lending controller.

17 So, for example, the 'pass the buck' culture, the finger pointing in which it is the role of the 'other' team to sell or find new business can be presented. Similarly the fierce unit loyalties, the 'them and us' attitude (where 'them' is any other organisational unit) in which 'they don't understand the pressure/procedures we're working under' becomes a common refrain, and where communication across the organisational divide is rare, can also be identified and discussed.

18 Although there was some early consideration of the use of the DNP 'in the field' it quickly became apparent that the DNP was best utilised as a support for the more traditional tools of the ethnographic trade (Calvey *et al.*, 1997).

10 Where the rubber hits the road: notes on the deployment problem in workplace studies

Bob Anderson

Generating technology innovation: the context

I approach workplace studies with a viewpoint shaped by the research and development needs of a technology provider. I recognise the validity and the importance of other points of view, especially what is often (dismissively) called 'the academic' or 'the theoretical'.[1] I support and enjoy the work which is done in their name. But in the end, what drives my interest is the contribution which workplace studies should make to ensuring the commercial success of the work systems that my company might bring to market. Clearly, I do believe that they can and have made such a contribution. Moreover, because for a number of reasons I think this contribution could well be vital in the future,[2] I want to see workplace studies not only continued but also supported and managed in ways which will maximise their impact on the whole design and commercialisation process. In all that follows, then, I am arguing from this strongly positive position. I want to promote workplace studies within research and development. I want to secure their representation and voice in the design process. And of course I want to maximise the opportunity which their presence in design might give for improving both the process itself and the artefacts so designed, that is, the products we take to market. None of these, though, should be taken as a demand that all our workplace studies, let alone all studies of the workplace, should be reconstituted according to the framework I shall outline. As I say, my concern here is with studies carried out as part of a clearly defined R&D process.

To achieve all of the objectives I have just outlined, I believe we have to go beyond simply building on the successes we have gained so far. We have to create a new sub-genre of sociology, a genre which, for want of a better term, I have been calling Practical Sociology.[3] This chapter is about some of the things required to establish this genre as a real engineering discipline.[4]

The R&D garbage can[5]

Before we get to specifics, it might be just as well to sketch the current state of play within corporate R&D. I do this first because I suspect it may not be very well appreciated or understood outside that domain and second because it forms the context within which Practical Sociology will have to find its feet and place. By 'state of play', I do not mean the provenance of such generalised motivational exhortations as 'maximising return on assets' and 'increasing shareholder value', 'growing profitable revenue streams', which derive from the 'corporate' part of corporate R&D. Rather, I have in mind current sets of concerns about the relationships between the 'R' and the 'D' of R&D and the ways they should be framed. It is into these that corporate-sponsored studies of the workplace, at least, will have to fit.

From my perspective, corporate R&D appears to be being carried out within a highly charged force field. The components of that force field are associated with a number of transformations. The most prominent are discussed below.

From 'voodoo innovation' to customer-centred research

In economics, theories of innovation are, by and large, versions of or adaptations to Adam Smith's 'hidden hand'. In the long run, entrepreneurial profits will tend to be eradicated in perfect markets. This is because where 'surplus' profits are being made, suppliers will enter the marketplace and being willing to accept lower profits (there is always someone willing to be worse off than yourself!) compete on price. Thus is the stability of 'normal' profits reasserted in the marketplace. In his classic work *The Theory of Economic Development*, Schumpeter (1934) described how, against such a background of stability, economic innovation and hence change occurs. In essence, this is the theory of mousetrap profits. If you are smart enough or lucky enough to invent, find, steal an innovative idea, a new and better mousetrap, the world will, for a short while at least, beat a path to your door. And you will become rich. Then as others in the 'de-moussification' business notice your competitive advantage, they will attack your market by copying or improving on your product. Your surplus profits will decline; stability will be returned. The iron law of the marketplace, the hidden hand of competitive forces, will have moved things back into place once more.

As with mousetraps, so with silicon. Or so it has been proposed, especially by defendants of the free range of market forces such as Gilder

(1991) in his analysis of high technology businesses. There is no predicting where or how innovation will arise, nor who will gain advantage from it. The only thing to do, it seems, is to put enough bright people in a dark room, throw them resources and money, and leave them alone. If you are lucky and can wait long enough, a new idea, a radical innovation (the digital mousetrap?) will emerge and sweep the marketplace.

In a coruscating reply to Gilder, Ferguson (1988) called this 'a voodoo theory of R&D' because it places all the explanatory and causal weight on processes which are non-rational and beyond our control. Ferguson points out that inventing the mousetrap is less than half the task. As every corporation knows only too well, it is not enough to have the invention. You have first to be able to recognise it *is* an innovation, and second, see how to turn it to business effect. Xerox discovered with the Alto, Ethernets, object-oriented programming (but not, interestingly, laser printing) that focusing only on the technology in hand and failing to understand the opportunities it offers can cause one to 'fumble the future' (D. K. Smith and Alexander, 1988).

This realisation is now taking the form of a demand for 'customer-focused research', a strategy which both narrows horizons, in that it targets activity, and increases the probability that what is targeted can be brought to commercial success. These days, before an R&D project can be consecrated, it is increasingly necessary to demonstrate just how the proposed product and its related technology will fit within the business and work processes found in customer settings (Grady and Fincham, 1990).

From pipelines to scrums

Not only is our conception of innovation being transformed, so too is our model of how to manage it. Because we no longer believe in voodoo R&D, we no longer seek to maintain a ritually purified boundary between research and the commercialisation process. The old model we have jettisoned was essentially that the R&D process is a pipeline constantly being filled a long way upstream with ideas and inventions (in research) and from which products emerge downstream to be carried off to the marketplace. The boundary was felt to be important to maintain because otherwise research might get polluted by short-term demands from current product teams. At Boeing, the boundary maintenance took the form of creating small teams which were hidden from top level management and focused on advanced research. These became known as 'skunk works'. A similar process was at work in the early design of the Alpha Chip at Digital (Leonard-Barton, 1992).

Currently, no clear alternative is being promoted in place of the pipe-line image (which probably accounts for why it still has some lingering influence) but all of the ones currently being paraded (Roussell *et al.*, 1991) have a common form. They require research to be 'close coupled' and 'rapidly responsive' to the marketplace with, reciprocally, the R&D team loosely managed, fast moving, multidisciplinary and multifunc-tional (McGrath, 1995). Since many senior managers are terminally addicted to sporting metaphors, often they refer to the resulting organisa-tion as a 'scrum'. It is plain that what they expect is tight integration, rapid adaptation and the free flow of information.

From 'big bets' to investment options

As R&D has been drawn into the mainstream of the company (a response to both the need to control the asset and the realisation of its strategic value), so the ways of thinking there have leaked back into research. Nowhere is this more visible than in the emergence of a new rationalisa-tion for R&D decision-making. If you like, instead of seeing R&D as a kind of *prospecting* for ideas, some of which will require major gambles and promise equally significant pay-offs (what in the R&D literature are called 'bet the company' decisions), the approach now is to distribute and manage risk by treating R&D as a series of *investment options* (Dixit and Pindyck, 1995). During its lifetime, any individual project is treated as part of a structured portfolio of more or less 'risky' options to invest. As the project proceeds, the investor (i.e. the company) can choose whether to exercise the option. When seeking funding for any project, then, the R&D manager is less likely to argue in terms of the size of the opportunity (its big bang) and almost certainly not in terms of the novelty of the tech-nology (its whizziness) (Quinn, 1987). Rather it is the structure of care-fully laid down points at which information will be fed back to enable the company to make the decision to 'call' or 'put' the option which will be emphasised.

From 'killer apps' and point products to sustainable competitive advantage

What the options model does is to militate against betting the company on a single throw, or, relatedly, to assume that success can be achieved only through the serial discovery of new services or usages which capture customers' imagination (often called 'killer apps' – or applications). To put it the other way around, it demands that R&D be configured to ensure that there is a continuity of success. The reason for this is a larger shift in strategic thinking which has gone on in corporations. Rather than viewing their 'product set' as a series of individual forays into a market or series of markets, corporations plan only to enter markets where they can maintain sustainable competitive advantage. By definition, a one-off success is not sustainable and hence not strategic. Since one of the primordial sources of success is the differentiation produced by continuous innovation within the product set, R&D is now being looked to to provide such sustainable strategies. What R&D provides the corporation is called (in the jargon) *innovative product platforms* (Myers and Rosenbloom, 1996).

All of the tendencies illustrated above have a common concern to integrate 'upstream R&D' with 'downstream market understanding'. It is hardly surprising, then, that some research managers have seen the social sciences, especially those elements which concern themselves with work and the work setting, as a powerful resource to draw upon in achieving this aim. What they have seen, though, may not necessarily be what social science thinks it is actually offering, or capable of offering, or indeed what it is best at. (I have been round this one before: Anderson, 1997). What R&D managers would like to have could probably be most succinctly described as marketplace intelligence and socio-ergonomics. And what they are looking for is its distillation into forms which the engineering and design disciplines can first accommodate and second deploy.

There is one obvious response to all this. Begin a campaign of re-education to show R&D managers how much they have misunderstood social science. There are lots of arguments in favour of such a strategy and several crucial ones against. For me, probably the most telling is that, should we be successful, not only do we risk strangling the golden goose (so to speak), but also we shall have lost an opportunity to try for something really interesting. So, rather than insisting that Muhammad go to the mountain by getting engineering to accommodate social science, I would propose the opposite tack. Let us see what we can do to take the mountain to Muhammad, social science to engineering. Let us see what it would take to build an engineering discipline which would fulfil the functions which market intelligence and socio-ergonomics are shorthand for. Let us see, that is, if we can make a practical sociology.

The problem of institutionalisation

Several years ago, when musing upon much the same order of problem, Klein (1993) argued that it was first and foremost a matter of institutionalisation. It really is not all that difficult to get an arbitrary engineering group to talk with some random social scientists. By and large, engineers are pleasant and well-mannered people, and social scientists occasionally have surprisingly useful things to say (Sommerville *et al.*, 1993a). But the workaday world of engineering projects is such that unless the exchange (or the collaboration) is institutionalised it will always remain at the fleeting level of pleasantries and hallway conversation. To have impact, it has to be embedded in the design process and to do that it has to be legitimised, sanctioned and part of what some sociologists themselves call 'the moral order of design' (Harper, 1992). Klein (1993) proposes that this requires changes in the training of engineers (and social scientists), changes to the structure of funding and resourcing, and changes to the standards and codes of practice enforced with regard to designed artefacts. All of which sounds like a tall order. But to make matters worse, it will also require quite wide-ranging changes in the character and conception of the social science being done in order to bring it under the auspices (as we are prone to say) of the engineering rubric. If you think Klein's proposals were hard ones, wait till you see what the latter imply, for they determine the reshaping which social science will have to undertake to be an engineering discipline and to have the position and influence I believe it both aspires to and should have. For workplace studies in corporate R&D, to coin a phrase, they mark where the rubber hits the road.

The problem of deployment

I want to frame all this in terms of the problem of deployment. That is, I want to ask how we might envisage (or indeed expect) the growing body of work, findings and techniques associated with workplace studies could be shaped to be used by the predominantly practical engineering disciplines we are seeking to engage. To get the discussion going (actually to get it going yet again, because in fact it has come and gone several times in the general debates), I want to pose things from the viewpoint of the practising engineering project manager. I do this not because I think it the only way to position and scope the problems to be addressed, nor because I wish to dismiss the broader epistemological and methodological questions which the attempt to relate intellectual pursuits always throws up. Aligning the design, the engineering and the sociological outlooks is a deeply fascinating problem. For the moment, though, I shall impose a self-denying ordinance. Instead, I shall ask how we might fit the sociological stance (as evidenced in workplace studies) with the endemically praxeological orientation of the engineering project manager.

A final introductory word: this time one of caution. Some people will be disappointed that I do not have any immediate programmes to offer. There are no ready answers or cut and dried recommendations in my knapsack. This is not because I have not thought about these questions, nor grappled with them as practical matters, for I have. Indeed, it is precisely because I have thought about them and have grappled with them as matters of practical management in a research and development setting that I know one really has to be suspicious of ready answers (especially if you do not know how *rough* they might be) and cut and dried recommendations (no matter how *pressed* one is for them).

The project manager's perspective

Broadly and very briefly summarised, the engineering project manager's perspective is constituted by the need to provide a schedule of products or deliverables

- on time
- within budget
- to specification.

While there are very many other good engineering (and non-engineering) desiderata for the effectiveness of project management, management of the constraints of time, cost, specification and schedule is paramount.[6]

Put as broadly and briefly, this characterisation of the engineering project manager's outlook may seem both less than impressive and less than perceptive (though a brief consultation of Fred Brooks's *The Mythical Man-Month* (1972) might lead us to be somewhat more confident in the observation and its applicability). We need to dig a little deeper and excavate the implications (or explicate the imprecations if you prefer) behind these points. When I say the management of a schedule of deliverables is central to the project manager's perspective, I mean no more than that the role of the manager is called into being in virtue of the requirement to attend to the monitoring and scheduling of activities. Engineering projects are (literally) composites. Or, to put it another way, the engineering approach to any complex problem (and at some level all real design problems are complex) is to divide the problem into manageable (and hence simpler) parts (modules), bring the requisite and relevant skills to bear upon each part, and then recompose the solutions thus created into the designed or engineered artefact. Project management is approached in the same top-down/bottom-up/divide and conquer manner as any other engineering problem (Newell and Card, 1985). Problem decomposition and recomposition creates the need for coordination and control. That is the task of the project manager.

The impetus to modularisation which is (I claim) a, but not *the*, characteristic of the engineering outlook places a number of requirements upon

the disciplines which contribute to the production of the eventual artefact. Prime among these is concatenation. That is, each discipline is
viewed as under an obligation to integrate its results with those of others
in consistent, predictable, rule-governed, systematic (that is disciplined)
ways. The contributions line up and are 'plug compatible', as my engineering friends say.

There is an associated aspect of this which should not go unremarked.
For the engineering project manager, the solution is all. Disciplines are
viewed as resources, as means to ends, and the problems such disciplines
take up and take on in like manner. The engineering project manager is
not motivated by an interest in the problem or endeavour for its own sake.
This sharply contrasts, perhaps not surprisingly, with much of the current
raison d'être of workplace studies.

To be an engineering discipline, workplace studies will have to adapt to
modularisation for them to be deployed within project teams. Perforce,
then, we shall have to rethink some of what often appears to be definitive
of the present genre.

The questions of deployment

The primary considerations which a project manager would bring to the
deployment of social science skills within a specific engineering project
are

   1 access
   2 qualification
   3 implementation.

Each of these is, naturally, a dense mass of subsidiary issues. The most
prominent are:

1.1 Where do I get it?
1.2 What are the trade-offs between having my own and getting it shrink-
     wrapped off the shelf?
1.3 How much do I really need?
1.4 Can I reuse it in the future?
1.5 If it is not shrink-wrapped can I reuse someone else's?
2.1 How do I know what sort I need?
2.2 How do I estimate fitness for purpose?
2.3 What are the five key issues I should target it on?
3.1 Where does it fit and who should it report to?
3.2 When should I bring it in?
3.3 How do I know when what I have got is 'good enough'?

The point about these questions is not that they are hard to answer or that
answering them will pose undue stress on a fledgling sub-genre. It is just

that within workplace studies little or no attention has been paid to them as institutional matters. Unlike other disciplines to which we might look for analogies (e.g. psychology, ergonomics), workplace studies do not have a body of common-sense recipe knowledge on which they can draw to help the project manager answer these questions or to estimate how far has been gone in getting to answers. This does not mean that we *have* to find answers to these questions. Neither does it mean that since we might not like their answers, we have to find answers *before* others do it for us. Rather, it is that in answering these and similar questions, I believe workplace studies will begin to reshape themselves as a practical, engineering discipline.

What's going on here?

In case you had not spotted it, these managerialist questions imply trade-offs between costs as well as benefits. And you cannot get the benefits (funding, impact, influence) without settling for the costs (external direction, scoping and shaping). Let us walk through them and see what might be involved.

Access

Central to the question of access are the professional processes for the dissemination of method, technique and generalisability of results. Taking the last first. We have, by now, piled a fair heap of studies. What, in general terms, can we say they show us? To my mind, and I will rephrase the old systems engineer's apothegm, we have got back pretty much what we have put in, to wit extensive and robust demonstrations of the possibility of analyses of the social organisation of technological innovation and technology use. While this is definitely not garbage, I would hesitate to say that adding yet more demonstrations to those already in hand was actually building anything up in any way (other than the pile).

Of course, the analysis of why this might be so can go in many ways. Perhaps we still need an integrating theoretical frame of reference? Perhaps we have just sprinkle sampled the domain? Perhaps (and I for one feel that this is the most likely) the investigations we have undertaken were not designed to be generalisable (let alone cumulative)?

Let me be extremely careful here. I am not proposing that workplace studies have to adopt some simple or even simplistic version of inductive generalisability. What I am saying is that they have got to figure out how new and unknown problems can be brought under the auspices of known and solved ones.[7] For all I know, this might be a matter of fixing determinant criteria for the formation of a kind of Case-Based Reasoning rooted in ideal types.

Then there is the question of specification. If we are able to frame general statements, how do we reduce them to the specifics of each new instance? What, to coin another term, is our theory of 'the theory of the case'? What are our analogues to the psycho-physical 'laws' of ergonomics (Fitt's Law), or the 'regularities' of psychology (Miller's rule)? This is where my (perhaps too glib) reference to ideal types might actually have a grain of sense in it. Moving forward here will mean working out what the appropriate categorical system should be and how it might be extensible.

Method and technique are, of course, closely related. Do workplace studies have *methods* in the usual sense? Or are they more craft-like? And if so, does that have implications for whoever may be called upon to carry out a study (see the qualification issue below)? If I look across the body of work currently in place, I find it just as hard to see the use of *a* method (let alone a replicable one) as I do to see the build-up of cumulative findings.[8] Probably the two are associated. There are similarities (family resemblances, you might say) between studies of ground control facilities, air traffic control centres, underground railway control centres, engineering shops, print factories and the like. But the methods adopted in each go no further than that. And of course this variety is motivated as a matter of principle. Each study is (at least in ambition) designed to be *uniquely adequate* (more or less) to its phenomena. The net result is that not only do you have to learn by doing (which is probably the only way you can learn) but also there are no principles to be drawn out other than the unique adequacy one.

In effect, all this seems to mean that we must tell our engineering project manager 'you have no choice but to have one of your own'. And the trouble with that is that it will make workplace studies *very expensive* and very slow to be disseminated and assimilated.

Qualification

In one sense this too is about professionalisation.[9] What are the standards which you would expect a journeyman practitioner to have achieved? What should they know and be able to do? Is there (heaven help us) a basic 'tool box', 'kit bag', or 'medicine chest' (choose your favourite metaphorical domain together with its portmanteaux) of approaches, techniques and formats? Or does the work depend only on having someone with skills, flair, insight and extraordinary talent – your own shaman, so to speak? If so, we are looking for a 'genius' engineering discipline and that is an oxymoron. No one in their right mind builds an engineering discipline which can be populated only by geniuses (or genii, bottled or otherwise, for that matter).

One way of thinking about what is involved here, could be to ask how workplace studies would fare under something like the Software Engineering Institute's Capability Maturity Model (CMM). I say this in the full recognition that an issue of *IEEE Software* (July 1996) was given over to examining just why software engineering remains in such a relatively primitive state with regard to performance measurement systems such as CMM. So it is not that software engineering provides a strong model to follow. Rather that the practices (especially the project management practices) built into the CMM are those which any engineering discipline should be attempting to follow (or so it seems reasonable to claim).

When using the CMM, assessors look for:

- demonstration that a clear, integrated and consistent methodology is followed throughout the project
- demonstration that project tracking and risk analysis are built into the assessment processes
- demonstration that defined measures of progress are deployed
- demonstration that the requirements for the project have been clearly identified
- demonstration that quality of outputs is measured.

Just for the sake of sharpness, I shall rephrase these as a set of questions relevant to workplace studies.

1 What are their methodologies and against which problem sets have workplace studies been deployed and validated? What domains of problem are *not* amenable to treatment from this perspective? What are the criteria of integration and consistency for their use in large-scale and small-scale projects?
2 What are the key risks associated with schedule slippage and performance failure for workplace studies? Which critical components will be disabled and in what order?
3 How do workplace studies identify and order milestones? Can progress be assessed other than in categorial terms? What specific project management techniques have been endorsed for workplace studies?
4 What form does requirements specification for workplace studies take? What processes should be put in place to prevent requirements drift?
5 What are the forms of output? Can workplace studies contribute to the determining of benchmarks, scenarios, forms of solution and so on (Newman, 1996)? What are the criteria for determining levels of quality and how do workplace studies compare the quality of output from different contributions or from different sub-projects?

The last question is, of course, about the results which you can expect an investigation to provide. Do we know which critical parameters we should select (Newman, 1997)? Here there is an interesting tie-back to one of the earlier questions. Do we know how to map the requirements of a project on to the choice of an investigative approach in order to isolate a chosen set of critical parameters?

The tricky question with regard to qualification is not that we do not know how to tell a good analysis from a poor one. We have seen enough PhD theses and novice field reports to be able to do that. What we lack are standards for the application of the high quality reports and findings we have been compiling to the design of artefacts. That is, we lack standards by which to judge what contribution the reports and findings make to the improvement of the artefact. If I put it in terms which are becoming increasingly familiar to all of us, can we say, crisply and succinctly, what the value add of workplace studies is for the design of specific artefacts?

I recognise that in part this is an unfair question. Many examples of workplace studies are as much about the process of design as they are the specifics of design. But that is just where the CMM becomes so relevant. What do workplace studies offer in the way of direct and practicable advice for how to improve design and development processes against criteria of assessment such as those encapsulated in CMM?

Implementation

Three questions are paramount here. Where does it fit? When do I use it? Who does it report to? Answers to the first question are likely to turn on what we think is the main leverage the research offers. Are we talking about market intelligence? Are we excavating the 'unarticulated needs' of some market segment? Are we defining the requirements and specifications for some envisioned product? Are we collecting evaluations of some extant and potential products? The answers here (and this is not a complete list) will give fairly strong guidance to the selection of results required (what are we looking for and how important is it?) together with the investigative tools and techniques designed to provide them.

Once we have identified the points of leverage, we can then get a lot closer to answering the timing question. All product delivery processes have a phased structure with decision points or 'gates' through which the project has to pass to gain further funding. Which gate reviews are workplace studies best at supporting? Do we know? Does it matter? (The answer to the latter is very definitely 'yes' for both political and pragmatic reasons. Unless we can identify the contribution made to phase gate reviews, we shall never be able to answer the 'value add' question above.)

The stopping rule problem

Gate reviews are, of course, an organisational solution to the stopping rule problem. Pursuing any solution, fine-tuning it and gathering data can be endless tasks. We can always justify 'another pass', a 'further search' or 'an update'. The question is, though, what does the incremental information, experience or understanding actually give us? Can we see not just what we shall get from the work but what value it will contribute to the final goal? It follows that for workplace studies the stopping rule problem is not binary in form. It is not whether to have studies but how many to have and for how long and to what depth? Are the targets, the 'deliverables' and the 'requirements' for the studies specified clearly enough and at a level that will enable us to determine when or if we have the information required for the task in hand? If we are not yet in a position to do this, what would it take to get us there?

Management lines

Formal management and reporting processes fall out from the previous two issues in the sense that the data which are collected and the generalisations which they support have eventually to be directed towards some pragmatic product development concerns. In the past, for the most part we have attempted to include workplace studies generally within the ambit of usability analysis and more especially end-user requirements specification. While this was (and is) not wrong, it is not to my mind the most advantageous point of leverage to go after, simply because for requirements to be collected and usability to be assessed we must have already defined the product and its 'use architecture'.[10] More and more, I see it is just this definitional process to which workplace studies can make its most valuable contribution. The point of interception of the development process is not, then, usability but the formation of product and market vision. Workplace studies should contribute right up front to shaping the value proposition for an offering and its supporting technology. Indeed, workplace studies can and should be the owners of that process.

This may sound somewhat odd, since the generation of market and product visions and strategy is, usually, the domain of marketing groups rather than engineering ones. Under the old pipeline model, such reservations would have been justified. However, in all of the emerging models, these functional silos are being broken down and responsibility for all aspects is being shared across an integrated product planning group. Moreover, since marketing groups are concerned with fit of offerings into settings, take up by users and, of course, with capturing and understanding the voice of the customer, that makes them more than natural allies for workplace studies. In addition, since, as one development manager put it to me, 'Engineering gets its marching orders from marketing', contributing to the shaping of market and product vision is not just a natural leverage point; it is a critically important one.

Conclusion

Although the tradition of studying the use of technologies in actual workplaces goes back a long way, it is only relatively recently that we have started to think in explicit terms of drawing specific technology recommendations (as opposed to generalised ones or policy recommendations) from our analyses. And we have come a long way in a very short time. We have built up a substantial body of detailed investigations. We have honed a number of exploratory techniques. We are beginning to understand how to derive requirements from our findings. What we have not done, though, or better, what we have not done very much, is to think about the institutionalisation and associated professionalisation of workplace studies as a practical sociological contribution to an engineering effort. These are the lines of thinking I have been following in this chapter. I have argued that the processes of institutionalisation and professionalisation will require attention to be paid to questions which have not featured much in the discussions thus far. In particular, they will require practitioners to become much more explicit about issues of goodness of fit between studies and design problems, criteria of assessment of outputs from studies, and, of course, the form which such outputs should take for particular purposes. If I have done nothing else, my hope is that I have sketched the rough order of concerns which these throw up and indicated something of what would be needed to resolve them.

Acknowledgements

My thanks to Annette Adler, Ben Anderson, Sara Bly, Graham Button, William Newman, Wes Sharrock and the various participants at the Colloquium on Workplace Studies held at King's College London at which some of the ideas were first bruited and suitably challenged. I should also probably thank Tom Rodden for failing to turn up at the colloquium and thus giving me the opportunity to ramble on about my interests rather than act as discussant for his.

NOTES

1 Indeed it would be odd if I did not, since I spent most of my previous life labouring in precisely those vineyards.

2 The other chapters in this volume clearly demonstrate both the specific form and broad scope of these contributions. From my own company's viewpoint, reference should be made to Button and Sharrock (Chapter 3 in this volume) and Suchman (Chapter 2 in this volume).

3 Do not get hung up on this name 'Practical Sociology'. I invest nothing in it except in so far as it designates the intent and the domain. The practice could just as well be called Socio-Technical Systems Design – though others would then get equally outraged.

4 There is much which could be said justifying why I make this assertion. Why, that is, it has to be an engineering discipline. Additionally, there is already a whole paper which says what Practical Sociology is *not*. It is not an applied sociology. It is not a policy science. It is not operations research. It is certainly not market research and it is definitely not Chris Bryant's (1996) kind of practical sociology. I have neither space nor time to go into these now. So I shall default to the classical academic strategy of argument by assertion. I am telling you where I am coming from and, starting from there, it seems to me that an engineering sub-genre is what we need. Disagreeing with my assumption is not of itself a refutation of my argument. To do that, one would have to show how it will not give me what I am looking for.

5 I have taken the allusion from Jim March (March and Olson, 1989) who describes all modern organisations as exhibiting many of the characteristics of rapidly spinning garbage cans.

6 In fact, with colleagues I have examined some of these in the context of particular engineering projects (Sharrock and Anderson, 1996). Other related issues are raised in Bucciarelli (1994).

7 Continually emphasising the uniquely identifying characteristics of each contexture really gets in the way here. It is both distracting and unhelpful since it is often taken to imply (wrongly in my view) that comparison is impossible *tout court*.

8 Again, though, let me try and trap a distracting and very misleading hare before it gets away. I am not, definitely not, saying that workplace studies as workplace studies are deficient because they do not seem to display commonality of method and cumulation of findings. As forms of conventional social science, such attributes might well be improper ones for them to have. But as components of an engineering discipline, their lack certainly would be a handicap, to say the least. Second, while I am at it, I might as well scoop up a related and equally misleading distraction. A lack of universal method or cumulativity does not imply a lack of rigour, analytic systematicity or, should one aspire to it, scientificity. Universal method and cumulative findings are desiderata of certain forms of science, not of science itself.

9 Notice it is professionalisation *not* professionalism. It has to do with certification of the field not enforcing rules of conduct – though, of course, the two are related.

10 'Use architecture' is a term I am stealing quite unashamedly from Annette Adler. For closely related work, see Dourish *et al.* (1996).

11 Situating workplace studies within the human–computer interaction field

Liam J. Bannon

Introduction

Since the late 1980s, one can discern a 'turn to the social' in the field of computing. The increased attention being paid to ethnographic studies of work by various subgroups of the computing profession – requirements engineers, system designers – is but the most visible manifestation of this interest. While there has always been a small number of people involved in studying the social dimensions of computing, from the birth of the computing field (e.g. Kling, 1980), this more recent phenomenon has been led by a rather different set of concerns, which, although quite heterogeneous in their origins, have all contributed to a shaping of the discourse on the social embeddedness of technology. Human–machine relationships more generally have become problematised in new ways, moving beyond human factors and cognitivist human–computer interaction frames to include participatory approaches to system design, and ethnomethodological and actor-network accounts of heterogeneous human–machine complexes. The outcome of this reconceptualisation of the field is still unclear, yet at the very least it has enlarged the arena for discourse on the nature of software development, and has allowed the participation of a number of actors from disciplinary fields previously not included in the discussion. One result has been a questioning of the assumptions behind standard development processes, such as the prototypical waterfall model of software development, and an increased emphasis on such areas traditionally known as requirements analysis and user needs analysis. The workplace studies presented in this collection thus have a bearing on a number of overlapping interdisciplinary communities concerned with the relation between people and technology – specifically the areas of human–computer interaction (HCI), Computer Supported Cooperative Work (CSCW), participatory design (PD) and requirements engineering (RE). Given the limited space for this commentary, I shall confine my remarks mainly to the HCI field. In the first section

230

I provide a short historical overview of the HCI field, noting the rise in importance of the cognitivist perspective and subsequent debates about the empirical and conceptual adequacy of this approach. In the second section I discuss how the field has now enlarged its object of interest, with an increased emphasis on 'social' factors, and the role that workplace studies have in this enlarged field. I conclude with some suggestions as to issues for further investigation.

The evolution of HCI

The emergence of HCI

The field of HCI rapidly developed from the beginning of the 1980s as an interdisciplinary community focused on improving the design of computer systems through an understanding of human needs and capabilities. This area has become one of the most popular and influential in the whole computing community, as developers realised that, in a sense, the interface *is* the system, at least from the viewpoint of the users (for further discussion of this point, see Kuutti and Bannon, 1991, 1993). The HCI field did not emerge from a vacuum, and has an obvious progenitor in the field of human factors, or ergonomics, established early in the twentieth century, concerned with the 'fit' between people and machines. Much of this early work focused on physical or physiological measures – work rate, fatigue and so on. With the advent of the computer a much wider range of people than traditional ergonomists became interested in the problems experienced by 'users' of computer systems. Major influences in this expansion were cognitive psychologists, who argued that making a good computer interface was a matter not simply of physical, but increasingly of cognitive ergonomics, and software engineers, who were experimenting with the design of highly interactive interfaces, and wanted guidelines on how to conduct dialogues with users and how to present complex information to users effectively. The need to provide more adequate interfaces to computer systems grew with the rapid growth of discretionary users, people who saw themselves as having a job or profession that was not primarily geared to the computing medium itself, but wished to use it as a useful tool. Computer companies also realised how user-friendly interfaces could give significant competitive advantage and dramatically increase the market for their products, and so support for an applied cognitive psychology concerned with human–computer issues was forthcoming in the early and mid-1980s. (The first major HCI conference was held in 1982 in the USA.)

The role of cognitive psychology in HCI

Most of the significant early advances in user interface design came from insightful system developers rather than academics, so there is a legitimate question as to how might the field of cognitive psychology contribute to better system design? (For a good historical overview see Baecker *et al.*, 1987: chapter 1.) Landauer (1987b) attempted to address this issue. First, he noted that there might be stores of knowledge developed within cognitive psychology that could be directly used in the applied field. Unfortunately, this is rarely the case. Aside from some general findings, for instance regarding the relationship between movement time, accuracy and size of target (Fitt's Law) which has been useful in comparing performances of pointing devices such as mouse, joystick and step keys, the body of findings that can be applied directly is minimal. It is difficult to generalise findings from laboratory experiments – the traditional testing ground for cognitive psychology – to real-world contexts. Too much of importance has been left out in the effort to make for a 'clean' psychological study, as we shall examine later.

What about the theoretical frameworks we have developed in psychology? Can they provide new insights into how to design better human–computer interfaces? Part of the problem is that the gap between theory and application is too large. It is not at all easy to see how to 'ground' some of the more developed cognitive theoretical frameworks in system design issues. One model of the human as an information processing system that was developed specifically as an engineering, calculational model, which could be of use in a design context was that of Card *et al.* (1983). A model user could be constructed from a basic cognitive architecture – a model human information processor – together with a set of approximate measures of human performance based on earlier experimental data. In principle this allowed a designer to predict the time involved in performing various operations on a system, so quantifying the trade-offs that previously had to be guessed. While of some use in certain very limited contexts, this approach has not been shown to have the flexibility, coverage and ease of use necessary to make it a really useful instrument for designers. Its utility is more obvious for description of processes than understanding how to do things differently – which is what real design should be about.

A third possibility that Landauer (1987b) examines would be to utilise the sophisticated methods and techniques used in psychology to analyse user behaviour, so that designers could find out how users perform on different versions of a system, or different prototypes, and not have to rely on intuition. However, standard lab experimentation is too limited, costly and time-consuming. For example, Thomas and Kellogg (1989) discuss the 'ecological gaps' caused by bringing studies into the lab, both by omission of factors in the real world, and by the addition of new elements in the testing situation that do not correspond to real-world eventualities. They discuss the 'user gap', based on individual differences and motivations, which is often not addressed, and the 'task gap', where the laboratory task may not generalise to actual work situations. There is the 'problem formulation gap', which has to do with how the user realises that a particular tool is appropriate for a task. An 'artefact gap' exists if the application does not fit into other applications. The 'extensionality gap' refers to the difference between brief laboratory use of a tool in an experiment and continuing use over perhaps years in a work setting. There is a tendency to focus too much on novice users in cognitive HCI studies or user testing, generally, with a concomitant neglect of the growth of competence and the development of people's qualifications within work settings. Perhaps the most important kinds of gaps noted, in the present context, are what Thomas and Kellogg (1989) refer to as 'work-context gaps', concerning the omission of important factors in the actual work setting that would affect performance on the task. It is this lack of appreciation of the use setting that is a major problem with much of the cognitive science HCI work to date. For example, one can question the human–computer dyad as the standard unit of analysis for HCI, when one begins to pay attention to how people actually accomplish their work tasks with technology. This has lead to an increased interest in field study methods as distinct from laboratory studies, and to the rise of a new field – namely, CSCW, where explicit attention is paid to the sociality of the workplace (for a more extended treatment of this field, see K. Schmidt and Bannon, 1992). For several years, Landauer (1987a, 1987b) has criticised the poverty of many of our experimental manipulations in HCI, and has attempted to push psychology out of the lab setting in order to be more directly relevant to human needs in the workplace. He notes: 'There is no sense in which we can study cognition meaningfully divorced from the task contexts in which it finds itself in the world'. What is needed are both 'quick and dirty' methods that can give rapid feedback to designers about the utility and usability of their products, as well as more extensive field investigations of the workplace both before, during and after the adoption of new technologies in order to learn more about how to improve our analysis and design methods for developing appropriate technologies for the workplace. We are only beginning to develop instruments to assist in the 'quick and dirty' part, although versions of the 'thinking aloud' protocol from cognitive psychology have been developed and used very successfully in usability studies on software (e.g. Monk *et al.*, 1993). We return to the issue of field studies later in the chapter.

Alternative conceptual approaches to HCI

We have noted some of the concerns about the utility of the cognitivist approach in HCI that began to be heard in the late 1980s. The body of useful knowledge available for designers appeared minimal. Advances in HCI seemed to emerge from work groups without any clear lineage from the conceptual frameworks or empirical methods touted by cognitive science. As a result, there was a questioning of the dominant information-processing approach to the understanding of human behaviour in the world. Indeed, Donald Norman, an ardent advocate of this approach to HCI in the early days, had himself noted some of the limitations of the cognitivist stance as far back as 1980:

The problem seemed to be in the lack of consideration of other aspects of human behaviour, of interaction with other people and with the environment, of the influence of the history of the person, or even the culture, and of the lack of con-sideration of the special problems and issues confronting an animate organism that must survive as both an individual and as a species. (Norman, 1980: 2)

There have been a number of attempts to answer some of these criticisms in the context of HCI, both from within the cognitive tradition and outside it. So, for example, the work of Carroll and his colleagues on the 'task–artefact cycle' is an attempt to approach the issue of the co-evolution of artefacts and human tasks (Carroll and Campbell, 1989). Likewise, the insightful work of Hutchins (1995) on what he has termed 'distributed cognition' is an approach that is mindful of Lave's dictum that 'cognition observed in everyday practice is distributed – stretched over, not divided among – mind, body, activity and culturally organised settings (which include other actors)' (Lave, 1988: 1). The work of Hutchins is a bold attempt to keep many of the concepts from cognitive psychology – such as computation and representational systems – but apply them in novel ways to situations, showing how several human actors and artefacts can be viewed as 'propagating' representations. This work is also distinguished by insightful ethnographies of work practice. Rogers (1993) refers to this as a socio-cognitive approach. While it extends the traditional cognitive model into a social and cultural setting, the basic underpinnings of the approach are still computational.

Many other conceptual approaches from outside the cognitivist camp have also begun to be applied to HCI concerns since the mid-1980s. Winograd and Flores (1986) reject the commonly accepted Cartesian, rationalist position underlying most western theoretical frameworks, instead relying on the biological approach to cognition of Maturana and Varela (1980). Another conceptual frame brought into discussion at this time was that of cultural-historical activity theory, an approach based on earlier work of the Russian psychologists Vygotsky, Leont'ev and Luria. This approach provides a coherent, if somewhat complex, conceptual framework based on concepts of human activities, actions and operations, with a strong emphasis on evolution and development, and a powerful view of artefacts as mediators in human activities (Bannon and Bødker, 1991; Nardi, 1996). It was around this time that the field of social studies of science and technology also became influential, with the work of people like Woolgar and Latour prominent. This approach provides a view of humans and artefacts as being enmeshed in complex networks where artefacts could be viewed as social actants – actor-network theory (Bijker and Law, 1992).

Perhaps the most interesting alternative approach to HCI issues for our current concerns is that of ethnomethodology, specifically those ethno-methodologically informed ethnographies of work that focus on the situated nature of human action in workplaces and its consequences for models of the user and ultimately, software design. The publication of Lucy Suchman's book *Plans and Situated Actions* in 1987 can be seen as the landmark publication of this genre. It was Suchman's book which introduced many people involved in software development and human–computer interaction to ethnography and more specifically, arguments from the field of ethnomethodology. It is a powerful critique of plan-based models of human behaviour, much in vogue in the field of artificial intelligence at the time, and influential in both cognitive psychology and the HCI field. Suchman has given us a powerful critique of the cognitivist HCI conceptual framework, and the ethnographic studies of workplaces – where people work with, through and around technologies – have provided a rich corpus of empirical data that help illuminate the sociality of work and require us to reformulate many traditional HCI problems (Suchman, 1987). In the next section, we examine the current state of the HCI field as a result of the changes described above, which has of necessity enlarged its object of interest from the human–machine dyad and user interfaces to an understanding of workplace practices and the way in which computers become embedded in human activities.

HCI today: expanding the scope of HCI concerns

From interfaces to computer-mediated activities

As we have seen, the originally dominant cognitive perspective in HCI has been – augmented/diluted/replaced by (depending on one's biases) – a variety of other socio-cognitive, sociological and anthropological perspectives since the late 1980s. Certainly, the very conception of the field, as being concerned with 'users' and 'interfaces' has shifted (Bannon, 1997; Grudin, 1993). Kaptelinin (1996), from an activity theory framework, prefers the term 'computer-mediated activity' to HCI, and there is general cognisance of this mediating view of artefacts in human activity. Ethnographic studies have provided a set of exemplary accounts of everyday human activity involving the use of technologies that situate our discourse about people using computers within the social world. Design practices that involve users are now more common as a result of the HCI field having learned lessons from the work of Scandinavian researchers and practitioners employing system development techniques (e.g. Greenbaum and Kyng, 1991). Nevertheless, much of the mainstream HCI conferences continue to reflect an individualist, cognitivist, laboratory-based framework for analysing human interaction with computers. Why is this still the case? The HCI community is made up of people from a variety of academic disciplines as well as practitioners. For many academic researchers, their primary audience remains their disciplinary colleagues, and this informs their research agenda and methodology. There is still tension within the community as to what are the appropriate metrics for assessment of research quality beyond those of experimental psychology. Workplace studies have contributed to 'consciousness-raising', and shifted attention to more general design questions and away from traditional evaluation methods. Nevertheless, the more radical reappraisal of the very foundations of the HCI enterprise that is implicit in much (ethnomethodological) ethnographic work has not, in my opinion, been debated within the HCI community, and so these workplace studies sit uneasily beside more traditional psychological theorising and experimental studies at many HCI conferences. While there is some acceptance of the legitimacy of the ethnographic approach, or at least its toleration, there is little engagement with it by many academic researchers in HCI. The background assumptions of different disciplines concerning the nature of science, the role of the observer, or description versus interpretation, for example, create serious difficulties. The problem of incommensurate world-views is not amenable to simple persuasion or argumentation, so I do not envisage any breakthrough in communication across these disciplinary divides. However, at a practitioner level, there is evidence of change. The emphasis on observing people in their actual work settings in ethnographic studies is an obvious plus from the point of view of practitioners. Likewise the need to involve users in the design process more fully, and the possible benefits of such an approach, could be easily grasped by practitioners working in HCI and computer systems development.

Relations between ethnography and systems development processes

The relationship between ethnographic studies and system design is still problematic, however (cf. Plowman *et al.*, 1995). We have had papers expressing several opinions on this, from a view of these studies as simply 'informing' design in some general way, through to attempts to develop design guidelines, to reflections on 'what ethnography is all about'. The current situation could best be characterised as one where many in the field now accept such observations from workplace studies as the following: the artful ways in which people 'get the work done' in spite of breakdowns and crises of various kinds, people's ability to cope with constant interruption, the ways in which local knowledge is used to shape the work in a matter-of-fact and unremarked-on fashion, the importance of mutual awareness in many complex work settings, the need for people to 'gear into' work, and so on. All of these insights have become part of the background against which many members of the HCI, and more particularly, the CSCW community (see Schmidt, chapter 6 in this volume) discuss computer support. The field has now gone beyond earlier arguments over the relevance of these studies to design, accepting that they provide a perspective that has helped to illuminate work practices and should serve as a backdrop for anyone that wishes to develop computer systems. That said, however, we also need to be aware of possible serious misunderstandings between designers and social scientists as to their different motivations, interests and conceptualisations of the world.

Indeed, there is an issue as to whether the developing relations between such unlikely bedfellows as technical systems developers and social scientists, particularly ethnographers, and more narrowly, ethnomethodological ethnographers, should be seen as a virtuous coupling or a 'deadly embrace'. If we are to have a useful interplay between these two professions then perhaps we also need to be aware of their different agendas, so as to reduce confusions and misunderstandings. Indeed at some recent gatherings where these two groups have been in evidence, signs of these misunderstandings and frustrations were palpable. The developer may be hoping that the sociologist can first help produce better 'requirements', and second, possibly obviate the need for the developers to enter the field and be subjected to the messiness of workplace practices therein. Concerning the latter, and taking a slightly jaundiced view, one could argue that the recent interest in work studies is simply another mechanism by which designers can off-load their responsibility of working directly with users, through treating the ethnographer as a translator, or user surrogate, who can go out into the field and return with the material designers need to populate their requirements documents, thus obviating the need for the designers to become directly involved with workers or the workplace. For example, Sommerville *et al.* (1993a) explicitly describe sociologists as the 'user's champion' and also 'the designer's conscience'. Such an approach is problematic, to say the least. As argued eloquently by Button (1993b) and Shapiro (1994) the descriptive language and sociologically generated analytical categories constructed in ethnographic studies are likely to be of little relevance to the practical problem of designing computer systems. Those ethnographers who attempt to mould their observations to fit the language of requirements analysis may find that in the process of translating their detailed accounts into more formal requirements, the richness and significance of their work gets lost, distorted or misconstrued. But if researchers find it problematic reconceptualising their findings, what is it like, on the other hand, for designers and consultants (whose job it is to implement new technology and redesign work) to translate descriptions of 'the sociality of work' into the language of design and workflow procedures?

The paper by Anderson (1994) concerning the relation between ethnographic field studies and requirements gathering puts forward a trenchant view on these confusions. While this is not the place to fully engage in detailed discussions on his arguments, a few points need to be made here. Certainly, it is a good thing that developers learn more about how to do fieldwork, interviewing, observing and documenting, and this should help them in drawing up their requirements. But, as Anderson points out, this does not exemplify what ethnography is really about. Whether the central feature of ethnography – the fact that it is an interpretative activity, and not simply 'data collection' – is understood by practitioners is more open to question. Some of the comments by computer scientists about the value of ethnography display significant problems in this regard, as we have just noted. Doubtless, it is helpful for designers to be made more aware of the nature of work itself and the role current and future technology plays in it. Indeed, the general list of precepts for a sociology for system design enunciated by Hughes and King (1992), for example, can serve as a useful set of heuristics for designers:

assume from the outset that the world is socially organized; see the world as socially organized from within the setting; understand the work and its activities in terms that members understand and use; go into the work setting and examine work activities in all their detail; treat work activities as part of the flow of work; don't treat domains as equivalent; don't draw a distinction between expert knowledge and practical knowledge; don't draw a sharp distinction between activities and technology; don't classify users. (Hughes and King, 1992)

The problem occurs in attempting to translate these guidelines into practical actions, especially if the actions are being performed by systems analysts or developers who do not have much training in performing field studies. Even if trained ethnographers are employed to do the observations, serious questions arise as to the value of the resulting material in the system development process. As Anderson (1994) notes, the particular analytic form of reportage characteristic of ethnography is not necessarily of direct relevance to the requirements gathering process *per se*. Also, the notion that this turn to the social can produce yet another 'method' in the armoury of systems analysis and development methodologies is mistaken. Just as, some years earlier, there was a misconception about the nature of the work done by people in participative design, which I have noted elsewhere (Bannon, 1995),[1] so the same misunderstanding is apparent here. What ethnographers are about is *not* simply some method for data collection, and viewing it solely in this light is the source of some of the current confusions. If both sides in the courtship are clearer about their interests and concerns, then, there is the possibility of opening up the design discourse, at a 'higher' level, to different 'sensibilities of design': 'The contribution that ethnography may make is to enable designers to question the taken-for-granted assumptions embedded in the conventional problem-solution design framework' (Anderson, 1994:170). But this is quite a different sort of endeavour to data collection.

Conclusion

In my final comments, I would like to look outward and to the future concerning the kinds of ethnographic approaches highlighted in this volume and their role in an enlarged HCI community. One approach attempts to bridge the gaps between psychologically oriented and sociologically oriented approaches to HCI by developing interdisciplinary theoretical frameworks, and the work of Shapiro (1994) on 'hybrid forms' is worth noting in this regard. In a provocative and somewhat neglected paper from CSCW'94, Shapiro attempts to walk a fine line between the traditions of ethnomethodology, psychology and participative design, in an effort to show how these different approaches and methods could possibly be mutually informing and made to work together for certain design purposes. Taking the idea of satisficing from design, he argues against disciplinary Puritanism. He notes: 'disciplines are the custodians of certain core perceptions which anyone setting out to achieve success in the design of certain kinds of system would ignore at their peril' (Shapiro, 1994:442). As an example of the kinds of results one might be able to put together from such a frame, he mentions such points as:

1) activities are socially organized and flexibly situated in context. 2) organizations make deliberate strategic changes; these engage highly differentiated interest. 3) users can easily be alienated from a system for reasons of presentation, interface, and usability. 4) using a system imposes a variety of cognitive loads; these can be assessed only in relation to practice and training. 5) sociotechnical systems are mutually constituting and adaptive. 6) users are the ultimate custodians of and experts in their own practices. 7) organizations and activities are continuously evolving. 8) the cost-benefit of systems should be optimized. (Shapiro, 1994: 423)

While the extent to which it is possible to bring together concepts from possibly incommensurable conceptual viewpoints is debatable, there certainly is room for the further investigation of Shapiro's syncretic approach.

Second, in commenting on the impact of workplace studies above, I have been focusing on their impact within interdisciplinary communities that include computer scientists and software engineers, but these are still primarily research-oriented communities. What about the impact of these studies on the extended software development community working in the commercial world? Can we see any impact of these studies there? The short answer is no, not to any significant degree at the moment, though some of the social science analyses of software disasters have been noted, and one can see increased interest concerning problems of requirements gathering in research and development projects within large companies, and an openness to alternative approaches. Most of the ethnographies referred to above have been done within a social science research frame, or occasionally as technology-focused advanced research projects, rather than as part of an 'industrial-strength' software development process. As a result, it is not surprising that there are difficulties in determining how one could 'fit in' these studies into an everyday software development project. While some might argue that hiring an ethnographer as a consultant for a brief period in the early stages of design might be useful, to open up design possibilities, my own preference would be to form an interdisciplinary development team, which includes ethnographers, who would be involved in the complete design process, from concept development and requirements right through to testing and evaluation. This would allow their perspective to be brought to bear at all stages of the design process, as well as allow them to develop an understanding of the perspectives of their technical colleagues and the everyday constraints in the design process brought on by budgetary considerations. Blomberg *et al.* (1993) provide an initial account of how this process might work, and Anderson (chapter 10 in this volume) provides some grist for the mill in his advice to his fellow social scientists as to the steps required to translate their ethnographic work into a form that can be handled successfully in software engineering project management. While the latter approach may be a step too far for many researchers in the field of workplace studies, it can be seen as defining one end of a continuum concerning the relationship between workplace studies and the design process.

To conclude, while misunderstandings are inevitable in interdisciplinary communities, it is my view that despite the differences in disciplinary backgrounds and orientations among both HCI researchers and practitioners, significant progress has been made in expanding the object of interest in the HCI community – from a concern with interfaces and the human–computer dyad to an awareness of the subtleties of workplace practices and the meshing of individual and cooperative work with and through computers (cf. Bannon, 1991). The new field of CSCW can be viewed as one manifestation of the increased interest in understanding the role of computers in the workplace. Workplace studies, whether they are inspired by ethnomethodology, by activity theory, by symbolic interactionism, by the Francophone 'course of action', or by distributed cognition, to name just a few of the theoretical orientations, have enriched the corpus of material available to researchers and practitioners involved in the design of more usable and useful computer artefacts, and can be mined 'as-is' for insights. Looking to the future, my own personal view is that the integration of ethnographers into design teams from the outset of the development process may ultimately have a more lasting impact on both the process and products of computer systems development. Given that the latter is only beginning, we shall have to wait a few years to see the results.

NOTE

1 In commenting on Kyng (1995) I note that he is not simply providing a 'method' or bag of tricks for how to do 'cooperative design'. Rather he is highlighting how he and his colleagues have evolved a set of design practices that have helped to ensure that system designers understand the work situation and design for and with end-users.

12 Analysing the workplace and user requirements: challenges for the development of methods for requirements engineering

Marina Jirotka and Lincoln Wallen

Introduction

This chapter discusses the relationship between workplace studies and requirements engineering for computer systems, focusing primarily on user requirements. Superficially, the two activities have much in common. Though an exact definition of the term 'requirements engineering' is still to be agreed upon, various perspectives reveal that requirements engineers must understand a domain well enough to determine requirements for computer systems intended for use in that setting. For example, Davis (1993) proposes that requirements engineering is the analysis, documentation and ongoing evolution of both user needs and the external behaviour of the system to be built; Loucopoulos and Karakostas (1995: vii) suggest that 'requirements engineering deals with activities which attempt to understand the exact needs of the users of a software intensive system and to translate such needs into precise and unambiguous statements which will subsequently be used in the development of the system'. Determining the needs of users will necessarily involve understanding the activities certain users are performing in order to accomplish their work, most particularly as the new technology might be intended to replace, transform or support existing work practices. Indeed, further definitions have sought to make such a perspective explicit in order to focus the debate on both social and technical concerns in requirements. Thus, Goguen (1994: 1) states that 'requirements are properties that a system should have in order to succeed in the environment in which it will be used'.

Workplace studies' central focus is the naturalistic understanding of a setting. However, the various studies that are embraced by this term differ in their analytic orientation; thus, rather than provide an overview of the different orientations that would detract from the main focus of the chapter, we consider one particular orientation that has proved useful to the requirements process. This orientation attempts to reveal the practices and procedures that participants themselves use to organise their activities in a setting and focuses on the ways in which workplace activities are produced in real time through talk and visual conduct. Such studies utilise video recordings of naturally occurring events in various settings to examine the interactional production and coordination of activities and the ways in which participants make use of artefacts, like documents and computer technologies (C. Goodwin, 1994; Greatbatch *et al.*, 1993; Heath *et al.*, 1994–5; Whalen, 1992).

In the following sections of this chapter we explore what lessons may be drawn for requirements engineering from such investigations, focusing particularly on methods employed in both the capture and analysis of data. We then consider the challenges that such an orientation poses for the practice of requirements engineering.

Background to requirements engineering

Requirements specifications for computer-based systems are expected to serve a number of purposes. The requirements must first inform system design and procurement, second, postulate the relationship between the system design and system performance when deployed, and third, do all this in a transparent and accountable way to a number of interested parties with different motivations and attitudes to innovation in the workplace. Requirements specifications which achieve these goals contribute substantially to the contractual, developmental and managerial processes involved in system design, procurement and maintenance, and as such are seen as crucial elements of the system life-cycle. This is despite a continuing unease over the practical methods available for the production and management of such specifications. A major part of requirements capture is to analyse both the domain – the environment in which the system will be deployed – and putative aspects of system behaviour. The product of this activity is typically a written specification of the external behaviour of the system to be built. In theory, the specification should contain 'a complete description of what the system will seek to achieve within the domain, without describing its behaviour in detail'. In practice, this amounts to a description of system behaviour using domain specific terms and notions, rather than using purely technological terms. Although this distinction can become problematic (Davis, 1993), it is nevertheless seen as a useful guide in ensuring that technological options are not eliminated too early in the process.

To the extent to which the putative system will interact with or affect work practices, the requirements engineer requires an understanding of the domain as a socially ordered environment. Unlike the sociologist or anthropologist, however, the requirements engineer looks at the existing social organisation of the workplace with a view to its transformation through technology. The widely accepted view of the goal of requirements engineering is not to produce a carefully warranted analysis of the existing social organisation. Instead, the aim is to produce a (necessarily partial) description of a hypothetical social system in terms of the functionality of some technological innovation. This account is designed to gain acceptance among those who have responsibility for innovation in the domain itself, and those responsible for producing the instrument of innovation: the technology designers. This emphasis on transformation leads to the requirements engineer being entreated to focus immediately on the hypothetical social organisation they wish to bring about, treating the extant order only as a source of terminology and points of reference. The customer is considered to be primarily interested in the hypothetical, the new, and definitely not in a detailed description of what exists.

In addition, the requirements engineer looks into one domain with a view to identifying aspects of technologies that may be introduced into many others. With an eye to mass production, technologists are required to design systems that are sufficiently generic to be useful in different domains, yet also adaptable for specific users in local circumstances. In order to achieve this, processes that specialise products to particular domains are used and involve marketing, installation and maintenance practices. Thus, when requirements engineers examine a domain they seek requirements as transportable items that may eventually be specialised, or at least used to provide an account of the technology as suitable for use in another environment. The need to be able to predict how work will change in the context of technological innovation is therefore fundamental. Such prediction is currently based on generalisations that the domain will have certain resources, and consequently, various hypotheses may be put forward about how the technology will work under new circumstances.

In general, workplace studies, with their emphasis on analysing naturally occurring activities, are also concerned to produce descriptions of the rich interrelationships between work and technology. These descriptions, and the techniques utilised in their production, are potentially usable by the requirements engineer to understand existing domains through their technological and organisational elements. Nevertheless, several methodological issues have yet to be resolved.

Workplace studies for requirements engineering

Workplace studies could influence requirements engineering in a number of ways and raise a number of methodological issues when studying the workplace, both in the initial production of requirements and in the evaluation of technological innovation. We shall concentrate below on two issues: how to see into a domain and what to look for, and how to justify statements about the domain.

Treating work as an achievement results in a documentation of the communicative resources people use in practice. In such studies it is important to observe and analyse work as it occurs. However, in general, requirements engineers' exposure to the workplace is very limited. Though observation of particular activities may be recommended in various requirements methods and an understanding of organisational issues seen as important for requirements analysis, engineers are more often encouraged to rely on (un)structured interviews, questionnaires, verbal protocols and personal experience in order to elicit the necessary information. Such techniques are currently employed in a context where requirements specifications are produced with little or no access to the domain in which the system will eventually be placed. Since 1990 there have been a number of critiques of these elicitation techniques within computer science (Goguen and Linde, 1993; Luff et al., 1993; Suchman and Jordan, 1990), and it is true to say these approaches have also been heavily criticised in the social sciences where they have a long history of use. A major justification for observing naturalistic activity is that the researcher cannot know in advance of the study what the relevant features of a particular setting might be in order to isolate and manipulate such features in interviews or questionnaires. Of course, the economic need to produce accounts of how existing technology can be used fruitfully in a domain does create an orientation from which the elicitation techniques mentioned can be constructed with only superficial regard to the domain; this might be called 'technology push'. It is worth noting that in such circumstances radical innovation may be stifled.

In addition, requirements practice must consider the contrast that may occur between what individuals believe happens in an event and what actually happens. This contrast severely limits the extent to which answers to questionnaires and interviews provide valid characterisations of what is taking place. The difference in accounts may occur not only because people have selective or defective memories, but also because many activities are performed repeatedly and become tacit in nature; they are seen but not noticed. For this reason workplace studies place great emphasis on 'making work visible' (Heath and Luff, 1992a; Suchman, 1995). In an ethnographic study of London City Dealing Rooms (Heath et al., 1994–5; Jirotka et al., 1993) it was found that technology designers' original assumptions about the dealing activity were greatly impoverished due to a lack of awareness of the tacit activities of dealing in stocks and shares. The proposed technology was intended to support the recording of deals, and the motivation for the system was to reduce the impact of increasing costs, effort and time that dealers took to record deals. Many of the requirements for the technology were determined by ex-dealers who were employed as business consultants, and though they were most familiar with certain activities of dealing, other more tacit activities were not taken into consideration. Thus, the close coordination of activities between two or more dealers in setting up a deal was left unanalysed. The ethnographic study supported by video analysis revealed that this coordination relied on the mutual monitoring of activities – the overseeing and overhearing of others as they perform their tasks. This overseeing and overhearing is seen by others but crucially, for requirements practice, is also unnoticed. Thus, when attempting to elicit information through more traditional requirements techniques, these types of 'hidden' activities are not readily accessible. They may not always be accessible to traditional observation techniques either, as it is difficult to capture the detail and complexity of activities either through casual observation or in fieldnotes.

Similarly, traditional techniques used in requirements analysis cannot reveal the interactional organisation of activities. Many seemingly individual tasks are accomplished in collaboration with others and more 'traditional' methods do not give the analyst access to information about the ways in which work activities are coordinated to this level of detail. Naturalistic inquiry in conjunction with the repeated scrutiny of video fragments allows examination of the location of a particular activity within a developing situation; that is, the analyst can consider the sequential development of that activity with respect to the previous actions. Such an analysis can begin to determine how each action displays a participant's understanding of the prior action and how the next action displays an understanding of the current action. The dealing room study revealed that while dealers may be engaged in a seemingly individual activity such as making a deal, they will also simultaneously be monitoring the local environment, including the activities of colleagues. Dealers not only are expected to remain sensitive to the local environment and to discriminate what may be relevant for them, but also are required, while engaged in one task, to participate simultaneously in other colleagues' activities. Thus, for example, a dealer may be apparently talking on the phone, and making suggestions to colleagues about what to buy or sell. A single utterance may be designed in such a way that it not only secures a deal on the telephone but also at the same time advertises the deal within the trading room itself, engendering the necessary currency arrangements to be made by another dealer in the local environment. These findings had important consequences for the proposed technology for recording deals in that designers reconsidered their original assumptions and altered their designs accordingly. For requirements engineers, such an analysis provides a way of looking into the domain and focuses the analysis to provide an assessment of what is going on. More importantly, it can also provide a warrant for the characterisation through consideration of the ways participants treat each other's activities.

This illustrates a further important methodological issue for requirements engineering. Currently in requirements practice, there is little provision for analysts to give warrants for particular analyses of domains. Standards may require that certain requirements can, for example, be traced to their sources of origin (for example, government white papers or system level requirements). However, requirements engineers, at present, have few resources through which to ground and warrant their analyses of work. Such information may be crucial for understanding at a later date why certain design features were or should be incorporated. Thus, techniques for warranting analysis can provide a justification for the role technology of all sorts plays in the creative achievements of people at work, as well as the investigative biases set up when seeking such information in the first place. An orientation to workplace studies that views work as an achievement suggests that events, actions and objects in the real world should be treated as practical accomplishments organised by the members who are party to these events. Work is accomplished through interactions with others as they coordinate a range of activities and make use of different tools and resources. This orientation toward the collaborative is quite different to the individualistic conceptions of work and activity embodied in many of the traditional methods for requirements engineering. These events, actions and objects are then seen as depending upon a social organisation which provides for a publicly available set of practices and reasoning. In this sense these practices are available for scrutiny not only to colleagues and other individuals in the setting but also to the analyst who can then 'reveal' these details in the investigation. Such an approach to looking into a domain can be contrasted with techniques suggested by requirements methods, where analysts' preconceptions of a domain and the ways in which work is accomplished often determine how the analysis proceeds.

Video recordings enrich the fieldwork in that they provide access to the details of language use and interaction that may not be revealed in fieldwork alone. The recordings themselves can be subjected to repeated scrutiny outside the setting and can then be used to inform any further fieldwork. The orientation of the study is also closely connected to the methods for capturing data. In order to describe the details of work activities and the ways in which they are coordinated it is necessary to have access to audio-visual data that can be viewed repeatedly at various times. Thus, the video data and analysis can provide requirements engineers with a resource through which they can begin to understand the organisation of the activities they are interested in supporting or transforming with technology.

In addition, the audio-visual data may provide access to 'sensitive' domains for others in the software life-cycle, or indeed in some cases to requirements engineers who have encountered difficulties gaining entry to the setting. The analysis can also easily be reproduced and re-presented for others in the software design process at various times and in different locations. The power of video data to give access to the working environment also provides opportunities to ensure a link to the domain throughout the software design process, and thus can inform what has been termed 'traceability'. Thus, video may be a useful resource to provide a trace to an original warrant for a requirement and is a preliminary step in grounding requirements within empirical materials gathered in particular settings. However, the full integration of analysed video fragments into the practice of requirements capture and the process of software development is yet to be developed.

Challenges

Perhaps a more exciting possibility is to use some of the analytic orientations of workplace studies to address the status of the engineer's description of a hypothetical social organisation, that is related to, but only partially reflective of, the existing workplace. The requirements engineer is attempting to understand the instrumental nature of the technology in the existing social organisation, and this may not be at all the same thing as describing the social order from any particular social scientific orientation. Indeed, the engineer is attempting to project that technology-based understanding of social organisation into a technology-based description of a hypothetical social organisation. Success in this venture must of course rest on a delicate, yet thorough, understanding of the ways in which technology configures, and is configured by, participants in their daily work. So once again the concerns of workplace studies, the experience of the rich and varied ways in which technology and people interact, may prove indirectly useful. Nevertheless, the central challenge of how to warrant statements/predictions about an as yet non-existent social organisation remains.

Once both workplace studies and requirements exercises have been completed a critical feature they share in common is the necessity to communicate the results to interested parties. With their background in anthropology and sociology and the problems of transferring experience from one context to another, workplace studies must seek to communicate information about a social order to others whose experience does not extend to the setting in question. Problems of interpretation and warrant are crucial here, but for the requirements engineer arise in relation to a hypothetical social organisation. The results of the requirements study must also be presented to various audiences who have a greater or lesser experience of the setting and include designers, testers, contractors, managers and users. However, the engineer has a different interest from the anthropologist or sociologist in communicating the information to others outside the domain. The results of this study now possess a transformational capacity: the requirements engineer must seek to describe how the technology might transform the social organisation while at the same time providing some warrant or justification for the analysis. Contrary to describing a piece of work as the outcome of a set of activities, various analytic orientations taken to workplace studies provide descriptions of the ways in which various resources are utilised in the workplace to achieve the activity at hand. In theory, this may be ideal for revealing what remains fixed when those resources are changed. Much of the innovation that occurs in a domain as a result of introducing computer systems may be seen to transform not the activity *per se* but the resources through which the activity is accomplished.

Consider telephone banking as an example of a technologically inspired innovation. The innovation is brought about by transforming the resources available for conducting banking transactions, not by transforming banking itself. Bills are paid, money transferred, balances listed, in short, all the transactions of the modern bank are reproduced. The authorisation check conducted physically by the bank clerk by testing the customer's ability to produce a signature and a distinguished bank card is transformed into the customer's ability to produce keywords and recall selected personal details; the GIRO form brought to the bank by the customer is replaced by the pre-signed bill payment order, resulting in a reduction in flexibility, but an increase in convenience; the receipt is replaced by the transaction code, unfortunately as difficult to retain as the small counterfoil. If our knowledge of the relation between banking transactions and our lives were rendered useless by the transformation of resources, the telephone bank would cease to function properly as just that – a bank; it would have no place in our lives. It is precisely the careful preservation of the structure of banking while at the same time transforming the resources required to bank that gives the innovation its power. We suggest that this may be the norm rather than the exception. While innovation in technological resources may be bounded only by our imagination and technical capabilities, innovation in the structure of activity is bounded by communal social organisation which must be recognised implicitly in the design of technological support. This is not to say that a workplace study of traditional banking would reveal those aspects of banking that should be preserved in general, as the focus of such studies is typically much more localised. However, in describing the interactive resources used when people actually interact with bank clerks, such a study should contribute to an evaluation of the adequacy of the new technological facilities.

From the point of view of the requirements exercise, communicating the results of the investigation to all interested parties is critical to its perceived success. The requirements engineer's analysis of technological structure is paramount to the requirements specification and consequently many techniques are currently available to support the engineer in this activity. However, workplace studies do not lay emphasis on describing technological structure. Consequently, current research is focused on how to present and communicate the results of ethnographic studies to software engineers in order to inform the design process. Some researchers have described the interaction between ethnographers and software designers in terms of a questions and answers approach attempting in the process to locate the boundaries of the ethnographer's activities and concerns (Randall *et al.*, 1994). The presentation of ethnographic material has also been considered in terms of viewpoints such as the context of the setting, views of work and workflow and incorporated in a general tool for designers (Hughes *et al.*, 1995). More recently, Pycock *et al.* (1998) consider current work practice and the envisionment of future work practices through the use of virtual technologies. Though such tools may be useful for presenting ethnographic observations, a critical issue for research lies in determining ways of transforming the ethnographic material in such a way that remains sensitive to the practices of designers themselves and thus can be readily used by them in the design process. The challenge of this research lies in describing technologically relevant requirements that reflect and are empirically supported by naturalistic analyses.

Requirements engineers may also look into specific domains for requirements for technologies that transcend any one particular setting and may be applicable to many. Workplace studies may also be seeking generic features, and analyses of different workplace studies are beginning to reveal interactional practices that occur across settings. However, the generalisation that requirements engineers are pursuing may not be characterised in the same way as sociological generalisation. Requirements engineers seek such generality based on the ability to provide an account of how technology can meet the requirements of a particular domain. In a business case for the customer, such requirements will be specific to the setting. However, the business case for marketing may also stress the range of domains in which a technology may be successfully applied. This might account for the general dissatisfaction requirements engineers perceive with the lack of discussion of generalisable findings arising from workplace studies. A further question remains, therefore, as to how requirements engineers can draw on workplace studies in pursuit of more generalisable requirements. It might be worth stating at this point that requirements engineers often account for the need for generalisable findings in terms that appeal to a more formal scientific approach. Such practice needs further investigation, not least because of the open criticism of qualitative studies and assumption of the possible mathematisation of social organisation.

Though workplace studies may be useful for highlighting systematic, robust features of work practices, they do not and perhaps cannot conclude either that these features *should* be preserved or that they *will* be preserved when new technology is introduced. Yet this is precisely the type of information that is tantalisingly suggested by these studies and fundamental to the requirements exercise. Determining which resources of the activity at hand must be preserved, either in their current form or supported by technology, and which might be safely transformed or discarded is the province of different interested parties of which the requirements engineer is only one.

To conclude, there are various issues and challenges for both requirements engineering and workplace studies to address in order to fulfil the potential of their relationship. Certainly, research is already under way to address some of these areas. However, it may be worth considering a final point. Both workplace studies and requirements engineering are concerned with formulating descriptions of social organisation which are transportable. For the requirements engineer, such communication is central to the division of labour in the technological activity. But a workplace study also seems to make an implicit claim to some universality beyond mere anecdote. Detailed consideration of questions such as how such universality is attained, of what it consists and where it resides may point the way for requirements engineering, since universal principles are the bedrock on which predictive sciences are based.

13 Supporting interdisciplinary design: towards pattern languages for workplaces

Thomas Erickson

Introduction

I am concerned with design, particularly with the issue of how to design systems that mesh gracefully with the practices and activities of particular workplaces. This concern gives rise to a number of questions: how do designers come to understand a new workplace? How do they get a sense of the sorts of activities that occur within it, and with which their design must coexist? How do designers avoid or minimise disruptions caused by the inevitable changes a new system will introduce? How do they figure out how to design things that are useful, and not just usable?

Workplace research is a vital part of any answer to these questions. However, from my vantage point as a practitioner of design, it seems very unlikely that a thorough research phase will become a standard part of design practice. Systems design and implementation typically takes place under considerable limitations of time and resources; it seems unlikely that this will change. To me, this suggests a clear conclusion: we need ways of allowing the results of workplace studies to be reused in new and different situations.

But in what form should the results of workplace studies be presented? This is a difficult problem because most designers are not versed in the disciplines and assumptions that underlie workplace research; workplace studies are not accessible to those who need them the most. The problem is compounded by the fact that those involved in systems design lack *any* core discipline. Systems are being designed by computer scientists, anthropologists, psychologists, visual designers and industrial designers; furthermore, the advent of new technological domains such as multimedia and virtual spaces are creating roles for architects, interior designers, musicians and film-makers. Even end-users (who are actually no more homogeneous in their backgrounds than 'designers') are involved in design.

I suggest that we are faced with a problem of representation. We need ways of representing knowledge about the workplace so that it is accessible to the increasingly diverse set of people involved in design. Ideally, we want not only to represent workplace knowledge, but to provide a framework within which it can be discussed, explicated, extended and generalised. In the absence of a shared discipline or conceptual framework, I believe that this means that knowledge must be embodied in a concrete, recognisable form, in the terms of the design's target domain: the workplace. This brings us to pattern languages, which, I suggest, deserve serious consideration as a representational mechanism for workplace design.

Pattern languages

The concept of a pattern language has been developed by Christopher Alexander and his colleagues in architecture and urban design (Alexander, 1979; Alexander *et al.*, 1977). In brief, a pattern language is a network of patterns of varying scales; each pattern is embodied as a concrete prototype, and is related to larger scale patterns which it supports, and to smaller scale patterns which support it. The goal of a pattern language is to capture patterns in their contexts, and to provide a mechanism for understanding the non-local consequences of design decisions.

Alexander's pattern language is more than an engaging theory. It has been in use since the late 1970s, and has been applied to the design of everything from rooms to communities (see Fromm and Bosselmann (1985) for references to a number of published accounts). Alexander's approach has a relatively small following among architects, many of whom are hostile to his methods or alienated by his rhetoric. Most of its use appears to be by those outside the mainstream of the architecture profession – designer-builders, and people with no design training who simply wish to expand or build their own houses, either by themselves or in collaboration with pattern-language-friendly architects.[1] A piece of corroborating evidence is that Alexander's book of design patterns, *A Pattern Language* (Alexander *et al.*, 1977), continues to be a best selling architecture book after two decades on the market, even though it is available only as a rather expensive hardback.

Since the late 1980s the pattern language approach has attracted a lot of interest in the field of object oriented software design. There is an active software patterns community with an annual conference, mailing lists and web sites (see the patterns home page).[2] Software patterns have been receiving increasing attention from mainstream computer science, with a special issue of *Communications of the ACM* on software patterns (D. Schmidt *et al.*, 1996) joining the growing number of books on the subject (e.g. Coplien, 1995; Gabriel, 1996; Gamma *et al.*, 1995). In contrast, the approach discussed in this chapter is very much in its exploratory phase; to my knowledge, no workplace pattern languages have been published.

It is important to note that the approach discussed in this chapter differs from those taken both by Alexander and the software design community. The principal difference is that this chapter emphasises the use of pattern languages as a descriptive device, a lingua franca for creating a common ground among people who lack a shared discipline or theoretical framework. In contrast, both Alexander and the software patterns community tend to use patterns more prescriptively. The software patterns community focuses on using patterns to capture accepted practice and support generalisation; Alexander's central concern is using patterns to achieve the ineffable 'quality without a name', which characterises great architecture. But these are differences of emphasis; in spite of my focus on patterns as a lingua franca, generalisation, reuse of design knowledge, and increased quality of design all seem to me to be possible and desirable outcomes of pattern languages for workplaces.

The Alexandrian pattern language

Alexander's pattern language is described in two books, one of which provides the theory and usage model (Alexander, 1979) and the other a language for planning and building which consists of a network of 253 patterns (Alexander *et al.*, 1977). The patterns range in scale from a pattern for the distribution of towns and cities down to a pattern for walls. The patterns are loosely connected across scales: any given pattern typically points to smaller scale patterns which can support it, and larger scale patterns in which it may participate. For example, the *Identifiable Neighbourhood* pattern (aimed at creating neighbourhoods with their own sense of place) invokes smaller scale patterns such as *Street Cafe*, *Individually Owned Shops* and *Corner Grocery*, and participates in larger scale patterns such as *Mosaic of Subcultures* which specify characteristics of communities.

The pattern language is *not* intended to be a book of patterns that is followed by rote. It is actually a meta-language which is used to generate languages for particular sites. For any particular situation a subset of existing patterns is selected; in addition, designers modify existing patterns and create new patterns that reflect the culture, environment, history, customs and goals of the site's location and inhabitants. These patterns – old, modified and new – form a site-specific language which is used to guide reflection and discussion about the relationships among the site, the proposed design and the activities of the inhabitants.

Each pattern is presented in a standard form. For example, the *Street Cafe* pattern (Alexander *et al.*, 1977) begins with its name, number and a photograph of a street café. The first paragraph describes some of the larger scale patterns of which it is part (e.g. *Activity Node*). Next is a statement of the essence of the pattern which illustrates the various forces responsible for the existence and nature of the pattern. This is followed by an often lengthy rationale section which describes the background of the pattern, evidence for its validity, ways in which the pattern can be manifested and so on. For *Street Cafe*, the rationale ranges from a careful description of the experience of being in a café, to an analysis of the elements of successful street cafés, to a discussion of a survey on the role played by student-oriented cafés in educational settings. *Street Cafe* concludes with a diagram and short statement describing how to implement the key features discussed in the rationale and with a paragraph describing smaller scale patterns (e.g. *Opening to the Street*, *A Place to Wait* and *Sitting Wall*) which may be used to strengthen this pattern.

Pattern languages as representational systems

Alexander's pattern language has a number of attributes that make it an interesting candidate for a lingua franca.

- **Concrete Prototypes:** Alexandrian patterns are embodied as concrete prototypes, rather than abstract principles. Every pattern comes with a name (generally sufficient to evoke an image), a picture of an archetype of the pattern and a diagram of how it is implemented. This is true for patterns at large scales (e.g. *Agricultural Valleys*; *Ring Roads*) and at small scales (e.g. *Thick Walls*; *Child Caves*). Whereas abstract principles require users of the principles to understand some conceptual framework and to be able to map the principles on to their domain of concern, the concrete prototypes in pattern languages make direct contact with the user's experience. Anyone who has experience with the situation can quickly understand, discuss and contest Alexandrian patterns.

- **Grounded in the Social:** Another characteristic is that the patterns tend to focus on the interactions between the physical form of the built environment and the way in which that inhibits or facilitates various sorts of personal and social behaviour within it. Thus, *Street Cafe* emphasises the importance of the café being located along a busy path because this facilitates casual meetings, people watching and so on. This linkage between the design components and usage reinforces the concrete, grounded nature of the pattern language.

- **Expresses Values:** Alexander's pattern language is not value neutral. Patterns such as *Individually Owned Shops, Bike Paths and Racks, Farmhouse Kitchen* and *Old Age Cottage* all manifest particular values in their names alone (and more explicitly in their rationales). While this aspect of *A Pattern Language* can alarm those who mistakenly believe it to be a universal prescription for architecture, I see its ability to explicitly express values as part of its representational power and as yet another way the language becomes grounded for its users.

Towards a workplace pattern language

An important aspect of Alexander's pattern language is that its aim is to support the design of the built environment. In contrast, a pattern language for describing workplaces has to embrace considerably more than the physical architecture. What else should such a pattern language include? What would it look like? How would it be used? The best way to answer such questions would be to develop a workplace pattern language; however, this is far beyond the scope of this chapter. Nevertheless, I believe it is instructive to make a small beginning in order to get a feel for what a language might be like and how it might be used.

An example: a consulting firm

My point of departure will be a study of a design consulting firm by Bellotti and Bly (1996). The company works with many clients at the same time and provides a wide range of services. Its designers and engineers work on project-oriented teams (often more than one at a time), which form and reform as new projects begin and old ones end. The company culture encourages kibitzing (unsolicited commentary offered by onlookers) and informal collaborations across team boundaries. The consulting firm is geographically distributed and it is not unusual for the members of a project team to be located in different buildings, or even in different cities. While Bellotti and Bly (1996) did a general study of the company, their report focused on what they called 'local mobility' (the tendency of workers to be away from their desks) and its impact on collaboration with local and remote co-workers. What I propose to do is recast some of their results into pattern language form.

In recasting the results of this study as patterns, a couple of issues immediately arise. First, it turns out that some of the patterns from Alexander's architectural pattern language are relevant. For example, the Alexandrian patterns *The Flow Through Rooms* and *Office Connections* discuss the way in which the interconnection of rooms and the traffic through them can facilitate or inhibit spontaneous interaction – something that is an issue in Bellotti and Bly's study. Thus, a workplace pattern language might be able to build on some of the work that Alexander and his colleagues have already done. However, it is also clear that new patterns need to be added to describe the consulting firm offices; for example, a pattern language for this site would need to include patterns for *Model Shop*, *Central Scanning Station* and *Open Plan Offices*, all spaces which play important roles in the life of this workplace.

In addition to new patterns describing spatial components of the workplace, new patterns are needed to describe two other entities: activities and roles. Activities range from formal events like a *Client Presentation*, to informal activities such as *Kibitzing*. Roles found in this workplace include *Manager, Engineer, Designer, Receptionist* and so on. As with spatial patterns, patterns for roles and activities would describe the role or activity itself, its context and rationale and its relationship to other patterns.

A sketch of a consulting firm pattern language

Let us look at some of the patterns that could describe the consulting firm. Because space is limited, I shall summarise the patterns; normally a pattern takes up several pages and has a well-defined canonical structure. After describing a few patterns and alluding to others, I shall discuss some of the ways in which a consulting firm pattern language might be used.

The largest scale pattern might be called *Consulting Firm*: its goal would be to characterise the consulting business by describing the various forces which shape it. Thus the pattern would depict the firm's need to act quickly and flexibly to get, keep and complete projects, balanced with its need to do this with a relatively fixed set of human resources and limited amounts of time and materials. *Consulting Firm* would also describe the multiple clients, simultaneous projects, loose teams and informal collaborations that occur in the firm. It would end with pointers to the smaller scale patterns which support *Consulting Firm*.

These patterns would include the following:

- **Maintaining Mutual Awareness**

  Bellotti and Bly (1996) observed that it was important for designers and engineers to keep up-to-date with what was going on, regardless of the projects with which they were involved. This practice helped the company bring a wide range of expertise to bear on problems and was a good counterbalance to the potential inflexibility of project-oriented teams. *Maintaining Mutual Awareness* is supported by a number of smaller scale activity patterns, ranging from *Blanket Email* (the custom of addressing email messages with questions or answers to large groups) to *Kibitzing*, to what one engineer called *Doing a Walkabout* (i.e. wandering through the work areas just to see what others were up to). *Maintaining Mutual Awareness* was also supported by spatial patterns such as *Open Offices*, *Model Shop* and *Central Scanning Station*.

- **Locally Mobile Worker**

  This pattern captures the fact that many engineers and designers spend considerable time away from their desks, but are still in the general vicinity. On the one hand, workers are pulled away from their desks by the need to get access to immobile shared resources such as *Model Shop* and *Central Scanning Station*, or to find local co-workers with whom they need to collaborate. On the other hand, they are pulled back to their desks by the need to use desk-based personal resources (PCs, telephones, voice mail) or to collaborate with remote colleagues. Thus, the engineers and designers spend considerable time moving about, a fact which – as Bellotti and Bly note – has considerable consequences for how they accomplish their work. To the extent that locally mobile workers encounter others (determined, in part, by *Open Offices*), this pattern supports *Maintaining Mutual Awareness*, at least for co-workers in the same locale.

Another pattern that goes hand in hand with *Locally Mobile Workers* is:

- **Receptionist as Hub**

  The mobility of many workers produces a need for coordination, a way for one person to locate another when the need arises. In this workplace Bellotti and Bly discovered that the receptionist played an important role in keeping track of people. This arose because her location and continuous presence at the entrance enabled her to observe the arrivals and departures of people. This was facilitated by her role as the conference room coordinator, which resulted in her being aware of the time, location and composition of meetings. Finally, some employees, recognising her role as *de facto* coordinator, had adopted the practice of informing her of their anticipated whereabouts.

Many other patterns could be described – *Open Offices*, *Shared Resources*, *Kibitzing*, *Blanket Email* and *Doing a Walkabout* – but this is enough to give a flavour of what the consulting firm pattern language would be like.

Discussion

Let us stop and look at what is emerging here.

First, even in this fragment of a pattern language, we are seeing the basic characteristics of the Alexandrian language for built environments. We see the growth of a set of interrelated patterns at multiple scales: *Maintaining Mutual Awareness* is supported by *Locally Mobile Workers*, *Kibitzing* and *Blanket Email*; *Locally Mobile Workers*, in turn, is supported by *Receptionist as Hub*. These patterns also focus on the interplay between the social and the physical, as in *Receptionist as Hub* being facilitated by the need for a person to coordinate the conference rooms. We also see that this language embodies values: *Kibitzing* and *Doing a Walkabout* are positive patterns that are supported by this firm's culture; it is easy to imagine workplaces in which such activities would be frowned upon.

Now let us look at some of the ways a consulting firm pattern language might be used. One use could be to better anticipate the impact of new systems on the consulting firm. For instance, imagine that the consulting firm is considering the purchase of an automatic scheduling system. While the first order effects of this might be to reduce the receptionist's workload and to provide employees with more immediate access to room scheduling, *Receptionist as Hub* suggests that such a change might have less beneficial second order effects: reducing the receptionist's involvement in meeting scheduling might well reduce her effectiveness in keeping track of employees' whereabouts. Similarly, switching from open offices to closed ones would clearly have an impact on *Maintaining Mutual Awareness* and *Kibitzing*. The point here is not that these patterns and their relationships should be used to reject or approve changes, but rather that they can be used as a language for discussing changes and reflecting on their possible impacts.

Another use of the consulting firm pattern language would be as a starting point for understanding a different type of workplace. Patterns from the consulting firm language can be sought in other types of workplaces. For example, a design team charged with implementing a new system in a hotel might, beginning with the consulting firm language, investigate the extent to which *Locally Mobile Workers* was present. If so, the workplace pattern language developed for consulting firms becomes a rich source of questions and hypotheses. What are the forces that sustain the *Locally Mobile Workers* pattern in this context – are they similar to those in the consultancy domain? In the consulting firm language, *Locally Mobile Workers* is supported by *Receptionist as Hub* – how do workers in the hotel domain achieve coordination? And so on.

Finally, we can see how, over time, the consulting firm pattern language might be generalised. For example, the design team studying the hotel might find that hotel workers achieve coordination primarily by means of shared objects, like bulletin boards and work sheets, rather than by relying on a person. The design team might devise a *Coordination Object* pattern that captures their findings and also the findings of other researchers; for example, other coordination objects in the literature are flight strips in air traffic control (Harper *et al.*, 1991), navigation charts in ship piloting (Hutchins, 1990) and timetables in control rooms for the London Underground (Heath and Luff, 1991). Over time we might see the development of a large-scale pattern, *Activity Coordination*, that can be supported by either artefacts (*Coordinating Objects*) or by social roles (*Coordinator*).

Conclusion

Design is becoming increasingly interdisciplinary. Neither 'designers' nor 'end-users' are homogenous groups; they lack common disciplines, practices and conceptual frameworks. All that we can realistically expect those involved in design to share is access to the situation for which they are designing. As a consequence, pattern languages, with their emphasis on embodying design knowledge as a network of concrete prototypes, have the potential to serve as a lingua franca for workplace design.

One question that might be posed is what advantages pattern languages offer over the more traditional means of presenting the results of workplace studies. In the course of this chapter, I have suggested the following:

- Patterns, especially smaller scale patterns, are more concrete, more tightly bound to the situation at hand and thus more accessible to an audience that lacks a common disciplinary framework.
- Recasting the results of workplace studies as a network of interrelated patterns results in the modularisation of workplace knowledge and thus makes it easier to take a subset of a pattern language and apply it to a new type of workplace.
- This modularisation also makes pattern languages more amenable to generalisation across workplaces.

However, the most important advantage is a side-effect of the form of representation. I believe that patterns are most likely to be created, developed and utilised by an audience that is largely distinct from those who read and write research papers.[3] The fact is that the communicative goals of pattern languages and research papers are quite different. The values that underlie research and lead to the publication or rejection of workplace studies, have to do with accuracy, careful examination and analysis of particular cases and new contributions to the literature. However, design teams faced with a new workplace and a short schedule have considerably more pragmatic needs. They need information that can be mastered quickly, applied to new situations and used as a basis for dialogue with their users. While researchers may, with full justice, be wary of the simplification and generalisation encouraged by casting workplace research as patterns – this is precisely what design teams need. If pattern languages can assist design teams in communicating effectively with their users, noticing connections between activities and artefacts that would have been otherwise missed, or simply decrease the time between encountering a workplace and being able to ask useful questions, they will be a boon to design.

Acknowledgements

Thanks are due to Victoria Bellotti, Paul Dourish, Beki Grinter, Don Norman, Lucy Suchman, John Thomas, Mike Tschudy and David Warren for comments on and discussions of various aspects of this chapter. I am indebted to two architects, Dale Mulfinger and Robert Boylin, who spent considerable time providing me with practising architects' perspectives on Alexander's pattern language, as well as helping me to understand its reception and use by lay folk and by professional architects. Finally, discussions in the CHI '97 Workshop on Interaction Pattern Languages deepened my understanding of these issues.

NOTES

1 D. Mulfinger, personal communication, in a conversation on 12 July 1996, Minneapolis, Minnesota, USA.
2 http://hillside.net/patterns/patterns.html
3 For links to such activity see the Interaction Design Home Page at: http://www.pliant.org/personal/Tom_Erickson/InteractionPatterns.html

Bibliography

Abel, M. J. (1990). Experiences in an Exploratory Distributed Organization, in *Intellectual Teamwork: The Social and Technological Foundations of Cooperative Work*, Kraut, R. E., Galegher, J. and Egido, C. (eds.), pp. 489–510. Hillsdale, NJ: Lawrence Erlbaum.

Agre, P. E. (1997). *Computation and Human Experience.* Cambridge: Cambridge University Press.

Agre, P. E. and Chapman, D. (1987). Pengi: An Implementation of a Theory of Activity, in *Proceedings of the Sixth Conference of the American Association for Artificial Intelligence (AAAI)*, pp. 268–72. Seattle, WA.

Alexander, C. (1979). *A Timeless Way of Building.* Oxford: Oxford University Press.

Alexander, C., Ishikawa, S., Silverstein, M., Jacobson, M., Fiksdahl-King, I. and Angel, S. (1977). *A Pattern Language: Towns, Buildings, Construction.* Oxford: Oxford University Press.

Anderson, R. J. (1994). Representation and Requirements: The Value of Ethnography in System Design, *Human–Computer Interaction* 9(2): 151–82.

(1997). Work, Ethnography, and System Design, in *The Encyclopedia of Microcomputing*, Kent, A. and Williams, J. G. (eds.), pp. 159–83. New York: Marcel Dekker.

Anderson, R. J., Hughes, J. A. and Sharrock, W. W. (1989). *Working for Profit: The Social Organisation of Calculation in an Entrepreneurial Firm.* Aldershot: Avebury.

Baecker, R. M., Grudin, J., Buxton, W. A. S. and Greenberg, S. (eds.) (1987). *Readings in Human–Computer Interaction: Towards the Year 2000*, 2nd edn. San Mateo, CA: Morgan Kaufmann.

Bannon, L. J. (1991). From Human Factors to Human Actors: The Role of Psychology and Human–Computer Interaction Studies in Systems Design, in *Design at Work: Cooperative Design of Computer Systems*, Greenbaum, J. and Kyng, M. (eds.), pp. 25–44. Hillsdale, NJ: Lawrence Erlbaum.

(1995). The Politics of Design: Representing Work, *Communications of the ACM.* 38(9): 66–8.

(1997). Dwelling in the "Great Divide": The Case of HCI and CSCW, in *Social Science, Technical Systems and Co-operative Work: Beyond the Great Divide*, Bowker, G., Leigh Star, S., Turner, B. and Gasser, L. (eds.), pp. 355–78. Mahwah, NJ: Lawrence Erlbaum.

Bannon, L. J. and Bødker, S. (1991). Beyond the Interface: Encountering Artifacts in Use, in *Designing Interaction: Psychology at the Human–Computer Interface*, Carroll, J. M. (ed.), pp. 227–55. Cambridge: Cambridge University Press.

Barley, S. and Orr, J. (eds.) (1997). *Between Craft and Science*. Ithaca, NY and London: IRL Press/Cornell University Press.

Barnard, P. (1991). Bridging between Basic Theories and the Artifacts of Human–Computer Interaction, in *Designing Interaction: Psychology at the Human–Computer Interface*, Carroll, J. M. (ed.), pp. 103–27. Cambridge: Cambridge University Press.

Beach, K. (1988). *The Role of External Mnemonic Symbols in Acquiring an Occupation, Practical Aspects of Memory 1*. Chichester: John Wiley.

Bellotti, V. and Bly, S. (1996). Walking Away from the Desktop Computer: Distributed Collaboration and Mobility in a Product Design Team, in *Proceedings of CSCW '96*, pp. 209–18 Cambridge, MA.

Benford, S. and Greenhalgh, C. (1997). Introducing Third Party Objects into the Spatial Model of Interaction, in *Proceedings of ECSCW '97*, pp. 189–204. Lancaster.

Bentley, R. and Dourish, P. (1995). Medium vs Message: Supporting Collaboration through Customisation, in *Proceedings of ECSCW '95*, pp. 133–48. Stockholm, Sweden.

Bentley, R., Hughes, J. A., Randall, D., Rodden, T., Sawyer, P., Shapiro, D. and Sommerville, I. (1992). Ethnographically Informed System Design for Air Traffic Control, in *Proceedings of CSCW '92*, pp. 123–9. Toronto.

Berkenkotter, C. and Ravotas, D. (1997). Genre as Tool in the Transmission of Practice over Time and across Professional Boundaries, *Mind, Culture, and Activity*. 4: 256–74.

Bijker, W. E. and Law, J. (eds.) (1992). *Shaping Technology/Building Society: Studies in Technological Change*. Cambridge, MA: MIT Press.

Blomberg, J. L., Giacomi, J., Mosher, A. and Swenton-Wall, P. (1993). Ethnographic Field Methods and their Relation to Design, in *Participatory Design: Principles and Practices*, Schuler, D. and Namioka, A. (eds.), pp. 123–55. Hillsdale, NJ: Lawrence Erlbaum.

Blomberg, J. L., Suchman, L. and Trigg, R. (1996). Reflections on a Work-Oriented Design Project, *Human–Computer Interaction* 11: 237–65.

   (1997). Back to Work: Renewing Old Agendas for Cooperative Design, in *Computers and Design in Context*, Kyng, M. and Mathiassen, L. (eds.), pp. 267–87. Cambridge, MA: MIT Press.

Bly, S. A., Harrison, S. and Irwin, S. (1992). Media Spaces: Bringing People Together in a Video, Audio and Computing Environment, *Communications of the ACM* 36(1): 28–47.

Blythin, S., Rouncefield, M. and Hughes, J. A. (1997). Never Mind the Ethno' Stuff, What Does All This Mean and What Do WE Do Now: Ethnography in the Commercial World, *Interactions* 4(3): 38–47.

Bourgine, P. and Varela, F. J. (1992). Introduction: Towards a Practice of Autonomous Systems, in *Towards a Practice of Autonomous Systems*, Varela, F. J. and Bourgine, P. (eds.), pp. xi–xvii. Cambridge, MA: MIT Press.

Bowers, J. (1994). The Work to Make a Network Work: Studying CSCW in Action, in *Proceedings of CSCW '94,* pp. 287–98. Chapel Hill, NC.

Bowers, J. and Button, G. (1995). Workflow from Within and Without: Technology and Cooperative Work on the Print Industry Shop Floor, in *Proceedings of ECSCW '95,* pp. 51–66. Stockholm.

Bowers, J. and Pycock, J. (1994). Talking Through Design: Requirements and Resistance in Cooperative Prototyping, in *Proceedings of CHI '94,* pp. 299–305. Boston, MA.

Bowers, J., Pycock, J. and O'Brien, J. (1995). Talk and Embodiment in Collaborative Writing Environments, submission to CHI '96, Department of Psychology, University of Manchester.

Bowers, J., O'Brien, J. and Pycock, J. (1996). Practically Accomplishing Immersion: Cooperation in and for Virtual Environments, in *Proceedings of CSCW '96,* pp. 380–9. Cambridge, MA.

Bowker, G. and Star, S. L. (1991). Situations vs. Standards in Long-term, Wide-scale Decision-making: The Case of the International Classification of Diseases, in *Proceedings of Twenty-Fourth Annual Hawaii International Conference on System Sciences,* pp. 73–81. Kauai, Hawaii.

(1994). Knowledge and Infrastructure in International Information Management: Problems of Classification and Coding, in *Information Acumen: The Understanding and Use of Knowledge in Modern Business,* Bud-Friedman, L. (ed.), pp. 187–213. London: Routledge.

Brooks, F. P. (1972). *The Mythical Man-Month.* Reading, MA: Addison-Wesley.

Brooks, R. (1987). *Planning is Just a Way of Avoiding What to do Next.* Working Paper, MIT AI-Lab, Cambridge, MA.

(1990). Elephants Don't Play Chess, in Designing Autonomous Agents, special issue of *Robotics and Autonomous Systems.* 6(1–2): 3–16.

(1991). Intelligence without Representation, i, Foundations of Artificial Intelligence, special volume of *Artificial Intelligence* 47: 139–59.

Brown, J. S. and Duguid, P. (1994). Borderline Issues: Social and Material Aspects of Design, *Human–Computer Interaction* 9(1): 3–36.

Bryant, C. (1996). *Practical Sociology, Post Empiricism and the Reconstruction of Theory as Application.* Oxford: Polity Press.

Bucciarelli, L. L. (1984). Reflective Practice in Engineering Design, *Design Studies.* 53: 185–90.

(1988). An Ethnographic Perspective on Engineering Design, *Design Studies* 9(3): 159–68.

(1994). *Designing Engineers.* Cambridge, MA: MIT Press.

Button, G. (1993a). The Curious Case of the Disappearing Technology, in *Technology in Working Order,* Button, G. (ed.), pp. 10–28. London: Routledge.

(ed.) (1993b). *Technology in Working Order: Studies in Work, Interaction and Technology.* London: Routledge.

Button, G. and Dourish, P. (1996). Technomethodology: Paradoxes and Possibilities, in *Proceedings of CHI '96,* pp. 19–26. Vancouver, BC.

Button, G. and Sharrock, W. (1994). Occasioned Practices in the Work of Software Engineers, in *Requirements Engineering: Social and Technical Issues,* Jirotka, M. and Goguen, J. (eds.), pp. 217–40. London: Academic Press.

(1995). On Simulacrums of Conversation: Towards a Clarification of the Relevance of Conversation Analysis for Human–Computer Interaction, in *The Social and Interactional Dimensions of Human–Computer Interfaces*, Thomas, P. (ed.), pp. 107–25. Cambridge: Cambridge University Press.

(1996). Project Work: The Organisation of Collaborative Design and Development in Software Engineering, *Computer Supported Cooperative Work: Journal of Collaborative Computing*, 5(5): 369–86.

(1998). The Organisational Accountability of Technological Work, *Social Studies of Science* 28(1): 73–102.

Button, G., Coulter, J., Lee, J. and Sharrock, W. (1995). *Computers, Minds and Conduct*. Cambridge: Polity Press.

Caines, E. (1997). A Health Lesson I Never Wanted: Need for National Health Service Reforms, *New Statesman* 9 May.

Calvey, D., Hughes, J. A., O'Brien, J., Rodden, T. and Rouncefield, M. (1997). On Becoming a DNP User: Some Reflections on the Developing Use of a Computer Support Tool, in *Proceedings of IRIS '20*, pp. 215–236. Oslo.

Carasik, R. P. and Grantham, C. E. (1988). A Case Study of CSCW in a Dispersed Organisation, in *Proceedings of CHI '88* pp. 61–5. Washington, DC.

Card, S. K., Moran, T. and Newell, A. (1983). *The Psychology of Human–Computer Interaction*. Hillsdale, NJ: Lawrence Erlbaum.

Carroll, J. M. (ed.) (1991). *Designing Interaction: Psychology at the Human–Computer Interface*. Cambridge: Cambridge University Press.

Carroll, J. M. and Campbell, R. (1989). Artifacts as Psychological Theories: The Case of Human–Computer Interaction, *Behaviour and Information Technology* 8: 247–56.

Clancey, W. J. (1997). *Situated Cognition: On Human Knowledge and Computer Representations*. Cambridge: Cambridge University Press.

Clarke, A. and Fujimura, J. (eds.) (1992). *The Right Tool for the Job: At Work in Twentieth Century Life Science*. Princeton, NJ: Princeton University Press.

Clement, A. (1993). Looking for Designers: Transforming the 'Invisible' Infrastructure of Computerized Office Work, *Artificial Intelligence and Society*. 7: 323–44.

Collins, H. M. (1990). *Artificial Experts: Social Knowledge and Expert Systems*. Cambridge, MA: MIT Press.

Collins, T. and Bicknell, D. (1997). *Crash: Ten Easy Ways to Avoid Computer Disaster*. London: Simon & Schuster.

Comic Deliverable 2.3 (1995). *Tool Support for CSCW Requirements*. Esprit Basic Research Project 6225. Lancaster University.

Comic Deliverable 2.4. (1995). *CSCW Requirements Development*. Esprit Basic Research Project 6225. Lancaster University.

Cooper, G., Hine, C., Rachel, J. and Woolgar, S. (1995). Ethnography and Human–Computer Interaction, in *The Social and Interactional Dimensions of Human–Computer Interfaces*, Thomas, P. (ed.), pp. 11–36. Cambridge: Cambridge University Press.

Coplien, J. O. (1995). A Generative Development-Process Pattern Language, in *Pattern Languages of Program Design*, Coplien, J. O. and Schmidt, D. C. (eds.), pp. 183–237. Reading, MA: Addison-Wesley.

Coulter, J. (1983). *Rethinking Cognitive Theory*. London: Macmillan.

(1989). *Mind in Action*. Cambridge: Polity Press.

(1991). Logic: Ethnomethodology and The Logic of Language, in *Ethnomethodology and the Human Sciences: A Foundational Reconstruction*, Button, G. (ed.), pp. 20–50. Cambridge: Cambridge University Press.

Dandeker, C. (1990). *Surveillance, Power and Modernity*. Cambridge: Polity Press.

Davis, A. M. (1993). *Software Requirements: Objects, Functions and States*, 2nd edn. Englewood Cliffs, NJ: Prentice-Hall.

Dixit, A. and Pindyck, R. (1995). The Options Approach to Capital Investment, *Harvard Business Review* (May–June): 105–15.

Dourish, P., Adler, A., Bellotti, V. and Henderson, H. (1996). Your Place or Mine? Learning from Long-Term Use of Video Communication, *Computer Supported Cooperative Work: Journal of Collaborative Computing* 5(1): 33–62.

Dreyfus, H. L. ([1972] 1992). *What Computers Still Can't Do: A Critique of Artificial Reason*. Cambridge, MA: MIT Press.

Ellis, C. A., Keddara, K. and Rozenberg, G. (1995). Dynamic Change within Workflow Systems, in *Proceedings of COOCS '95 Conference on Organizational Computing Systems*, pp. 10–21. Milpitas, CA.

Engeström, Y. (1987). *Learning by Expanding: An Activity-Theoretical Approach to Developmental Research*. Helsinki: Orienta-Konsulit.

(1993). Developmental Studies of Work as a Testbench of Activity Theory: The Case of Primary Care Medical Practice, in *Understanding Practice: Perspectives on Activity and Context*, Lave, J. and Chaiklin, S. (eds.), pp. 3–31. Cambridge: Cambridge University Press.

(1995). Objects, Contradictions and Collaboration in Medical Cognition: An Activity-Theoretical Perspective, *Artificial Intelligence in Medicine*. 7: 395–412.

(1996). Development as Breaking Away and Opening up: A Challenge to Vygotsky and Piaget, *Swiss Journal of Psychology* 55: 126–32.

Engeström, Y. and Escalante, V. (1996). Mundane Tool or Object of Affection? The Rise and Fall of the Postal Buddy, in *Context and Consciousness: Activity and Human–Computer Interaction*, Nardi, B. A. (ed.), pp. 325–73. Cambridge, MA: MIT Press.

Engeström, Y. and Middleton, D. (eds.) (1996). *Cognition and Communication at Work*. Cambridge: Cambridge University Press.

Erickson, T. (1996). Design as Storytelling, *Interactions*. 3(4): 30–5.

Evans, C. (1979). *The Mighty Micro: The Impact of the Micro-Chip Revolution*. Sevenoaks: Hodder & Stoughton.

Ferguson, C. H. (1988). From the People Who Brought You Voodoo Economics, *Harvard Business Review*. (May–June): 55–62.

Filippi, G. (1994). La Construction collective de la régulation du trafic du R.E.R.: Etude ergonomique dans une perspective de conception de situations d'aide à la coopération. thèse de doctorat d'ergonomie. Université Paris XIII.

Filippi, G. and Theureau, J. (1993). Analysing Cooperative Work in an Urban Traffic Control Room for the Design of a Coordination Support System, in *Proceedings of ECSCW '93*, pp. 171–86. Milan.

Finkelstein, A., Kramer, B., Nuseibeh, B. and Goedicke, M. (1992). Viewpoints: A Framework for Integrating Multiple Perspectives in System Development, *International Journal of Software Engineering and Knowledge Engineering* 2(1): 31–58.

Fitzpatrick, G., Kaplan, S. and Mansfield, T. (1996). Physical Spaces, Virtual Spaces and Social Worlds: A Study of Work in the Virtual, in *Proceedings of CSCW '96*, pp. 334–43. Cambridge, MA.

Fromm, D. and Bosselmann, P. (1985). Mexicali Revisited: Seven Years Later, *Places* 1(4): 78–91.

Fuchs, L., Pankoke-Babatz, U. and Prinz, W. (1995). Supporting Cooperative Awareness with Local Event Mechanisms: The GroupDesk System, in *Proceedings of ECSCW '95*, pp. 245–60. Stockholm.

Gabriel, R. P. (1996). *Patterns of Software: Tales from the Software Community*. New York: Oxford University Press.

Galison, P. (1997). *Image and Logic: A Material Culture of Microphysics*. Chicago: University of Chicago Press.

Gamma, E., Helm, R., Johnson, R. and Vlissides, J. (1995). *Design Patterns: Elements of Reusable Object-Oriented Software*. Reading, MA: Addison-Wesley.

Garfinkel, H. (1967). *Studies in Ethnomethodology*. Englewood Cliffs, NJ: Prentice-Hall.

(ed.) (1986). *Ethnomethodological Studies of Work*. London: Routledge & Kegan Paul.

Garfinkel, H. and Sacks, H. (1970). On Formal Structures of Practical Actions, in *Theoretical Sociology*, McKinney, J. C. and Tiryakian, E. A. (eds.), pp. 338–66. New York: Appleton-Century-Crofts.

Garfinkel, H., Lynch, M. and Livingston, E. (1981). The Work of a Discovering Science Construed with Materials from the Optically Discovered Pulsar, *Philosophy of the Social Sciences* 11: 131–58.

Gaver, W. W., Moran, T., Maclean, A., Lovstrand, L., Dourish, P., Carter, K. A. and Buxton, W. (1992). Realizing a Video Environment: EuroPARC's RAVE System, in *Proceedings of CHI '92*, pp. 27–35. Monterey, CA.

Gaver, W. W., Sellen, A., Heath, C. C. and Luff, P. (1993). One is Not Enough: Multiple Views in a Media Space, in *Proceedings of INTERCHI '93*, pp. 335–41. Amsterdam.

Gay, J.H. and Cole, M. (1967). *The New Mathematics and an Old Culture: A Study of Learning among the Kpelle of Liberia*. New York: Holt, Rinehart & Winston.

Geertz, C. (1973). *The Interpretation of Cultures*. New York: Basic Books.

(1983). *Local Knowledge: Further Essays in Interpretative Anthropology*. New York: Basic Books.

Gilder, G. (1991). Into the Telecosm, *Harvard Business Review* (March–April): 150–61.

Goffman, E. (1961). *Encounters*. Harmondsworth: Penguin.

(1964). The Neglected Situation, *American Anthropologist* 6(2): 133–6.

Goguen, J. A. (1994). Requirements Engineering as the Reconciliation of Social and Technical Issues, in *Requirements Engineering: Social and Technical Issues*, Jirotka, M. and Goguen, J. (eds.), pp. 165–200. London: Academic Press.

Goguen, J. A. and Linde, C. (1993). Techniques for Requirements Elicitation, in *Proceedings of RE '93: IEEE International Symposium on Requirements Engineering*, pp. 152–65. San Diego, CA.

Goodwin, C. (1994). Professional Vision, *American Anthropologist* 96(3): 606–33.

(1995). Seeing in Depth, *Social Studies of Science* 25(2): 237–74.

Goodwin, C. and Goodwin, M. H. (1996). Seeing as a Situated Activity: Formulating Planes, in *Cognition and Communication at Work*, Engeström, Y. and Middleton, D. (eds.), pp. 61–95. Cambridge: Cambridge University Press.

Goodwin, M. H. (1990). Announcements in their Environment: Back-To-Back Interaction in a Multi-Activity Work Setting, in *Proceedings of the Twelfth World Congress for Research on Activity Theory*, Lahti, Finland.

Grady, D. and Fincham, T. (1990). Making R & D Pay, *McKinsey Quarterly* 3: 22–9.

Gray, B. H. (1991). *The Profit Motive and Patient Care: The Changing Accountability of Doctors and Hospitals*. Cambridge, MA: Harvard University Press.

Greatbatch, D., Luff, P., Heath, C. C. and Campion, P. (1993). Interpersonal Communication and Human–Computer Interaction: An Examination of the Use of Computers in Medical Consultations, *Interacting with Computers* 5(2): 193–216.

Greenbaum, J. and Kyng, M. (eds.) (1991). *Design at Work: Cooperative Design of Computer Systems*. Hillsdale, NJ: Lawrence Erlbaum.

Grint, K. and Woolgar, S. (1997). *The Machine at Work: Technology, Work and Organization*. Cambridge: Polity Press.

Grønbæk, K. and Mogensen, P. (1997). Informing General CSCW Product Development through Cooperative Design in Specific Work Domains, *Computer Supported Cooperative Work: Journal of Collaborative Computing*. 6(4): 275–304.

Grudin, J. (1988). Why CSCW Applications Fail: Problems in the Design and Evaluation of Organizational Interfaces, in *Proceedings of CSCW '88*, pp. 85–93. Portland, OR.

(1993). Interface: An Evolving Concept, *Communications of the ACM* 36(4): 110–19.

Grudin, J. and Grinter, R. (1995). Ethnography and Design, *Computer Supported Cooperative Work: Journal of Collaborative Computing* 3: 55–9.

Hall, P. (1988). *Cities of Tomorrow*. Oxford: Blackwell.

Hammond, K., Converse, T. and Grass, J. (1995). The Stabilization of Environments, Computational Research on Interaction and Agency, special issue of *Artificial Intelligence* 72(1–2): 305–22.

Hanlon, M. D., Nadler, D. A. and Gladstein, D. (1985). *Attempting Work Reform: The Case of "Parkside" Hospital*. New York: Wiley.

Harper, R. (1992). Looking at Ourselves: An Examination of the Social Organization of Two Research Laboratories, in *Proceedings of CSCW '92*, pp. 330–7. Toronto.

(1995). The Faces of Information Work: Collaborative Tools, Information, and Organisational Symbols, presented at the Colloquium on Workplace Studies, King's College London.

(1996). *Requirements Analysis in Support of Organisational Work.* Cambridge: International Monetary Fund and Rank Xerox Research Centre.

(1997). Gatherers of Information: Some Remarks on the Mission Process at the International Monetary Fund, in *Proceedings of ECSCW '97*, pp. 361–76. Lancaster.

(1998). *Inside the IMF: An Ethnography of Documents, Technology and Organisational Action.* London: Academic Press.

Harper, R. and Hughes, J. (1993). 'What a F-ing System! Send 'em All to the Same Place and then Expect Us To Stop 'em Hitting': Making Technology Work in Air Traffic Control, in *Technology in Working Order*, Button, G. (ed.), pp. 127–44. London: Routledge.

Harper, R. and Newman, W. (1996). Designing for User Acceptance Using Analysis Techniques Based on Responsibility Modelling, in *Proceedings of CHI '96*, pp. 217–18. Vancouver, BC.

Harper, R., Hughes, J. and Shapiro, D. (1989). *The Functionality of Flight Strips in ATC Work: The Report for the Civil Aviation Authority.* Lancaster Sociotechnics Group, Department of Sociology, Lancaster University.

(1991). Working in Harmony: An Examination of Computer Technology and Air Traffic Control, in *Studies in Computer Supported Cooperative Work. Theory Practice and Design*, Bowers, J. and Benford, S. D. (eds.), pp. 225–34. Amsterdam: North-Holland.

Hartland, J. (1993). The Use of 'Intelligent' Machines for Electrocardiograph Interpretation, in *Technology in Working Order*, Button, G. (ed.), pp. 55–80. London: Routledge.

Heath, C. C. and Hindmarsh, J. (1997) Les Objets et leur environnement local. La Production interactionnelle de réalités matérielles, in *Raison pratiques. cognition et information en société*. Etudes en Sciences Sociales, pp. 149–76. Paris: Editions de l'Ecole des Hautes.

Heath, C. C. and Luff, P. (1991). Collaborative Activity and Technological Design: Task Coordination in London Underground Control Rooms, in *Proceedings of ECSCW '91*, pp. 65–80. Amsterdam.

(1992a). Collaboration and Control: Crisis Management and Multimedia Technology in London Underground Line Control Rooms, *Computer Supported Cooperative Work: Journal of Collaborative Computing*. 1(1–2): 69–94.

(1992b). Media Space and Communicative Asymmetries: Preliminary Observations of Video Mediated Interaction, *Human–Computer Interaction* 7: 315–46.

(1996a). Convergent Activities: Line Control and Passenger Information on London Underground, in *Cognition and Communication at Work*, Engeström, Y. and Middleton, D. (eds.), pp. 96–129. Cambridge: Cambridge University Press.

(1996b). Documents and Professional Practice: 'Bad' Organizational Reasons for 'Good' Clinical Records, in *Proceedings of CSCW '96*, pp. 354–63. Cambridge, MA.

Heath, C. C., Jirotka, M., Luff, P. and Hindmarsh, J. (1994–5). Unpacking Collaboration: the Interactional Organisation of Trading in a City Dealing Room, *Computer Supported Cooperative Work: Journal of Collaborative Computing* 3(2): 147–65.

Heath, C. C., Luff, P. and Sellen, A. (1995). Reconsidering the Virtual Workplace: Flexible Support for Collaborative Activity, in *Proceedings of ECSCW '95*, pp. 83–100. Stockholm.

Hekman, S. (1990). *Gender and Knowledge: Elements of a Postmodern Feminism.* Boston, MA: Northeastern University Press.

Henderson, A. and Kyng, M. (1991). There's No Place Like Home: Continuing Design in Use, in *Design at Work: Cooperative Design of Computer Systems*, Greenbaum, J. and Kyng, M. (eds.), Hillsdale, NJ: Lawrence Erlbaum.

Hindmarsh, J., Fraser, M., Heath, C. C., Benford, S. and Greenhalgh, C. (1998). Fragmented Interaction: Establishing Mutual Orientation in Virtual Environments, in *Proceedings of CSCW '98*, pp. 217–26. Seattle, WA.

Høeg, P. (1994). *Borderliners.* New York: Farrar, Straus & Giroux.

Hudson, S. E. and Smith, I. (1996). Techniques for Addressing Fundamental Privacy and Disruption Tradeoffs in Awareness Support Systems, in *Proceedings of CSCW '96*, pp. 248–67. Cambridge, MA.

Hughes, J. A. and King, V. (1992). Sociology for Large Scale System Design, in *Proceedings of Paper for Software and Systems Practice: Social Science Perspectives, CRICT (Centre for Research into Innovation, Culture and Technology, Brunel University) Conference*, Reading.

Hughes, J. A., Shapiro, D. Z., Sharrock, W. W., Anderson, R. A., Harper, R. R. and Gibbons, S. C. (1988). *The Automation of Air Traffic Control.* Final Report, Department of Sociology, Lancaster University.

Hughes, J. A., Randall, D. and Shapiro, D. (1993). From Ethnographic Record to System Design: Some Experiences from the Field, *Computer Supported Cooperative Work: Journal of Collaborative Computing* 1: 123–41.

Hughes, J. A., King, V., Rodden, T. and Andersen, H. (1994). Moving Out of the Control Room: Ethnography in System Design, in *Proceedings of CSCW '94*, pp. 429–40. Chapel Hill, NC.

Hughes, J., O'Brien, J., Rodden, T., Rouncefield, M. and Sommerville, I. (1995). Presenting Ethnography in the Requirements Process, in *Proceedings of Second IEEE International Symposium on Requirements Engineering*, pp. 27–35. University of York.

Hughes, J., O'Brien, J., Rouncefield, M. and Rodden, T. (1996). "They're Supposed to be Fixing It": Requirements and System Re-design, in *CSCW Requirements and Evaluation*, Thomas, P. (ed.). London: Springer-Verlag.

Hughes, J., O'Brien, J., Rodden, T., Rouncefield, M. and Blythin, S. (1997). Designing with Ethnography: A Presentation Framework for Design, in *Proceedings of Designing Interactive Systems '97*, pp. 147–58. Amsterdam.

Hutchins, E. L. (1990). The Technology of Team Navigation, in *Intellectual Teamwork: The Social and Technological Foundations of Cooperative Work*, Kraut, R. E., Galegher, J. and Egido, C. (eds.), pp. 191–221. Hillsdale, NJ: Lawrence Erlbaum.

(1991). Organizing Work by Adaptation, *Organization Science.* 2(1): 14–39.

(1995). *Cognition in the Wild.* Cambridge, MA: MIT Press.

Ilyenkov, E. V. (1982). *The Dialectics of the Abstract and the Concrete in Marx's Capital.* Moscow: Progress.

Ishii, H. (1990). TeamWorkStation: Towards a Seamless Shared Workspace, in *Proceedings of CSCW '90*, pp. 13–26. Los Angeles.

Ishii, H., Kobayashi, M. and Grudin, J. (1992). Integration of Inter-Personal Space and Shared Workspace: Clearboard Design and Experiments, in *Proceedings of CSCW '92*, pp. 33–42. Toronto.

Jessor, R., Colby, A. and Shweder, R. A. (1996). *Ethnography and Human Development: Context and Meaning in Social Inquiry*. Chicago: University of Chicago Press.

Jirotka, M., Luff, P. and Heath, C. (1993). Requirements for Technology in Complex Environments: Tasks and Interaction in a City Dealing Room, special issue of *SIGOIS Bulletin* in Do Users Get What They Want? (DUG '93), 14(2): 17–23.

Kaplan, S. M., Tolone, W. J., Bogia, D. P. and Bignoli, C. (1992). Flexible, Active Support for Collaborative Work with Conversation Builder, in *Proceedings of CSCW '92*, pp. 378–85. Toronto.

Kaplinsky, R. (1995). Patients as Work in Progress: Organisational Reform in the Health Sector, in *Europe's Next Step: Organisational Innovation, Competition and Employment*, Andreasen, L. E., Coriat, B., den Hertog, F. and Kaplinsky, R. (eds.). Ilford: Frank Cass.

Kaptelinin, V. (1996). Computer-Mediated Activity: Functional Organs in Social and Developmental Contexts, in *Context and Consciousness: Activity and Human–Computer Interaction*, Nardi, B. A. (ed.), pp. 45–68. Cambridge, MA: MIT Press.

Kirsh, D. (1995). The Intelligent Use of Space, Computational Research on Interaction and Agency, special issue of *Artificial Intelligence* 72(1–2): 31–68.

Klein, L. (1993). On the Collaboration between Scientists and Engineers, in *The Social Engagement of Social Science*, Trist, E. and Murray, H. (eds.), pp. 369–84. Philadelphia, PA: University of Pennsylvania Press.

Kling, R. (1980). Social Analyses of Computing: Theoretical Perspectives in Recent Empirical Research, *ACM Computing Surveys* 12(1): 61–110.

Kolodner, J. (1993). *Case-Based Reasoning*. San Mateo, CA: Morgan Kaufmann.

Kotonya, G. and Sommerville, I. (1992). Viewpoints for Requirements Definition, *Software Engineering Journal* 7(6): 375–87.

Kuutti, K. (1996). Activity Theory as a Potential Framework for Human–Computer Interaction Research, in *Context and Consciousness: Activity and Human–Computer Interaction*, Nardi, B. A. (ed.), pp. 17–44. Cambridge, MA: MIT Press.

Kuutti, K. and Bannon, L. J. (1991). Some Confusions at the Interface: Re-conceptualising the "Interface" Problem, in *Proceedings of Human Jobs and Computer Interfaces Conference*, pp. 3–19. Tampere, Finland.

(1993). Searching for Unity Among Diversity: Exploring the Interface Concept, in *Proceedings of ACM/IFIP Conference InterCHI '93, Human Factors in Information Systems*, pp. 263–8. Amsterdam.

Kyng, M. (1995). Making Representations Work, *Communications of the ACM* 38(9): 46–55.

Landauer, T. K. (1987a). Psychology as a Mother of Invention, in *Proceedings of CHI+GI '87, Human Factors in Computing Systems and Graphics Interface*, pp. 333–5. Toronto,

(1987b). Relations between Cognitive Psychology and Computer Systems Design, in *Interfacing Thought, Cognitive Aspects of Human–Computer Interaction*, Carroll, J. M. (ed.), pp. 1–25. Cambridge, MA: MIT Press.

Latour, B. (1990). Drawing Things Together, in *Representation in Scientific Practice*, Lynch, M. and Woolgar, S. (eds.), pp. 19–68. Cambridge: MIT Press.

Lave, J. (1988). *Cognition in Practice: Mind, Mathematics and Culture in Everyday Life*. Cambridge: Cambridge University Press.

(1993). The Practice of Learning, in *Understanding Practice*, Lave, J. and Chaiklin, S. (eds.), pp. 3–31. Cambridge: Cambridge University Press.

Lave, J., Murtaugh, M. and de la Rocha, O. (1984). The Dialectic of Arithmetic in Grocery Shopping, in *Everyday Cognition*, Rogoff, B. and Lave, J. (eds.), pp. 67–94. Cambridge, MA: Harvard University Press.

Law, J. (1991). Introduction: Monsters, Machines and Sociotechnical Relations, in *A Sociology of Monsters*, Law, J. (ed.), Sociological Review Monograph 38, pp. 1–25. London: Routledge.

Leonard-Barton, D. (1992). Core Capabilities and Core Rigidities: A Paradox in Managing New Product Development, *Strategic Management Journal* 13: 111–25.

Leont'ev, A. N. (1978). *Activity, Consciousness, and Personality*. Englewood Cliffs, NJ: Prentice-Hall.

(1981). *Problems of the Development of the Mind*. Moscow: Progress.

Loucopoulos, P. and Karakostas, V. (1995). *System Requirements Engineering*. London: McGraw-Hill.

Luff, P. and Heath, C. C. (1993). System Use and Social Organisation: Observations on Human Computer Interaction in an Architectural Practice, in *Technology in Working Order*, Button, G. (ed.), pp. 184–210. London: Routledge.

Luff, P., Jirotka, M., Heath, C. C. and Greatbatch, D. (1993). Tasks and Social Interaction: the Relevance of Naturalistic Analyses of Conduct for Requirements Engineering, in *Proceedings of RE '93: IEEE International Symposium on Requirements Engineering*, pp. 187–90. San Diego, CA.

Lynch, M. (1991). Method: Measurement – Ordinary and Scientific Measurement as Ethnomethodological Phenomena, in *Ethnomethodology and the Human Sciences*, Button, G. (ed.), pp. 77–108. Cambridge: Cambridge University Press.

(1993). *Scientific Practice and Ordinary Action: Ethnomethodology and Social Studies of Science*. Cambridge: Cambridge University Press.

Lynch, M. and Bogen, D. (1996). *The Spectacle of History: Speech, Text and Management at the Iran-Contra Hearings*. Durham, NC and London: Duke University Press.

McDonald, J. C. (1994). Inpatient Flow Management: A Collaborative Approach, in *Case Management for Healthcare Professionals*, Howe, R. S. (ed.). Chicago: Precept Press.

McGrath, M. (1995). *Product Strategy for High-Technology Companies*. Burr Ridge, IL: Irwin Professional.

Mackenzie, D. and Wajcman, J. (eds.) (1985). *The Social Shaping of Technology: A Reader*. Milton Keynes: Open University Press.

MacLean, A., Young, R. M., Bellotti, V. M. E. and Moran, T. P. (1996). Questions, Options, and Criteria: Elements of Design Space Analysis, in *Design Rationale: Concepts, Techniques and Use*, Moran, T. P. and Carroll, J. M. (eds.), pp. 53–105. Mahwah, NJ: Lawrence Erlbaum.

Malone, T. W., Lai, H.-W. and Fry, C. (1992). Experiments with Oval: A Radically Tailorable Tool for Cooperative Work, in *Proceedings of CSCW '92*, pp. 289–97. Toronto.

Mantei, M., Baecker, R., Sellen, A., Buxton, W., Milligan, T. and Wellman, B. (1991). Experiences in the Use of a Media Space, in *Proceedings of CHI '91*, pp. 203–8. New Orleans, LA.

March, J. G. (1991). How Decisions Happen in Organizations, *Human–Computer Interaction* 6: 95–117.

March, J. and Olson, J. (1989). *Rediscovering Institutions: The Organisational Basis of Politics*. New York: Free Press.

Marvin, C. (1988). *When Old Technologies Were New*. Oxford: Oxford University Press.

Maturana, H. R. and Varela, F. J. (1980). *Autopoiesis and Cognition: The Realisation of the Living*. Dordrecht: Reidel.

Mead, G. H. ([1931] 1980). The Physical Thing, in *The Philosophy of the Present*, pp. 119–39. Chicago: University of Chicago Press.

Miller, R. A., Pople, H. E. and Myers, J. D. (1984). INTERNIST-I, an Experimental Computer-Based Diagnostic Consultant for Gereral Internal Medicine, in *Readings in Medical Artificial Intelligence*, Clancey, W. J. and Shortliffe, E. H. (eds.), pp. 109–209. Reading, MA: Addison-Wesley.

Modell, J. (1996). The Uneasy Engagement of Human Development and Ethnography, in *Ethnography and Human Development: Context and Meaning in Social Inquiry*, Jessor, R., Colby, A. and Shweder, R. A. (eds.). Chicago: University of Chicago Press.

Monk, A., Wright, P., Haber, J. and Davenport, L. (1993). *Improving Your Human–Computer Interface: A Practical Technique*. London: Prentice-Hall.

Moran, T. P. and Anderson, R. J. (1990). The Workaday World as a Paradigm for CSCW Design, in *Proceedings of CSCW '90*, pp. 381–94. Los Angeles.

Moran, T. P. and Carroll, J. M. (eds.) (1996). *Design Rationale: Concepts, Techniques and Use*. Mahwah, NJ: Lawrence Erlbaum.

Myers, M. and Rosenbloom, R. (1996). Re-thinking the Role of Research, in *Engines of Innovation: U.S. Industrial Research at the End of an Era*, Rosenbloom, R. S. and Spencer, W. J. (eds.), pp. 14–18. Boston, MA: Harvard Business School Press.

Nardi, B. A. (ed.) (1996). *Context and Consciousness: Activity and Human–Computer Interaction*. Cambridge, MA: MIT Press.

Nardi, B. A., Schwartz, H., Kuchinsky, A., Leichner, R., Whitakker, S. and Sclabassi, R. (1993). Turning Away from Talking Heads: The Use of Video-as-Data in Neurosurgery, in *Proceedings of INTERCHI '93*, pp. 327–34. Amsterdam.

Newell, A. and Card, S. K. (1985). The Prospects for Psychological Science in Human–Computer Interaction, *Human–Computer Interaction*. 1(3): 209–42.

Newman, W. (1996). The Place of Interactive Computing, in *Tomorrow's Computer Science: Computing Tomorrow*, Wand, I. and Milner, R. (eds.). Cambridge: Cambridge University Press.

(1997). What Application Designers Know: Some Thoughts on Innovation in Interactive Systems, in *Proceedings of Software Ergonomie '97*, Dresden.

Norman, D. (1980). Twelve Issues for Cognitive Science, *Cognitive Science* 4: 1–32.

Norman, D. A. (1983). Some Observations on Mental Models, in *Mental Models*, Gentner, D. and Stevens, A. L. (eds.), pp. 7–14. Hillsdale, NJ: Lawrence Erlbaum.

(1988). *The Psychology of Everyday Things*. New York: Basic Books.

(1991). Cognitive Artifacts, in *Designing Interaction: Psychology at the Human–Computer Interface*, Carroll, J. M. (ed.), pp. 17–38. Cambridge: Cambridge University Press.

Norman, D. A. and Draper, S. W. (eds.) (1986). *User Centered System Design: New Perspectives on Human–Computer Interaction*. Hillsdale, NJ: Lawrence Erlbaum.

Nunberg, G. (1996). Farewell to the Information Age, in *The Future of the Book*, Nunberg, G. (ed.), pp. 103–39. Berkeley, CA: University of California Press.

Ogden, C. K. and Richards, I. A. (1923). *The Meaning of Meaning*. London: Routledge & Kegan Paul

Olson, G. M., Olson, J. S., Carter, J. S. and Storrosten, M. (1992). Small Group Design Meetings: An Analysis of Collaboration, *Human–Computer Interaction*. 7: 347–74.

Olson, G. M., Olson, J. S., Storrosten, M., Carter, M., Herbsleb, J. and Rueter, H. (1996). The Structure of Activity during Design Meetings, in *Design Rationale: Concepts, Techniques and Use*, Moran, T. P. and Carroll, J. M. (eds.) pp. 217–39. Mahwah, NJ: Lawrence Erlbaum.

Olson, J. S., Olson, G. M., Mack, L. A. and Wellner, P. (1990). Concurrent Editing: The Group Interface, in *Proceedings of Interact '90 – Third IFIP Conference on Human–Computer Interaction*, pp. 835–40. Cambridge.

Olson, M. H. and Bly, S. A. (1991). The Portland Experience: A Report on a Distributed Research Group, *International Journal of Man–Machine Studies* 34: 211–28.

Ombredane, A. and Faverge, J. M. (1955). *L'Analyse du travail*. Paris: PUF.

Orlikowski, W. J. (1992). Learning from Notes: Organizational Issues in Groupware Implementation, in *Proceedings of CSCW '92*, pp. 362–9. Toronto.

Orr, J. E. (1996). *Talking about Machines: An Ethnography of a Modern Job*. Ithaca, NY: ILR Press.

Page, D., Williams, P. and Boyd, D. (1993). *Report of the Inquiry into the London Ambulance Service*. London: South West Thames Regional Health Authority.

Payne, S. J. and Green, T. R. G. (1986). Task-Action Grammars: A Model of the Mental Representation of Task Languages, *Human–Computer Interaction*. 2(2): 93–133.

Pinsky, L. (1979). Analyse du travail de Saisie-Chiffremont, in *Le Travail de Saisie-Chiffremont sur terminal d'ordinateur*, Pinsky, L., Kandaroun, R. and Lantin, G. (eds.), pp. 1–257. Collection de Physiologies du Travail et d'Ergonomie du CNAM, no. 65, Paris: CNAM.

Pinsky, L. and Theureau, J. (1982). *Activité cognitive et action dans le travail. Tome 1: Les mots l'operatrice*. Paris: CNAM.

(1992). Analyse du travail de Saisie-Chiffremont, in *Concevoir pour l'action et la communication: essias d'ergonomie cognitive*, Pinsky, L. (ed.), pp. 1–257. Berne: Peter Lang.

Plowman, L., Rogers, Y. and Ramage, M. (1995). What are Workplace Studies for?, in *Proceedings of ECSCW '95*, pp. 309–24. Stockholm.

Potts, C. and Newstetter, W. C. (1997). Naturalistic Inquiry and Requirements Engineering: Reconciling their Theoretical Foundations, in *Proceedings of Third IEEE International Symposium on Requirements Engineering*, pp. 118–27. Annapolis, MD.

Pougès, C., Jacquiau, G., Pavard, B., Gourbault, F. and Champion, M. (1994). Conception de collecticiels pour l'aide à la prise de décision en situation d'urgence: La Nécessité d'une approche pluridisciplinaire et intégrée, in *Systèmes coopératifs: De la modélisation à la conception*, Pavard, B. (ed.), pp. 351–75. Toulouse: Octares Editions.

Pycock, J., Palfreyman, K., Allanson, J. and Button, G. (1998). Representing Fieldwork and Articulating Requirements through VR, in *Proceedings of CSCW '98*, pp. 383–92. Seattle, WA.

Quinn, J. B. (1987). Technological innovation, entrepreneurship, and strategy, in *Generating Technological Innovation*, Roberts, E. (ed.), pp. 117–31. New York: Oxford University Press.

Randall, D., Hughes, J. and Shapiro, D. (1994). Steps towards a Partnership: Ethnography and System Design, in *Requirements Engineering: Social and Technical Issues*, Jirotka, M. and Goguen, J. (eds.), pp. 241–58. London: Academic Press.

Randall, D., Rouncefield, M. and Hughes, J. A. (1995). Chalk and Cheese: BPR and Ethnomethodologically Informed Ethnography in CSCW, in *Proceedings of ECSCW '95*, pp. 325–40. Stockholm.

Richards, T. and Richards, L. (1991a). The NUDIST Qualitative Data Analysis System, *Qualitative Sociology*. 14(3).

(1991b). The Transformation of Qualitative Method: Computational Paradigms and Research Processes, in *Using Computers in Qualitative Research*, Fielding, N. and Lee, R. (eds.), pp. 38–53. London: Sage.

Robertson, T. (1997). 'And It's a Generalisation. But No It's Not': Women, Communicative Work and the Discourses of Technology Design, in *Women, Work and Computerization: Spinning a Web from Past to Future*, Grundy, A., Köhler, D., Oechtering, V. and Petersen, U. (eds.), pp. 263–76. Berlin: Springer-Verlag.

Rodden, T. (1996). Populating the Application: A Model of Awareness for Cooperative Applications, in *Proceedings of CSCW '96*, pp. 87–96. Cambridge, MA.

Rodden, T. and Blair, G. (1991). CSCW and Distributed Systems: The Problem of Control, in *Proceedings of ECSCW '91*, pp. 49–64. Amsterdam.

Rodden, T., Mariani, J. A. and Blair, G. (1992). Supporting Cooperative Applications, *Computer Supported Cooperative Work: Journal of Collaborative Computing* 1(1–2): 41–68.

Rogers, Y. (1992). Ghosts in the Network: Distributed Troubleshooting in a Shared Working Environment, in *Proceedings of CSCW '92*, pp. 346–55. Toronto,

(1993). Coordinating Computer-Mediated Work, *Computer Supported Cooperative Work: Journal of Collaborative Computing*. 1: 295–315.

(1997). Reconfiguring the Social Scientist, Shifting from Telling Designers What to do to Getting More Involved, in *Social Science, Technical Systems and Co-operative Work: Beyond the Great Divide*, Bowker, G., Leigh Star, S., Turner, B. and Gasser, L. (eds.), pp. 57–78. Mahwah, NJ: Lawrence Erlbaum.

Roseman, M. and Greenberg, S. (1996). TeamRooms: Network Places for Collaboration, in *Proceedings of CSCW '96*, pp. 325–33. Cambridge, MA.

Rosenschein, S. (1987). *Formal Theories of Knowledge in AI and Robotics*. Technical Report, Center for the Study of Language and Information, Stanford, CA.

Roussell, P., Saad, V. and Erickson, T. (1991). *Third Generation R&D Managing the Link to Corporate Strategy*. Cambridge, MA: Harvard Business School Press.

Sabbagh, K. (1989). *Skyscraper: The Making of a Building*. London: Macmillan.

Sacks, H. (1972). An Initial Investigation of the Usability of Conversational Data for Doing Sociology, in *Studies in Social Interaction*, Sudnow, D. (ed.), pp. 31–74. New York: Free Press.

(1992). *Lectures in Conversation: Volumes I and II*. Oxford: Blackwell.

Salomon, G. (ed.) (1993). *Distributed Cognitions: Psychological and Educational Considerations*. Cambridge: Cambridge University Press.

Sandor, O., Bogdan, C. and Bowers, J. (1997). Aether: An Awareness Engine for CSCW, in *Proceedings of ECSCW '97*, pp. 221–36. Lancaster.

Schegloff, E. A. and Sacks, H. (1973). Opening Up Closings, in *Semiotica Selected Readings*, Turner, R. (ed.), pp. 233–64. Harmondsworth: Penguin. Reprinted in *Ethnomethodology*: 7: 289–327, .

Schmidt, D., Fayad, M. and Johnson, R. (1996). Special issue on Software Patterns, *Communications of the ACM* 39(10).

Schmidt, K. (1991). Riding a Tiger, or Computer Supported Cooperative Work, in *Proceedings of ECSCW '91*, pp. 1–16. Amsterdam.

Schmidt, K. and Bannon, L. (1992). Taking CSCW Seriously Supporting Articulation Work, *Computer Supported Cooperative Work: Journal of Collaborative Computing* 1(1–2): 7–40.

Schmidt, K. and Rodden, T. (1996). Putting It All Together: Requirements for a CSCW Platform, in *The Design of Computer Supported Cooperative Work and Groupware Systems*, Shapiro, D., Tauber, M. and Traunmüller, R. (eds.), pp. 157–76. Amsterdam: North-Holland Elsevier.

Schmidt, K. and Simone, C. (1996). Coordination Mechanisms: Towards a Conceptual Foundation of CSCW Design, *Computer Supported Cooperative Work: Journal of Collaborative Computing* 5(2–3): 155–200.

Schumpeter, J. (1934). *The Theory of Economic Development*. Cambridge, MA: Harvard University Press.

Schutz, A. ([1932] 1967). *The Phenomenology of the Social World*. Evanston, IL: Northwestern University Press.

([1943] 1964). The Problem of Rationality in the Social World, in *Collected Papers II: Studies in Social Theory*, Broderson, A. (ed.), pp. 64–90. The Hague: Martinus Nijhoff.

([1953] 1962). Common-sense and Scientific Interpretations of Human Action, in *Collected Papers I: The Problem of Social Reality*, Natanson, M. (ed.), pp. 3–47. The Hague: Martinus Nijhoff.

(1964). On Multiple Realities, in *Collected Papers II: Studies in Social Theory*, Broderson, A. (ed.). The Hague: Martinus Nijhoff.

Scribner, S. (1984). Studying Work Intelligence, in *Everyday Cognition*, Rogoff, B. and Lave, J. (eds.), pp. 9–40. Cambridge, MA: Harvard University Press.

Seidel, J. and Clark, J. (1984). The Ethnograph: A Computer Program for the Analysis of Qualitative Data, *Qualitative Sociology* 7(1–2): 110–25.

Seidel, J., Kjolseth, R. and Seymour, E. (1988). *The Ethnograph: A User's Guide*. Salt Lake City, UT: Qualis Research Associates.

Sellen, A. and Harper, R. H. R. (1996). *Can Workflow Tools Support Knowledge Work? A Case Study of the International Monetary Fund*. Technical Report, Rank Xerox Cambridge EuroPARC, Cambridge.

Shapin, S. (1989). The Invisible Technician, *American Scientist* 77: 554–63.

Shapiro, D. (1994). The Limits of Ethnography: Combining Social Sciences for CSCW, in *Proceedings of CSCW '94*, pp. 417–28. Chapel Hill, NC.

Sharples, M. (ed.) (1993). *Computer Supported Collaborative Writing*. London and Berlin: Springer–Verlag.

Sharrock, W. W. and Anderson, R. J. (1996). Organisational Innovation and the Articulation of the Design Space, in *Design Rational Concepts, Techniques and Use*, Moran, T. and Carroll, J. (eds.), pp. 429–51. Mahwah, NJ: Lawrence Erlbaum.

Sharrock, W. W. and Button, G. (1997). Engineering Investigations: Practical Sociological Reasoning in the Work of Engineers, in *Social Science, Technical Systems and Co-operative Work: Beyond the Great Divide*, Bowker, G., Leigh Star, S., Turner, B. and Gasser, L. (eds.), pp. 79–104. Mahwah, NJ: Lawrence Erlbaum.

Shepherd, A., Mayer, N. and Kuchinsky, A. (1990). Strudel: An Extensible Electronic Conversation Toolkit, in *Proceedings of CSCW '90*, pp. 93–104. Los Angeles.

Simone, C. and Bandini, S. (1997). Compositional Features for Promoting Awareness within and across Cooperative Applications, in *Proceedings of GROUP '97: ACM SIGGROUP Conference on Supporting Group Work*, pp. 358–67. Phoenix, AZ.

Simone, C. and Schmidt, K. (1998). Taking the Distributed Nature of Cooperative Work Seriously, in *Proceedings of the Sixth Euromicro Workshop on Parallel and Distributed Processing*, pp. 295–301. Madrid.

Simone, C., Divitini, M. and Schmidt, K. (1995). A Notation for Malleable and Interoperable Coordination Mechanisms for CSCW Systems, in *Proceedings of COOCS '95, Conference on Organizational Computing Systems*, pp. 44–54. Milpitas, CA.

Smith, D. E. (1993). *Texts, Facts, and Femininity: Exploring the Relations of Ruling.* London: Routledge.

Smith, D. K. and Alexander, R. C. (1988). *Fumbling the Future: How Xerox Invented, then Ignored the First Personal Computer.* New York: William Morrow.

Sommerville, I., Rodden, T., Sawyer, P. and Bentley, R. (1993). Sociologists can be Surprisingly Useful in Interactive Systems Design, in *People and Computers VII*, Monk, A., Diaper, D. and Harrison, M. (eds.), pp. 341–53. Cambridge: Cambridge University Press.

Sommerville, I., Rodden, T., Sawyer, P., Bentley, R. and Twidale, M. (1993). Incorporating Ethnography into Requirements Engineering, in *Proceedings of RE '93: IEEE International Symposium on Requirements Engineering*, pp. 165–73. San Diego, CA.

Star, S. L. (1989). The Structure of Ill-structured Solutions: Boundary Objects and Heterogeneous Distributed Problem Solving, in *Distributed Artificial Intelligence Vol. II*, Gasser, L. and Huhns, M. N. (eds.), pp. 37–52. London: Pitman.

  (1991). Invisible Work and Silenced Dialogues in Knowledge Representation, in *Women, Work and Computerization: Understanding and Overcoming Bias in Work and Education*, Ericksson, I. V., Kitchenham, B. A. and Tijdens, K. J. (eds.), pp. 81–91. Amsterdam: Elsevier North-Holland.

Stefik, M., Foster, G., Bobrow, D. G., Kahn, K., Lanning, S. and Suchman, L. (1987). Beyond the Chalkboard: Computer Support for Collaboration and Problem Solving, *Communications of the ACM* 30(1): 32–47.

Strauss, A., Schatzman, L., Bucher, R., Ehrlich, D. and Sabshin, M. (1964). *Psychiatric Ideologies and Institutions.* London: Free Press.

Strauss, A. L., Fayerhaugh, S., Suczek, B. and Weiner, C. (1985). *The Social Organisation of Medical Work.* London: University of Chicago Press.

Suchman, L. A. (1982). Systematics of Office Work: Office Studies for Knowledge-Based Systems, in *Proceedings of Office Automation Conference*, pp. 409–12. San Francisco, CA.

  (1983). Office Procedures as Practical Action: Models of Work and System Design, *ACM Transactions on Office Information Systems* 1(4): 320–8.

  (1987). *Plans and Situated Actions: The Problem of Human–Machine Communication.* Cambridge: Cambridge University Press.

  (1993a). Do Categories Have Politics? The Language/Action Perspective Reconsidered, in *Proceedings of ECSCW '93*, pp. 1–14. Milan,

  (1993b). Technologies of Accountability: On Lizards and Aeroplanes, in *Technology in Working Order*, Button, G. (ed.), pp. 113–26. London: Routledge.

  (1995). Making Work Visible, special issue on Representations of Work, *Communications of the ACM* (September): 56–64.

  (1996a). Constituting Shared Workspaces, in *Cognition and Communication at Work*, Engeström, Y. and Middleton, D. (eds.), pp. 35–60. Cambridge: Cambridge University Press.

  (1996b). Supporting Articulation Work, in *Computerization and Controversy: Value Conflicts and Social Choices*, 2nd edn, Kling, R. (ed.), pp. 407–23. London: Academic Press.

Suchman, L. A. and Jordan, B. (1988). Computerization and Women's Knowledge, in *Women, Work and Computerization: Forming New Alliances*, Tijdens, K., Jennings, M., Wagner, I. and Weggelaar, M. (eds.), pp. 153–60. Amsterdam: North-Holland.

(1990). Interactional Troubles in Face-to-Face Survey Interviews, *American Statistical Association* 85(409): 232–41.

Suchman, L. A. and Wynn, E. (1984). Procedures and Problems in the Office, *Office: Technology and People*. 2: 133–54.

Tallerico, M. (1991). Application of Qualitative Analysis Software: A View from the Field, *Qualitative Sociology* 14(3).

Tatar, D. G., Foster, G. and Bobrow, D. G. (1991). Designing for Conversation: Lessons from Cognoter, *International Journal of Man-Machine Studies* 34(2): 185–209.

Theureau, J. (1991). Etude du cours d'action et relation du source, in *A Quoi servent les usagers?*, Paris: RATP.

(1992). Le Cours d'action: Analyses Sémio-Logique. Berne: Peter Lang.

Theureau, J., Jeffroy, F., Bonpays-Le Guilcher, B., Bouzit, N., Filippi, G., *et al.* (1994). *Ergonomie des situations informatisées: La Conception centrée sur le cours d'action des utilisateurs*. Toulouse: Octares Editions.

Thomas, J. and Kellogg, W. A. (1989). Minimizing Ecological Gaps in User Interface Design, *IEEE Software*. (January): 78–86.

Toulmin, S. and Gustavsen, B. (eds.) (1996). *Beyond Theory: Changing Organizations through Participation*. Amsterdam: John Benjamins.

Turner, R. (ed.) (1974). *Ethnomethodology: Selected Readings*. Harmondsworth: Penguin.

Trevor, J., Rodden, J. and Blair, G. (1995). COLA: A Lightweight Platform for CSCW, *Computer Supported Cooperative Work: Journal of Collaborative Computing* 3(2): 197–224.

Varela, F. (1980). *Principles of Biological Autonomy*. New York: Elsevier North-Holland.

Varela, F., Thomson, E. and Rosch, E. (1991). *The Embodied Mind: Cognitive Science and Human Experience*. Cambridge, MA: MIT Press.

Vinkhuyzen, R. E. (1997). Expert Systems in Practice: Two Case-Studies. PhD dissertation, University of Zurich.

Vogel, D. R. and Nunamaker, J. F. (1990). Design and Assessment of a Group Decision Support System, in *Intellectual Teamwork: The Social and Technological Foundations of Cooperative Work*, Kraut, R. E., Galegher, J. and Egido, C. (eds.), pp. 511–28. Hillsdale, NJ: Lawrence Erlbaum.

Vygotsky, L. S. (1962). *Thought and Language*. Cambridge, MA: MIT Press.

(1978). *Mind in Society: The Development of Higher Psychological Processes*. Boston, MA: Harvard University Press.

Wagman, M. (1998). *The Ultimate Objectives of Artificial Intelligence: Theoretical and Research Foundations, Philosophical and Psychological Implications*. Westport, CT: Praeger.

Weick, K. E. (1995). *Sensemaking in Organizations*. Thousand Oaks, CA: Sage,

Whalen, J. (1992). Technology and the Coordination of Human Activity: Computer-Aided Dispatch in Public Safety Communications, in *Proceedings of Discourse and the Professions*. Uppsala, Sweden.

(1995a). Expert Systems vs. Systems for Experts: Computer-Aided Dispatch as a Support System in Real-World Environments, in *The Social and*

Interactional Dimensions of Human–Computer Interfaces, Thomas, P. (ed.), pp. 161–83. Cambridge: Cambridge University Press.

(1995b). A Technology of Order Production: Computer-Aided Dispatch in 9-1-1 Communications, in *Situated Order: Studies in the Social Organization of Talk and Embodied Activities*, Psathas, G. and ten Have, P. (eds.), pp. 187–230. Washington, DC: University Press of America.

Whalen, J. and Zimmerman, D. H. (1998). Observations on the Display and Management of Emotion in Naturally Occurring Activities: The Case of 'Hysteria' in Calls to 9-1-1, *Social Psychology Quarterly*. 61: 141–59.

Wieder, D. L. (1970). On Meaning by Rule, in *Understanding Everyday Life*, Douglas, J. D. (ed.), London: Routledge & Kegan Paul.

Winograd, T. (1988). A Language/Action Perspective on the Design of Cooperative Work, *Human–Computer Interaction* 3(1): 3–30.

Winograd, T. and Flores, F. (1986). *Understanding Computers and Cognition: A New Foundation for Design*. Norwood, NJ: Addison-Wesley.

Woods, D. D. and Roth, E. M. (1988). Cognitive Systems Engineering, in *Handbook of Human–Computer Interaction*, Helander, M. (ed.), pp. 3–43. Amsterdam: Elsevier North-Holland.

Woolgar, S. (1991). The Turn to Technology in Social Studies of Science, *Science, Technology and Human Values* 16(1): 20–50.

(1993). What's at Stake in the Sociology of Technology? A Reply to Pinch and Winner, *Science, Technology and Human Values* 18(4): 523–9.

Wynn, E. (1979). Office Conversation as an Information Medium. PhD dissertation, University of California, Berkeley.

Zimmerman, D. H. (1974). Fact as a Practical Accomplishment, in *Ethnomethodology*, Turner, R. (ed.), pp. 128–43. Harmondsworth: Penguin.

(1992). The Interactional Organization of Calls for Emergency Assistance, in *Talk at Work: Interaction in Institutional Settings*, Drew, P. and Heritage, J. (eds.), pp. 418–69. Cambridge: Cambridge University Press.

Zuboff, S. (1988). *The Age of the Smart Machine*. London: Heinemann.

Index